Words of the Grey Wind

Words of
the Grey Wind

Family and Epiphany in Ulster

Chris Arthur

BLACKSTAFF PRESS

BELFAST

'Kingfishers', 'Ferrule', 'Meditation on the Pelvis of an Unknown Animal' and 'Linen' are from *Irish Nocturnes* (ISBN-10: 1-888570-49-0 / ISBN-13: 978-1-888570-49-6) published by The Davies Group, Publishers, Aurora CO USA, 1999, and appear here by arrangement with the publisher.

'A Tinchel Round My Father', 'Table Manners' and 'Train Sounds' are from *Irish Willow* (ISBN-10: 1-888570-46-6 / ISBN-13: 978-1-888570-46-5) published by The Davies Group, Publishers, Aurora CO USA, 2002, and appear here by arrangement with the publisher.

'Witness', 'Miracles' and 'Swan Song' are from *Irish Haiku* (ISBN-10: 1-888570-78-4 / ISBN-13: 978-1-888570-78-6) published by The Davies Group, Publishers, Aurora CO USA, 2005, and appear here by arrangement with the publisher.

The photographs of the author's parents, on pages viii and 250, appear courtesy of Chris Arthur as does the photograph used on the inside back cover. This shows the boy mentioned in 'Kingfishers' (p. 5). He was to be among the hundreds who perished when the *Lusitania* was torpedoed in 1915.

First published in 2009 by
Blackstaff Press
4c Heron Wharf, Sydenham Business Park
Belfast BT3 9LE
with the assistance of the Arts Council of Northern Ireland

Typeset by CJWT Solutions, St Helens, Merseyside

Printed in England by Athenaeum Press

A CIP catalogue record for this book
is available from the British Library

ISBN 978-0-85640-843-4

www.blackstaffpress.com

Whether or not declared, all my writing
carries a dedication to the tribe. Without family, I'd
not be who I am. Beyond such blood-obligation,
I'd like to pay tribute to three important
influences on my life by dedicating this book
to the memory of

Hugh Gray Bass ('Uncle Jamesie')
An inspiring independent spirit

Arnold Benington
Who nurtured my love of nature

David Berwick Young
Who nurtured my love of literature

My cast of mind is such that I am moved by intuitions,
intimations, imaginative realisations, epiphanies,
which, after all, may not be the
worst way to face life…

JOHN HEWITT

CONTENTS

FOREWORD

Most of the essays in this splendid book have been chosen from three volumes originally published in Colorado: *Irish Nocturnes* (1999), *Irish Willow* (2002) and *Irish Haiku* (2005). In hindsight, there was something fitting about the quiet first appearance of these volumes in the American West – quiet in their pleasingly fine format (with their delicately suggestive titles) as well as in their unassuming arrival from an unsuspected source, a hitherto unknown Irish essayist. For like the essays themselves, the unassumingness was rather deceptive. The beginning may have been modest but since over thirty essays were collected in just three years, there was an impression of cumulating work having kept itself in reserve and the pressure of its contents under rein. (The inclusion of three new essays in *Words of the Grey Wind* is a welcome suggestion that the writer is now in mid-flow.) Moreover, just as the essays typically begin without fanfare or flourish, with what may even appear as casualness or arbitrariness, and then unfold themselves resolutely if elegantly, so this published selection signals an important stage in what I believe will be the widening spiral of Chris Arthur's reputation beyond discriminating readers of choice books published by a Colorado publisher and into the more robust British and Irish literary scene.

My own first acquaintance with Arthur's writings was accompanied by a trivial coincidence of the kind the author might himself have enjoyed and that added a personal note to the otherwise impersonal swim of a deeply impressive writer into this reader's ken. I was several pages into an offprint of Arthur's essay, 'Miracles', when its inspiring figure of Brother Erskine gradually lifted itself off the page and into sharp recognition, much like a photograph materialising in the developing tray. He became D.B. Erskine, one of the masters who in grammar school had quickened my love of literature. I thought that the essayist who had brought him back to life was an ex-schoolfellow of mine; I was wrong, but my acquaintance with a characteristically thoughtful essay led to my acquaintance with its author.

David Erskine, I learned, had left my Belfast grammar school, taken the cloth, and become chaplain at the college where Arthur was a pupil. Arthur, with his attraction to beginnings and unfoldings, might enjoy someone else's memories of Brother Erskine's pre-clerical career (a bare decade after the end of the Second World War) when this physically imposing, Clark Gableishly handsome ex-tank commander embodied the worldly-wise. I see him striding down our interminable corridors with an improbable number of books tucked under his impressive wingspan, with his gown flapping as if for flight. I see him perched precariously on a chairback (as Arthur does too) reading Arthur Conan Doyle to us in a sonorous voice, all the while smoothing an invisible moustache, perhaps in gestural memory of a suitable wartime adornment. (When some boy's books clattered off the desk, D.B. Erskine would mix his world wars and cry, 'Someone dropped a Mills bomb!') I see him, too, on dining hall duty, silencing a turmoil of working-class schoolboys with the clangs of a huge handbell and the bellowed observations – 'Bedlam! Chaos! Pandemonium!' Arthur's Brother Erskine, to which I leave the reader of this wonderful essay, is a figure unfolded in a new direction, one doing characteristically fertile philosophic duty, and my own memories merely add a caption to Arthur's chart, in this essay and elsewhere, of all our movements through time and space with their accompanying alterations in our opinions, in our bodies, and finally in our claims to identity and existence.

The movement of Arthur's mind is one of exfoliation. His

modus operandi, which after a few essays the reader begins with pleasure to anticipate, is a measured departure from a particular object, incident, word or memory, often commonplace but sometimes highly personal and sometimes intrinsically poetic – ferrule, table, mistletoe, swan's wing, one afternoon's occurrence – into its ramifying implications, symbolisms and meanings. An extended metaphor is often the required ignition. The pursuit of the subject is a 'long foray', to borrow an oxymoron from Seamus Heaney, and exemplifies not only the parsings, propositions and interrogations of analytic thought, but also its reservations, denials and reassertions, until, oddly, the essay's stages of argument seem to exist simultaneously, even though points along the way have been decisively made and conclusions reached. The alertly cognitive becomes something akin to reverie without loss of alertness or cognition. He may have used the term 'nocturne' for one of his titles, but 'fugue' seems closer to the development of an Arthur essay. The net result is metaphysical: Arthur's acute inquiry is accompanied all the while by an awareness that nothing, be it argument or the stuff of the world, comes to final rest.

I say 'net' advisedly, since 'tendril' in the suggestive sense of relentless reticulate growth is one of Arthur's favourite words and characterises his own procedure as much as the world and his experience of it that he chooses to ravel and unravel for us. In Arthur's world, everything is connected in shrinking degrees of separation. To display the restlessness of matter, Arthur typically tracks the things and thoughts of the world to their far reaches where they, like all transient particular existence, are dwarfed and contemplation itself is spent, the essay completed. When he speaks of 'the smoke of forms' that blows across each place over time and of 'the endless tundra of extinction', I am reminded of H.G. Wells' Time Traveller courageously taking his machine not to the ends but the end of the earth because he must see his scientific pilgrimage through. (The writing desk is Arthur's time machine.) This cosmic awareness of endless material motion has its dark aspect as though Arthur's essays were long and eloquent disappointments, with (at times) Larkinesque or even Beckettian accents. 'Swan Song', in which he contemplates his stillborn son, is unswervingly frank and to think this deeply sad event into its farthest implications, beyond fatherly grief and human loss, is an extraordinary feat.

The binaries we wrestle with, and usually shrink from, surface and submerge in these essays with an unfashionable candour: the metaphysical and the mundane, the commonplace and the miraculous, the physical and the spiritual, the accidental and the destined, the personal and the universal, the temporal and the eternal. Time and again the essayist seeks to resolve these oppositions as tie-breaks in the realm of some invisible other province. At the heart of the essays is a paradox: transcending of the self is sought through a relentless examination of the life. Heaney's word 'squarings' comes to mind when I think of the task of squaring or reconciling opposites in each Arthur essay, a task self-imposed from the outset but given all the appearance of a necessity freshly unfurling as the essay proceeds. Biology (especially Darwinism) helps, so too do physics, chemistry and astronomy. And a vestigial Christianity. Arthur shares his reading with us along the way, and from his essays I've taken note of fascinating-sounding studies I intend to read. But above all, Buddhism helps. Presumably as a result of his study and practice of Buddhism, his essays are courteous yet firm assaults on the Ineffable, part of a book-long, probably lifelong campaign to come to rest in some Truth where the commonplace and the epiphanic conjoin, because the miraculous can only exist in 'the stupendous fabric of the real'. There are some admissions of defeat in the essays, but even when Arthur's campaign loses heart or self-justification (if 'everything is ineffable', then why seek to know it?), it is still a worthwhile and courageous one.

Arthur's Northern Irishness has been part of the fabric of his reality: his quiet Belfast upbringing and schooling and the later, if indirect, impact of the so-called 'Troubles'. The latter were, in actuality, a disgraceful thirty-year record of cruelty, of violent rebellion, reprisal and counter-insurgency. In a writer much concerned with transcending the coordinates of time and place, it was a subdued coincidental pleasure to find a timely set of rhetorical but morally urgent post-Troubles questions in 'Witness': 'I often wonder what *ought* to be remembered from Ulster's years of agony and turmoil … should we recall the dates of dreadful crimes and what was done, the names of individuals slaughtered and those who did the slaughtering? Or would it be better to let a slow tide of forgetfulness accumulate and slowly buoy us toward healing, forgiveness and reconciliation?' We might be tempted to add one more Arthurian question: how does one square the requirements of morality with awareness of the inevitable extinction even of morality?

Ireland, of course, has produced its quota of essayists, from Oliver Goldsmith through (among others) Thomas Davis, Robert Lynd, Thomas Kettle, Stephen Gwynn and Filson Young to Hubert Butler. But if Lynd can be regarded as the Irish exponent *par excellence* of the English essay, it's clear that Arthur belongs to some other tradition, if he is not *sui generis*. His thought processes are too unconfined, his subjects at once too spacious and narrowly focused, his procedure too conceptually chaste, and his intention too severely tasking, for the English essay. His writing has some of the curiosity of Ciaran Carson's prose books, with their lodes of charming arcana, but does not have Carson's almost metaphysical wit. One thinks instead of Octavio Paz or Gaston Bachelard, at times of a soberer and longer-winded Borges. But this is trawling the academic net, as Seamus Heaney once remarked of such critical activity. If an Irish affinity must be sought, then the poetry of Michael Longley, with its finely-spun lyrical procedures, moral presence and its almost Eastern sensibility, comes to mind. In any case, Arthur's essays reveal a rarefied and rare, if not unique intelligence, and this selection from Blackstaff Press is a cause for congratulation and celebration.

JOHN WILSON FOSTER

INTRODUCTION

THE INFINITE SUGGESTIVENESS
of COMMON THINGS

For as long as I can remember, I've been captivated by *Birds of the Grey Wind*, Edward Armstrong's lyrical celebration of the bird-life of Ulster. As a child, my eyes used always to seek it out as I scanned the bookshelves at home. The title was like a beautiful feather fallen amidst rows of dreary plumage. For me, *Birds of the Grey Wind* contained – still contains – that alluring magic of natural poetry which some word-combinations possess. Even before I'd read the book, the title seemed imbued with a haunting music of its own. When I progressed to flicking through the photos and illustrations, scanning the chapter headings, picking out familiar locations on the inside cover's pictorial map, the title soon acquired a cargo it has never lost, one that floods the mind with images of Lough Neagh and Strangford, of sparrowhawks and owls, of Rathlin Island vistas and gannets diving into the sea off Larne. Armstrong's title acts like a little reliquary, into which is packed a treasury of Ulster scenes, the compelling spirit of place somehow distilled into five syllables.

My father's copy of the book has 'W.W. Arthur, Belfast, June 1946' written boldly in blue ink on the front endpaper. At that point he's forty-one, the war is recently ended and he's back in his peacetime occupation as a civil servant. He walks with a limp now, as he will for the rest of his life, after bomb shrapnel shattered his right leg during active service in Egypt. It's three years before his marriage, nine years before my birth. Ulster's quarter century of bitter internecine strife will not begin for another twenty years, though even now sectarian tensions are roiling not far below the surface. It's forty years until Dad's death, sixty-three until this book that lies open before you now will see the light of day. And, dwarfing all these little computations, it's some twelve or fourteen billion years since the moment of creation that sparked the universe into being; one hundred and fifty million years since the Archaeopteryx marked the advent of the birds; over three million years since early hominids left their evocatively familiar trail of footprints at Laetoli, Tanzania; five billion years until the death of the Sun.

I'm not sure why, but Dad's copy of *Birds of the Grey Wind* seems to crystallise a sense of time, a sense of history, a sense of the precariousness and mystery of existence. It's like a little depth-charge that shatters the calm waters of routine, alerting me to other lives and to the mysterious uncharted depths that lie all around us and across whose surfaces we skate, mostly oblivious to what underlies us. This slim, blue-grey volume, an oystercatcher embossed on its faded cover, offers a kind of portal into time, at once nostalgic and unnerving.

My appropriation and alteration of its title – an act of homage rather than mere theft or vandalism – stems largely from the sound of Armstrong's words alone, the way their cadences summon back places and people that I love. Beyond the immediate music of the title, though, there are other aspects of *Birds of the Grey Wind* that made me want to name this book after it. Armstrong's physical territory closely matches mine. The map at the start of *Birds of the Grey Wind*, dominated by Antrim and Down, encompasses my own homeland, my heartland. I also feel a strong answering resonance when he talks about being a 'minute philosopher'. He explains that this is someone 'who discovers in simple things material for reflection and investigation'. This is a description that fits me well. The fact that, like me, he studied

2

religion and philosophy and was acquainted with Eastern thought (having for a time lived in Kowloon), weaves another link between our writing. His love of literature – one of his books is *Shakespeare's Imagination* – strikes another chord. It seems strangely apt, given the impact of his verbal pentagram on me, that his study of the bard is focused on word-clusters. We were both born and schooled in Belfast, and our love of nature was nurtured by the Ulster countryside – though, as our lives turned out, we spent large parts of them living far away from the environs that shaped us.

Words of the Grey Wind begins and ends with birds – 'Kingfishers' and 'Waxwings' stand like totems marking out its territory. Its midpoint too is avian, with 'Swan Song' deliberately placed dead centre. But my take on birds is not the same as Armstrong's. I share his delight in their beauty, but my real interest lies not in any feathers, however lovely, but in the more fantastic plumage of ideas and the words that trace them out. The book's subtitle identifies my preoccupations and will, I hope, make clear that what follows is not ornithology. My concerns are with family, place, and what I've termed 'epiphany'. By this I mean those moments when we have a sense of discovering some special insight into the things around us, so that we better grasp their true nature. These epiphanies are not built on anything extraordinary, but take simple things as their point of departure. Alexander Smith – another 'minute philosopher', whose book *Dreamthorp* possesses a gentle lyricism akin to Armstrong's – talks about 'the infinite suggestiveness of common things'. I have taken some of the 'common things' that have emerged out of my Ulster origins – birds, walking sticks, books, flowers, empty rooms, photographs, the sound of trains – and found such infinite suggestiveness in them that they are soon transformed into peregrine-like rarities.

Words of the Grey Wind is dependent on Edward Armstrong for its title; dependent on three other books for much of its contents.

Although my *Irish Nocturnes*, *Irish Willow* and *Irish Haiku* have enjoyed a positive critical reception, they were published obscurely and are scarcely known in the place that inspired them and which I still think of as home. Given their unknownness, it does not seem inappropriate to set a selection from them before a wider readership. *Words of the Grey Wind*, therefore, presents ten essays from these collections, alongside three new pieces of writing.

I have tried to arrange what follows in a way that will facilitate a straight reading through from cover to cover. However, meandering often leads to more interesting journeys than following straight lines and I have every confidence that the kind of reader drawn to this book will be robustly independent and quite as likely to start midway through as at the beginning. There is no reason not to do so; the essays are individually intelligible without reference to each other – though I like to think that their arrangement and proximity will amplify and add to the ethos of any single piece.

Like any author, my hope is to be read. But I'd also be pleased if my title lodged like some benign splinter of the familiar in a child's mind as they stared at the volumes on their parents' bookshelves. Then, *Words of the Grey Wind* would become a part of their world, a private talisman of home and childhood and family carried secretly within, the words weaving the music of their notes into the invisible fabric of the mind, in the same way that *Birds of the Grey Wind* has been woven into mine, laden with a rich bounty of memories, dreams and imaginings.

CHRIS ARTHUR

KINGFISHERS

Their plumage is so richly iridescent, the blue and red so bright, that for my first few sightings of them, kingfishers seemed unnatural. They struck the eye as something artificial, synthetic, clad in all the arid shininess of plastic, rather than the subtler hues of life. To see them flash past constitutes such a discordant eruption of sudden metallic colour against the muted greens and browns of their riverside haunts, that it's not surprising if the mind reaches at first for man-made analogues in order to find some likeness for them. Having this little chromatic missile shoot into view without warning can even create an expectation of noise. It's as if one had been surprised by a tiny, secret, supersonic jet, roaring its intrusion through the world, the fly-past soon to be caught up with by the same ear-splitting barrage of sound that follows in the wake of low-flying fighter planes.

To anyone with an eye for birds, kingfishers are memorable. Not only because the brightness of their colours sets them apart from all other native species (the green woodpecker is their only serious rival), but also because, at least in an Irish setting, sightings are uncommon. Indeed even those with no ornithological leanings may find the kingfisher an exception to their normal indifference towards birds. It is likely to make a forced entry into their notice, its shimmering electric turquoise and burnished orange demanding that it is seen, in much the same way as those with no love of cars may yet find themselves staring at a Ferrari or a Porsche. Such things seem designed to arrest the eye.

After the surprise of those first few instances when, taken off guard, I was wrong-footed into thinking of bits of brightly coloured wind-blown plastic, or of impossibly miniature jets, king-fishers soon fell into recognition's line as something known, named, seen before. (How quickly we put even the brightest and most beautiful things into categories!) But they remained suffi-ciently rare for them to be exciting and memorable; they have never become commonplace. I can remember every time a king-fisher has flown across my life. And sometimes, on those odd occasions when I see them now, I think of the previous sighting, and the one before that, and before that again, and so on stretch-ing all the way back to my first encounter. This chain of bright occurrences dotted through the years has become like sporadic punctuation, offering another way to divide and marshal time and so facilitate another reading of the past, though the sentences thus marked out are long and complex, often hard to follow, some-times seemingly devoid of sense. Like all punctuation, it is some-what subjective, even arbitrary; like all readings, there are many alternative versions.

I don't want just to make a list. To detail every sighting might provide material for a local natural history of the bird, but it would shed no light on the mythic and symbolic status which I've grad-ually accorded to them. Looking at kingfishers now, I can under-stand why some animals come to be seen as sacred. Where the understanding fails is in unravelling the causes of that blindness, that deadness of vision, which sees no glint at all of their numi-nous, improbable beauty, and so treats them as entirely unimpor-tant. Mapping the occurrence of the species, its range and habitat, its breeding patterns and feeding behaviour, would help us to understand kingfisher ecology more minutely. And such an anno-tated log of sightings would, no doubt, paint a now accustomed picture of pollution, habitat destruction, a steep decline in popu-lation. All that is important, tragic, terrible. We should take note. But to understand the depth of loss we risk through letting such creatures edge towards rarity and extinction requires (I think) taking soundings in the less easily observed ecology of the psyche, attempting to assay the role given to them there. Without such things to dart along the waters of consciousness as it wrestles with the interminable puzzle of its being, what would we be left with to bear our dreams and imaginings, to ferry our half-formed ideas at the speed of thought towards some sort of more than merely mechanical understanding? Kingfishers can dive and retrieve from below the surface of the literal those sparkling images that go by there in too often unnoticed shoals. In doing so they help to save us from the colourless perspectives that threaten should the imagination fail.

The first kingfisher I ever saw was in Armagh, Ireland's ancient ecclesiastical capital, one warm Sunday afternoon in August, sometime in the mid-1960s. (At least, it was the first one I remember seeing, for who knows if before then kingfishers had crossed my infant eyes, inscribing a now indelible message on the lost vistas they looked out on, before all the framings of language established their vice-like grip on cognition.) And to say I *saw* it is misleading. I was aware of a bright streak of colour, my mother's surprised expression and, too late to be of any use, her cry of, 'Look! A kingfisher!' It had already vanished, leaving a memory, not of any bird, but of a tiny, fast-moving sapphire shape, almost like a bead of light, tracing an unlikely line a few inches above the muddy water of the stream we were walking beside. It left a mingled sense of astonishment, pleasure, disappointment and uncertainty. The sheer unexpectedness of it was astonishing. We were pleased to have even glimpsed so uncommon and beautiful a bird, but disappointed not to have had a better sighting. The uncertainty came because its speed and suddenness introduced an element of doubt. Had we really seen it at all? In some ways it seemed more like the stuff of fantasy, too exotic for the mundane world. And, I suppose, on that day, walking as we were in the grounds of what was then Armagh's asylum, we were predisposed to wonder about what was real and what imagined, alert to the possibility that some gleam of madness, bright and unexpected as a kingfisher, might suddenly manifest itself in the midst of the ordinary, ripping down sanity's still waters with a wild, disruptive incandescence.

The asylum (long since given over to other use) was a grim, stone-built Victorian edifice surrounded by high walls. The architecture inclined more towards the style of a penitentiary than anything more humane, its air of drabness, heaviness, imprisonment giving weight to the suspicion that something bright as quicksilver must be caged here. Within sight of the main building a stream ran through the grounds, its fluid sounds and shapes, the lushness of the vegetation on its banks, acting to gentle the impact of the brutal built façade. We were drawn to it as people always are to water.

I was maybe nine or ten. It was my first visit to an asylum, my first real brush with madness. I was apprehensive, scared, unsure what sudden explosions of terrifying derangement might issue from the dark forbidding buildings, or from the people we passed as we walked through the grounds. I looked at them uneasily, searching for clues, trying not to let them see that I was looking. Were they patients? Doctors? Nurses? Visitors like us? Were they normal? Harmless? Violent? The kingfisher's sudden streak of momentary colour, the complete unexpectedness of its appearance, underlined the sense of unpredictability that sat heavy on my boy's mind, ripe with all manner of fears and misconceptions, on that summer's afternoon all those years ago. It seemed to confirm the horrible suspicion which that place awoke, that anything could happen. That all the bulwarks of convention, custom, routine, what is accorded normal, could be ruptured without warning by a piercing blue-green spark – glittering, electric, unnatural – as the rogue ignition of insanity sparkled along the little rivers of the mind's amazing waterways, fusing and firing its delicate synapses into all manner of grotesque arrangements.

How much of any symbol resides in the thing itself, and how much is foisted on it by the preoccupations of those for whom it takes on a special significance? The question could be debated endlessly, with example and counter-example drawn from the whole panorama of human history. We are a symbol-making species *par excellence*, individually and collectively. There is scarcely anything that we cannot turn from literal to symbolic mode, thereby sometimes transmuting the profane into something close to sacred. Such transformation hugely increases the weight of significance something can be made to carry for us. Think of what we've made two crossed pieces of wood stand for! On the smaller scale of personal symbols, things that in an individual's life come to hold a heaviness of portent beyond the routine weight of everyday transaction, there is certainly much reading-in involved. Although some of the kingfisher's significance in my scheme of things derives from its intrinsic nature, from its colour, brightness, the speed and fleetingness of its appearances, as much if not more stems from the coincidence of sightings with particular moods and moments in my life.

We were visiting the asylum to see Auntie Carrie, my father's aunt. It was our first visit to her there. She had moved from the family farm near Dunfanaghy, a rambling, spacious house grown ramshackle over time, when it had become too hard for her two remaining sisters to look after her. First to an old folks' home, then to another, then a third, where she had caused some kind of trouble, and so to here. Washed up on the desolate shore of the asylum, beached and bereft, a reluctant survivor in the life-raft of her unwanted longevity, visited sporadically by nephews and nieces and, because of their age and the difficulties of the journey, scarcely at all by her sisters. I remembered her vaguely from our trips to Donegal, though to a child's perspective she was a marginal figure there, saying almost nothing, and quite eclipsed by her brother Willie, a bright-eyed, tousle-haired old man who we were told was 'odd', but who charmed us with unexpected gifts (a blown swan's egg, an empty tortoise-shell, polished flints he said were arrowheads) and stories so outrageously untrue they made us laugh. He died the year before Auntie Carrie left the farm. Whilst Uncle Willie had been labelled 'odd', little was said about Carrie, beyond the fact that some terrible tragedy had befallen her and that she 'hadn't been herself' since it had happened. Madness was never mentioned, but we knew, as children do, that something in her life had gone seriously awry, leaving her sad and broken. 'Don't worry if she cries,' my brother and I were warned before meeting her for the first time, 'sometimes children make her cry.' We were wary of her strangeness.

That first visit to her in Armagh had not gone well. We had taken her for a drive, offered sweets, asked about her room in the asylum. Was she comfortable? What was the food like? She didn't reply. I sat in the back seat with her and she held my hand tightly, staring at me with immense, fathomless, tear-filled eyes. As we approached the gates of the asylum again, she said in a perfectly normal, steady voice, 'Please don't take me back there.' These were the only words she spoke all afternoon. My father went back inside with her, leaving us to walk by the stream and see the kingfisher. 'It's a shame your father wasn't here to see it.' But he was left that afternoon to watch a sadder, slower flight, limping brokenly along the last stretches of a river of tears. The colour had all but left her life by then; she sat through the days drained and unhappy, letting time break over her, just waiting for submergence in its tides.

People have different ways of calibrating their lives, of taking stock of where they are and what they've done, of cutting notches on some personal totem that marks their progress through the years. Birthdays, Christmases, weddings, funerals, christenings, traditionally afford occasions when we can take such bearings. Or we may find revisiting a familiar place after long absence, or meeting someone we have not seen for years, acts to stimulate this kind of pause for thought. Sometimes, though, these periodic self-assessments, where we stop and take orientation beyond the immediate compass points of present preoccupation, may be sparked off by more idiosyncratic factors. In my own case, kingfishers have become an unlikely stimulus for such reflection. Each time I see them now makes me review previous sightings, think about where I was on each occasion, recall how the years have taken me down the stream of life between each technicolour appearance and, looking upstream, consider what the future seems to hold and how far it may stretch before all the quickness and colour of life vanishes and my waters dry into extinction.

Years separated the Armagh sighting from the next time I saw a kingfisher. In the intervening period Auntie Carrie had died, Ulster had lurched into terrible violence, my parents had aged and I had almost grown up. This is, of course, to view things through the pinhole of the familiar, that protective circumscription of awareness that prevents the full enormity of what happens from crushing our frail individual perception. The scale of time's passing, the weight of human sediment carried even in a second of its waters, is truly dwarfing. Between my first two sightings, billions of lives had forged their way forward, moment by moment, encountering all the pains and pleasures of existence. In the interval marked out by these two pinprick moments of sentience, many thousands of kingfishers had followed the life-patterns incised in their genes like indelible multicoloured tattoos. They had hatched and flown and fed and mated, leant their colour to countless river-bank moments, most unobserved by any human eye. The planets had wheeled in their gigantic orbits, the sea's tides had scoured a billion new erosive lines into the fabric of the land-masses. And the inner oceans of the blood that course through all of us had turned time's weathering cycles around countless different human seascapes, marking them with their passage as surely as the tide's coming and going is written on a coastline. How much water under how very many bridges! We delude ourselves daily with our hours and minutes, our records of what happens; the real arithmetic of time's passing is incalculable.

So, years later, with all that that entails, a second kingfisher was poised to burst across my notice. I was in Hillsborough, a small attractive County Down town with a cathedral, and what used to be the Governor's residence to give it ideas above its station. There is a popular forest park there, with a lake and pleasant walks. It was another Sunday, but it must have been September or October.

I remember a feeling of autumn in the air, leaves underfoot, a smell of dampness. My parents and I had just walked round the lake and were heading back to the car. I was cold, having had to match my pace to my father's steps, which were faltering by then. We paused, just where the path curved towards the car park, to look back at the lake. At that moment, with a loud *chee-chee, chee-chee* and a whirr of wings, a kingfisher flew low across the water, its momentary blue breathtakingly bright against the grey. Then it vanished again into the surrounding vegetation. We stood for a long while waiting, in case it might reappear, but we didn't see it again. Like a piece of shrapnel from a sudden chromatic explosion, it burst across our vision only once, a brief flash of colour, incandescent and then gone, like a momentary firework, blazing and then extinguished.

We came very close to not seeing it. The near miss made me think about coincidences, intersections, chance, what is versus what might have been. If we had taken a minute longer on our walk, if one of us had stopped to tie a shoelace, if we had not turned at that precise moment but had instead headed straight to the car, it would have passed us by. The nearly unseen kingfisher underlined the extent to which the merely accidental seems to plot the courses that our lives take, determine the paths we follow, the precise pinprick points at which we meet with love, laughter, death.

My mind was already tuned in to the question of causation, partly by reading those no doubt inadequate treatments of Chaos Theory that were so popular at the time. These sought to trace lines, weave links of intricate connection, between the micro-scale of tiny happenings – a butterfly's wings opening, a child laughing, a fish rippling the surface of some muddy pool, its dorsal fin, like some living pencil, marking a line across the water – and macro-scale events like storms and earthquakes. I had also begun to think about the great Buddhist theory of causation, *paticcasumupadda*, or interdependent origination, which likewise suggests, though in very different terms, how every action has a reaction; how the whole

complex network of what happens can be reduced to the princi-
ple of 'where this is, that becomes; where this ceases, that ceases
to be'. Endless skeins of consequence rippling back and back from
the point of every present alignment; everything explained by the
outcome of individual desires, attachments, and the actions stemming from them; an endlessly subtle mapping of the essential interdependence of things at every moment (which has been described
as 'the unique and central teaching of Buddhism'). But, weighing
far more heavily than such inchoate intellectual ventures, and
making me reach first for the analogy with shrapnel and explosion
on sighting my second kingfisher, was a much more direct
encounter with something that had almost happened.

I think about the explosion still, all these years later, and wonder what would have happened *if*. It had happened just a couple
of days before we went walking in Hillsborough. I felt the breath
of Ulster's terror on me that day. It came very close in the witnessing of other people's hurt and screams and blood, but it didn't
strike me directly. I am one of the lucky ones. I wasn't killed, or
maimed, or scarred. The blast left me unscathed; the injuries I saw
were minor. I don't think my mother or father realised how close
I'd been or how shocked I still felt. All the way round the lake, I
kept asking myself, what if I'd left the house a minute later,
stopped to tie my shoelace, walked just a little slower?

It was a small bomb, as such things go, one of three planted to
explode within minutes of each other. They were left in various locations in the centre of Lisburn, the sprawling market town in
which we lived, eight miles from Belfast. Warnings had been given,
but they were either deliberately misleading or just confused, and
were at very short notice. The police were unsure which streets to
close, where to shepherd people to safety. There were sirens,
shouts, an air of desperation and confusion. I was walking along
Railway Street as it was being emptied and taped off at either end.
I was one of the last people to leave it. Joining the crowd of frightened people who were milling about uncertainly behind the incident tape, I looked back down the eerily deserted street that I had

just walked up. And, as I turned to look, one of the bombs went off, blowing the windows out of the shop it had been left in, showering the pavement with glass, flame and debris. I had walked past it no more than a minute earlier. If the explosion had happened just a little sooner, I would have been caught in the full force of the blast.

In Armagh I was predisposed to think about unpredictability, the sudden eruptions of insanity in the psyche, and the kingfisher there came to take on something of this hue, helped to parse and define a sense of madness. In Hillsborough, the recentness of my escape made that kingfisher take on a far heavier mantle of coincidence and accident than anything just suggested by the bird's momentary appearance and our sighting of it. It became a kind of living totem, symbolising the fact of chance, how our lives intersect with events, places, people, moments, the way in which whole chains of happenstance lead to any particular coincidence of lifelines in time and space.

Why, out of the maelstrom of possibilities, does just this one particular outcome solidify into the reality of what happens? From the moment of our conception to our death, we are surrounded by a dense crowd of seemingly possible alternatives. Why our precise moment of beginning and not some other genesis? Why that sperm and not some other? Why this particular pairing of a couple? Why this particular second for their coupling, our conception? The bladed, razored edge of chance and causality cuts through what might have been to yield up our experience. The strangeness of things being just so, the way they are, can strike us with particular force when we come as close to a radically different outcome as I came to the bomb. Such only tiny alterations would be needed to change utterly the whole fabric of our lives.

If the bomb's timer had run down just a little faster, I might not be here. If the pilot of the German bomber above Alexandria, decades before that, had banked another degree before releasing the bomb whose shrapnel shattered my father's leg, I might not be here. If any of a thousand little kingfisher flashes streaking their trajectories of chance across the nerves of each moment were altered millimetrically, I might not be here. We seem suspended in an unlikely network of coincidences, fragile and improbable as the intricate detail of a spider's web beaded with dew on a winter's morning.

Auntie Carrie's life had been harrowed by a tragic and terrible intersection which, so family tradition supposed, had pushed her over that ever-present drop which edges sanity with madness. The web of her life had been brutally torn. In thinking about her madness, and what sparked it, and my own near miss with terrible injury or death, I've come to revisit often that ancient and no doubt interminable site of human inquiry, the extent to which our fates are immovably set, with us caught helpless as flies in the amber of time and space, and the extent to which we are free agents who can make things happen, who can mould things to our will. Is it possible for things to happen otherwise, for history to unfurl a different story, dance to a different tune? *Might* Auntie Carrie never have gone mad, *might* we never have seen that kingfisher, *might* I have been killed by that bomb? If a butterfly somewhere had failed to open its wings, if a child had cried instead of laughed, if a fish had altered by the merest fraction where it had swum, could everything have worked out differently? Or, does what happens happen the way it does and in no other manner because it is set rock-hard in an embrace of predetermination which dictates only one outcome, which demands that time carries only this one particular cargo?

There is a photograph of Auntie Carrie's son at home in Ireland, in a drawer containing the hundreds of photos that a family accumulates over time. We remember who he is but have forgotten his name, and my father and his four siblings, who would have known, are all dead now. There is no one left to ask. No doubt when the next generation looks through this cache of images they will have no idea who he is, or what his story was. The picture shows him as a boy of maybe five, with what is probably a new bike (perhaps a birthday present?). He is a serious-looking child, with his mother's dark, fathomless eyes staring unsmilingly at the camera. I suppose the fact of this single, unframed photo's survival down the years, and its intersection with my life, is as improbable in its own way, as nearly missed, as any kingfisher sighting. It was only years after our visit to Armagh that I found it and was told who he was, what had happened to him, given more than the usual euphemisms for Auntie Carrie's madness.

May 7, 1915, around 2.15 p.m. What, I wonder, was Auntie Carrie doing then? Was she sitting in the front room of the then not yet ramshackle farmhouse, sewing, reading, chatting with her sisters? Or was she outside, breathing in the sweet spring air, taking in the beautiful views across Sheep Haven Bay and Horn Head? Was she content? What sort of a person had she been before the moment that signalled the end of her composure? Why should it seem so strange to think that, had we been there watching, we could have seen, described, witnessed precisely what was happening there, at the self-same moment that we know exactly what was happening some 260 miles southwest, about eight miles off the coast at Kinsale? And on 7 May 1900, had what was going to happen fifteen years later already set and solidified out of the magma of possibilities which must course beneath every moment of our lives, ready to erupt into actuality? And on 7 May 1800? 800? 1,000 years before Christ? Or, if one of time's countless kingfishers had flown at a slightly different speed, dived instead of perched, could a whole new sequence of events have been nudged into history?

How only minutely things would have to have been altered to stop what happened from happening! The apparent provisionality, the utter contingency, of any moment can become haunting if it comes to carry a burden which, thereafter, we desperately wish was otherwise. Auntie Carrie's son, seventeen years old, is a crewman on the great Cunard liner *Lusitania*. In 1915 it's still the largest, fastest and most luxurious passenger ship in the world. Thirty-two thousand tons, capable of carrying over two thousand passengers, she had crossed between Liverpool and New York two hundred times since her maiden voyage in June 1907. On her second voyage she set a new speed record by completing the passage between Cobh (Queenstown) and New York in four days, nineteen hours, fifty-two minutes. People still vaguely associate the name 'Lusitania' with disaster, but few recall the details. It was torpedoed by a German U-boat, we even know which one (U-20) and the captain's name (Kapitan-Leutnant Walter Schweiger). The great ship sank in less than twenty minutes. Close to 1,200 people drowned, Auntie Carrie's boy among them. My father would have been the same age then as I was that Sunday afternoon in Armagh when we visited the asylum. I picture the news of his cousin's death winging its way towards him, news of her son's death winging its way towards Auntie Carrie, a piece of unfeathered shrapnel, clad in all the grim resplendence of the shocking, breaking upon their minds with the force of an explosion.

I've described kingfishers as red, as blue, as sapphire, as shimmering turquoise, as burnished chestnut, as blue-green. Depending on the light and the angle at which you see them, they can strike the eyes in different ways. Like some terrible monochrome kingfisher, capable of only a single interpretation, allowing only one seeing, catching the light from only one angle, U-20's unexpected torpedo shot out along precisely that disastrous trajectory which struck the *Lusitania* amidships. Schweiger's log records: '90 degrees travelling 22 knots. Single torpedo launched 2.12 p.m.' Was there no butterfly that might have shut its wings, shimmered a tiny alteration through the cobweb of events in which this disaster was embedded, changing the heading, speed, time, preventing it from ever happening?

There were approximately eight hundred survivors. One hundred and fifty rescued by *The Wanderer*, a Manx fishing boat which had seen the liner founder. To a mother who had lost her only child, though, such figures bring little comfort. Two of the saved were momentarily sucked into one of the *Lusitania's* four giant funnels as she sank and shot back out when the sea water caused a boiler to explode. To have been in precisely the place, at precisely the time, for that unlikely chain of happenings to grip and set one free again, makes visible for a moment the iron lace-work of causation on which we clamber, the torque noosed round each moment.

I visited the farm in County Donegal not long ago. The house has been abandoned, left to tumble down. The new owners live in a bungalow built in front of this abandoned hulk. I walked down to the lake, which the property encompasses, half expecting to see a kingfisher. Uncle Willie always said that they nested in the bank of one of the feeder streams. But all I saw were swans, maybe fifty or sixty, an enormous flock, perhaps among them de-scendants of the same birds whose blown egg I had been given and which still sits in a drawer at home, an icon of emptiness pro-viding a reminder of all the vanished lives once lived here.

The swans' whiteness made me think of blanking things out, of forgetfulness, of painting over, of the way in which, however foul and fierce life may be, alongside it other creatures (other peo-ple) sail along serenely, unaffected by the turbulence which has rocked us, impervious to the impact of things on others. No doubt there were swans swimming here, majestically, as they have swum for years, on that fateful May afternoon nearly a century ago; as they were swimming when poor mad, tormented Auntie Carrie was laid to rest at last; as they are swimming now, white, unperturbed, as these words are read and as unseen marine life further encrusts and invades the wreck of the *Lusitania*, still there, fathoms down, under the sea off Kinsale.

In fact, Auntie Carrie showed little of the madness that was talked about in whispered tones. 'She's never been the same since then, you know', 'She's not herself', 'It was just too much for her', 'She couldn't bear the loss', all the euphemisms for a mind pushed beyond its bounds of tolerance. Apart from her silence, her ten-dency to want to hold hands with children and to sometimes cry, and her staring, almost expressionless eyes, she showed no trace of anything as colourful as what 'madness' suggested to me. The only real madness I witnessed that day in Armagh came just after sighting the kingfisher, when we saw a woman walking along a path which ran parallel to the rear of the main asylum building. At first she seemed unremarkable, ordinary, just like us. But when she had walked maybe twenty paces she stopped abruptly, as if her path had been blocked by some invisible obstacle. Then she turned round, retraced her steps and, after going the same distance in the other direction, stopped abruptly again. Then she turned and re-started her pacing. The pattern was performed repeatedly. It was as if she inhabited an invisible cage and was boxed in by its immovable, undetectable constraints. At each turn, as she reached her glassy, invisible barrier, it was as if some fiery, terrible kingfisher dived into her bloodstream and tore from there whatever nerves control facial expression. Her face contorted in a massive, ghastly spasm as she performed each about-turn and then continued, expressionless, with her measured pacing. I still wonder about her sometimes, long dead by now, about what terrible forces forged the constraints she laboured under, about how the world looked from her perspective, about the fact that she too was part of the cargo of time that passed between two kingfisher sightings, that I was a small part of her story as she is of mine. That we are all, to some extent, boxed in. Who was she, I wonder, who mourned her, where is she buried? Has her story, her spirit, quite vanished from the cosmos?

As if in contrast to their astonishing beauty, kingfishers' nest holes will strike most people as utterly disgusting. Usually made in a riverbank, the holes lead maybe two feet in to a nest chamber, where the bird lays its clutch of half a dozen pure white eggs. The yolk shows through them pinkly when they're fresh, a blush betraying the fact that this little oval sepulchre is a chromatic time-bomb ready to crack and burst into colour. They hatch in about three weeks and the chicks are fed on fish, the remains of which gradually accumulate around them so that you can smell a nest hole from quite some distance off. That they are born and raised amidst the omnipresent, all-pervasive stench of decay somehow increases the bird's attractiveness. Why should this be so? Maybe it's the sense of contrast, the fact that such beauty, so alive a thing, can be so contiguous to such putrefaction. Or perhaps such an interdependence of beauty and ugliness is suggestive of redemption, so that we who are faced with the knowledge of our finitude can extract from it some little parable of resurrection that suggests the possibility of meaning beyond the ripe fish-smell of death. Does the bursting forth of so much colour, such vibrancy of life, from a foul-smelling hole in the earth comfort our terrible knowledge of our own eventual occupancy of the grave?

What is a kingfisher? (The same question can be put, with the same effect, to any life-form that strikes the imagination.) It's tempting to reach for naming's obvious answer, or the safe detail of ornithological specialisation. It's easy to think of it singly, individually, simplistically, bounded by the frames of individual sightings. But, if we widen the focus to take in the bird's life-story – from egg, to chick-amidst-the-fish-stink, to fledgling, to adult, to endless flights and dives, retrievals, matings, to its becoming a corpse, slowly settling with its own small fish-reek into the waters, its flesh pecked at by the minnows it used to feed on – we can move some way towards another answer. And, if we expand again in terms of time and in terms of scale, the picture acquires further definition. All the years of development, evolution, growth, this line of life stretching back from any bird today through the almost endless annals of geological time, through ancient fossils, to the earliest cellular stirrings, the first disturbance of life upon the planet's surface, the point of genesis from which we all began – bacteria, kingfishers, humans, dinosaurs. A bright line from there to here, a kingfisher flash from one end of life's river to the other, nudging the invisible barriers of evolution with possibility's warmth and colour. Thinking beneath the feathers, beneath the skin, beneath the bone, to the world of cells and nuclei and mitochondria and chromosomes, we can hear even more of the notes in the fantastic organic symphony that maintains and animates across time this wonderful, colourful bird-melody. Somewhere in the delicate runnels of the sub-visible, molecular, atomic level, branded into the finally incomprehensible stuff of being, are the replicative mechanisms to sustain the continuance of this species. These contain coded instructions to pace along this path, so far, no further; to turn, re-pace and turn again; to make these expressions, gestures, sounds. And such thinking back, and back again, can be paired with a movement forward, looking along the same bloodline to the future and the destinies it holds.

'Look! A kingfisher!' How little our language catches; how superficial our perception is! How quickly we categorise, frame, limit everything around us. Of course we need some shorthand, some familiar names, some abbreviations; the daily business of living would soon grind to a halt if we had always to confront the reality of things head on. Sometimes, though, language seems to cut the umbilical between perception and wonder too soon. We are so keen to proceed with namings that we end up forgetting what such abbreviations really stand for.

After the one at Hillsborough I saw kingfishers on various occasions in Ireland, mostly on the shores of Lough Neagh, once from a train between Antrim town and Lisburn, a sudden burst of colour unnoticed by the other passengers, and once on the beautiful Shimna ('River of the Bulrushes') near Newcastle. The last time I saw one was in Wales. In the space between that sighting and the one on the Shimna, I had left Ireland, changed jobs several times, travelled, married, had a daughter. So much water under so very many bridges; another massive tonnage of history between these two tiny punctuation marks. I'm not sure if Lucy saw it. She was only two and more interested in splashing in puddles than in seeing some incomprehensible bird. But perhaps its blaze of colour will have left some minute imprint on her nascent memory. Her name reminded me of Carrie's son, for the *Lusitania* was often fondly referred to as 'The Lucy.' My great-aunt's tragedy came into focus as I pointed out the kingfisher to my daughter, knowing that such a loss could well make sanity list and founder. What intersections will there be in Lucy's life? Are they already hatched and inevitable and set, beyond any hope of changing, or

21

is her path ahead more fluid, bound only by the ore of numerous laws' out-workings, rather than the iron of specific predetermined outcome? All the while, as she grows up, ages, dies, the parallel lives of kingfishers will happen. And on the lake behind a derelict farmhouse in Donegal, which will hold no meaning for her, the swans will glide serenely across the waters, as oblivious to all her pains and passions as she will be to all that happened there.

Sometimes I think of Carrie's son unborn, still nestling curled, warm, embryonic, in the soft twilight of her womb. I wonder if she walked, pregnant, by the lake, looking out at the swans, never imagining what emptiness and blankness would torpedo her life in the waters of the future. If my daughter's womb is ever filled with the load of life, what scenes, I wonder, will she look out on as she waits, what lies in store for my grandchildren? Will they look back down the stream of time that bore them and see there anything of the brightness of vanished lives? Mine? Auntie Carrie's? Her son's? The ancient people who occupied the area around that ramshackle farmhouse in Donegal long ago, who made Uncle Willie's flint arrowheads (for that is indeed what they were)? All part of the human line, pacing its continuing story across the millennia, side by side with kingfishers, swans, butterflies, living filaments of enormous length, of awesome complexity, stretching back to that moment of common conception when life first congealed, and on to who knows what destinations.

Although it may seem a grotesque, almost gruesome comparison, I now sometimes think of kingfishers as scalpels, their striking line of colour as they fly upstream is like a razor slash, a bladed incision into the ordinary, so that, for a moment, the bland skin of the present is torn open and time's secret innards spill out. The mundane is unzipped and zipped up again, revealing things below the surface that are shocking and beautiful and suggestive of another dimension to things beyond our everyday routines.

Sometimes I think of imagination as a kingfisher, diving into time's waters repeatedly, beading scores of ideas together and then disbanding them again. It's easy to imagine links between things that are sundered, to draw lines on the map of what happened that were never there. To weave a wordy mesh between me, now, the boy who perished in the sea just off Kinsale, his grief-maddened mother, my daughter, the mad woman pacing in Armagh, and all those others whose stories overlap and inter-connect and interpenetrate, or pass each other by with only the most feather-light breath of contact.

It's easy to thread through the lifeline of language a whole ship's manifest of memories – the ark of family, clan and species. But can we really salvage much from all that is past? We may be able to cast a net of words and save some sense of what hap-pened, but we are powerless to change history; its butterfly wings have closed as tightly as the jaws of a trap. So, to that extent at least, the present is already held in a vice that sets the scene for what can happen. But, if we let them, memory and imagination can plumb something of the depth of that present. Such sound-ings set the pitch of time to another key, allow us to discern a dif-ferent register of resonance, to hear the ultra-low frequency of something like eternity sounding mysteriously, like whale song, in the still unfathomed reaches of our bloodstream.

And, in the end, the impossible question: is our life punctu-ated by a flash of kingfisher colour as something transcendent im-pinges on us, or are we imprisoned in the world we see, earthbound and clumsy, shackled immovably to the chains of our finitude? Is there, behind the stink of fish in a dark hole in the earth, some hope of bright colour beyond it? I've looked hard for the fly-past that might herald such otherness. Sometimes I have been surprised by something unexpected, sudden, beautiful, seem-ingly like the stuff of fantasy, too exotic for the mundane world. But have I really seen it? Sometimes nothing much seems to stir above the waters of the ordinary. But has my vigil been sufficiently keen to catch that sudden flash of sapphire light? In the end, the final answer, if there is one, lies downstream, where all the cur-rents of water, air, flesh and feather are inexorably leading us.

FERRULE

Like almost everyone, I picked up language like a dog running through a field of burrs. Suddenly, without any effort or deliberation, you find yourself peppered with words. The first one or two will be noticed by those around you. After all, they spend a lot of time throwing them, hoping they will stick. But soon they cover you so completely that their continuing accretion goes unnoticed. Grammar, pronunciation, vocabulary, stealthily sink their hooks into the deepest furrows of the mind and take root there.

A burr-covered dog will roll and groom until his coat is clear. Language clings to us unshakeably, sending its tendrils to creep through us like ivy, finding some purchase in even the most intimate interstices of silence. So thorough is this subtle penetration, at once empowering and imprisoning, that, by the time we are equipped to think about it, it is impossible to imagine what life without language would be like. No exertion of memory can retrieve, intact and intelligible, the way in which we acquired this second skin of words. The genesis even of the most vital parts of our vocabulary is lost, hidden in that strange dead-ground which occupies so much of everyone's biography – time we have inhabited but have no memory of passing through, our presence here, articulate and grown, the only evidence of ever having been there.

Can anyone bring to mind that moment of epiphany when they realised they had a name, or when mute shapes on paper – 'mother', 'tree', 'dog', 'grass' – first spoke the burden of their meaning to us?

Who can remember when they first heard the sound of 'genocide' and took into mind all the terrible dimensions of its menacing enormity? Or when the eye first met 'redolent' on the page and translated its net of sound and sense into another gentle weapon in meaning's potent armoury? Who can recall that subtle loss of virginity when the mind and mouth and breath conspired together to send the erotic vocables of 'sensuous', 'lithe' and 'nubile' spinning into the realm of spoken desire? Such moments, however epochal, are lost as surely within our individual horizons as the first words spoken by *Homo sapiens* are lost in the dwarfing silence of prehistory and the ensuing centuries of endless chatter.

Strangely, though, I can remember with complete exactitude my first encounter with a seemingly far less important word – 'ferrule'. Perhaps this verbal burr was thrown so clumsily that I could not help but feel it landing on my consciousness, or maybe it came at a time when I was peculiarly sensitive to what it allowed me to feel and think. For whatever reason, its trajectory and impact have left an indelible impression.

My father walked with what he called a 'drop-foot'. This gave his steps a signature of their own, so that even if he was out of sight you could still recognise his approach along the ringing surface of the pavement which ran the full length of our street. Every alternate step slapped down harder on the ground than normal, sending out a simple two-beat rhythm: soft-*slap*, soft-*slap*, soft-*slap*. One of the few times I ever saw him really angry was when a gang of boys behind him imitated his footfalls. The soft-*slap*, soft-*slap*, soft-*slap* of his tune was almost drowned out by their crude exaggeration, a soft-*wham*, soft-*wham*, soft-*wham*, accompanied by raucous laughter. He rounded on them, a stern man in a rage, and they dispersed, startled that their simple parody had hit home so surely. The drop-foot was the result of a leg wound sustained in a German bombing raid on Alexandria during the Second World War. He had spent months recuperating on hospital ships, and in sanatoria in Egypt, South Africa and England. Sometimes he would let us run our fingers along his right shin. We cautiously explored the six-inch furrow left by the shrapnel, felt the out-of-kilter bone, and were mesmerised by the damage flesh could bear.

As children, my brother and I would sometimes wait for him to return from work in the evening, listening for his steps at the top of the street and then crouching behind the bushes in the front garden, giggling, our ears straining to measure his approach and time the moment when we would leap out in ambush. His suit always held the sweet aroma of tobacco and the smell of steam-trains, which in those days still ran on the commuter line between Belfast and our leafy suburb.

Often his soft-*slap*, soft-*slap*, soft-*slap* was accompanied by the regular staccato tap of a walking stick. The handle of his favourite ashplant was polished by his grip. The whorls and knots of the wood grain were like transplanted fingerprints. The intimacy of the grip was such that you could imagine a two-way transfer, with the wood's swirling lines and contours being echoed in the flesh. More than anything else I associated with him – coats, keys, cigarette case – the stick seemed imbued with my father's presence. It was as if his heavy leaning on it had somehow bled something of his substance into it. Whenever I saw the stick I thought of his walk and its unique sound-signature.

One evening his rhythm was subtly different. Soft-*slap*, rattle-tap, soft-*slap*, rattle-tap. Later I found him carefully examining the tip of his walking stick. Seeing my interest he explained, 'The ferrule's coming loose.' He wobbled the small brass cap that cupped the end of the stick. 'Look, it's worn out.' He showed me the tiny holes in the scratched metal of the base, worn wafer-thin by miles of contact with the ground. 'We'll get a new one on Saturday.'

The shop we visited the following Saturday remains one of the most vivid images of place which I retain from childhood. We took the train 'up to Belfast' as people always said then, as if the city were some sort of celestial region to which one had to ascend. From the dilapidated grandeur of the station at Great Victoria Street (long since vanished into rubble) we walked to Cornmarket, part of Belfast's old commercial heart. My father's steps beside me (soft-*slap*, soft-*slap*, soft-*slap*) were a reassuringly familiar presence. Visits to the city were rare and I was still awed by its bustle and scale, but thought myself too old at nine to consider holding hands. He carried the stick but didn't use it. Perhaps the rattle of the loose ferrule intruded a discordant note into the accustomed rhythm of his walk.

Braithwaite's (or 'R.W. Braithwaite & Son, Gentlemen's Accessories, Estab. 1887', to give the full wording on the faded gold lettering above the door) was old-fashioned even then. Its exterior was dull and understated, with a window display that in these brash days of self-advertisement would scarcely qualify for such a description. Inside it was dark and quiet and smelt of tobacco and leather. And always in the background, like some strange percussion instrument, the sound of wood hitting wood, as customers tried out, or staff rearranged, the racks of walking sticks. My father and Mr Braithwaite, Jr, a man of about his own age, were evidently acquainted and treated each other with that mutual respect which is born from a feeling of knowing and being content with your own place in the scheme of things and feeling no inferiority to anyone.

By 'Gentlemen's Accessories' Braithwaite's seemed principally to mean belts, wallets, walking sticks, umbrellas, cigarette cases, pipes and tobacco pouches. Yet, however genteel and dowdy the shop's appearance might have been, the vestiges of weaponry seemed somehow to cling to it indelibly. I had a sudden and irreverent image of the sombre Mr Braithwaite, decked out in skins and war paint, helping my father to choose a spear or club.

The variety of sticks was staggering. There were scores of different styles and shapes, in woods of different colours and textures, ranging from knobbly blackthorns to smooth ashplants like my father's. The handles could be plain or showy, straight or curved. Some were topped with bone or silver. And it was somehow impressively adult, evidence of a grown-up-ness I was years removed from, that my father knew of, and was known in, a place of such serious specialism. But more powerful than any other impression was astonishment that a word existed to describe the metal cap affixed to the end of a walking stick. It seemed to me amazing that there was a name for a device designed to perform so small a task as protecting the wood from damage every time it touched the ground.

Who had invented the object? Who had invented the word? Which had come first? Who had said it first? Why just that particular sound and shape, 'ferrule', and not some other? Since my father introduced me to it I had turned the word over in my mind and occasionally whispered it to myself. Prompted by its strangeness, I had reflected on the mysteries of language. Even within the modest lengths to which my childish vocabulary could carry such meditations, I was amazed at the delicate precision of naming and the enchanted possibilities that were opened up by talk. Standing in the sepulchral dimness of Braithwaite's, I thought of all the things that we have had to find words for and had a tribal sense of pride and belonging. I knew that I was being gradually initiated into the edifice of language which we have woven round our nakedness for centuries. (Though, at nine years old, I could not have found the right words, had not yet acquired the layers of language, to express such aboriginal sentiments.)

Walking back to the station my father's customary rhythm was restored: soft-*slap*, tap, soft-*slap*, tap, soft-*slap*, tap, over and over again as we made our way home. My mind beat time to each crisp tap of the newly repaired stick with a soundless recitation: 'ferrule', 'ferrule', 'ferrule', as the word slowly sunk its roots into the loam of my emergent vocabulary and became something known and familiar. Soon, of course, after its first appearance had inexplicably borne on the back of its novelty one of those startling little revelations that dot a life with unexpected moments of insight, 'ferrule' vanished into my word-store, only to be drawn out again at odd times, and then largely shorn of its strange initial numen.

Years later, though, it came back quite unexpectedly with all its potency restored. Some while after my father's death, I was sorting through some rubbish in the attic – books, photographs, old suitcases filled with the assorted oddments of a life – when, hidden in among some rusty golf clubs, I found his ashplant, cobwebbed and forgotten. It had long been displaced by crutches, then a wheelchair, and the rhythm of all our lives had been broken as my father's steps had faltered into illness and incapacity. Beneath the dust, the handle was still smooth and shiny from his grip, but the ferrule was loose and worn through, crudely symbolic of his final decrepitude (but then life is full of crude reminders). I wobbled it between my fingers and was taken straight back through the years to Braithwaite's, to the old rhythm of his steps, and to my discovery of 'ferrule'.

I thought about all the ferrules I'd developed and encountered since that moment of childhood awakening. I now know that people construct all sorts of bolstering devices and affix them to their lives, hoping that the ferrules of name, occupation, wealth, writing will sheath their awful vulnerability, somehow clothe their nakedness and protect them against the impact of all the hard surfaces they must daily encounter. And in the aftermath of decades of violence in Ulster, I realised that the scratch and tap of ferrules had grown almost deafening. But their sound held none of the easy innocence of utility that had issued from the one which had capped my father's walking stick. These metaphorical ferrules served a darker, masking function, a shoring up of old hatreds, a keeping together of sectarian splinters that, without them, might have gradually worked themselves free and simply disappeared – as today they show some signs of doing.

As I turned the stick in my hand and mused about the word, I remembered reading a romantic story once, where a crotchety old woman, soured by age and disappointment, is wooed back into the fold of life by a young friend. The point at which her rehabilitation is complete is marked when she abandons the stick that had become emblematic of her bitterness, planting it in a summer meadow bright with wildflowers and walking away unencumbered by it. Eventually it takes root there, green shoots spring from it and, in the years to come, it blossoms and bears fruit. There was no such life in the abandoned ashplant. Its deadness, like the death we all must face, was unambiguously complete. No seed for blossom here, yet, hoarded in its loose and worn ferrule, the little contours of its scratched and dented metal gravid with remembrance, lay a harvest of meaning richer by far, if also more troubling, than any merely happy ending.

MEDITATION ON THE PELVIS
OF AN UNKNOWN ANIMAL

Owl pellets were among the most prized possessions in the little hoard of natural treasures that I accumulated as a boy. The instincts of collector and beachcomber ran deep, so that my room was always littered with fir cones, feathers, bits of quartz, chestnuts, seashells, acorns and the like. Every walk would add to this scruffy, olid treasury. New finds (or swaps with friends) regularly revalued its exchange-rate, but, amidst all the fluctuations in this private economy, owl pellets held their value. In part, this was due to their scarcity – owls were rare in the countryside around us – in part, it was because they were forbidden. Few parents warm to the idea of an owl's rank, rodent-filled disemboguement and mine were no exception. But in addition to the allure of rarity and the appeal of thwarting parental prohibition, the pellets bore within them something of the mystery of killing and of death.

Owls tend to swallow their prey whole and cough up what can't be digested. Their pellets are large, slug-shaped compressions of fur and bones, spat out as the owl perches in its roost tree, digesting after a night's successful hunt. When fresh, or wet, they are repellent objects, reeking of decay and infested with worms and parasites. But, once dried out completely, they become hard, inert and odourless. In this state they are like globules of once molten granite, their densely packed ceratoid cargo swelling out their grey surface with all the promise of half-exposed fossils. Dissecting them reveals a treasure-trove of remains. Like little sarcophagi they bear within them a plenum of bones reaped from the owl's victims. Scarab-studded on the outside with shiny splinters from the exoskeletons of beetles, inside are the skulls and tiny bones of mice, shrews, frogs and small birds, embedded in a tangle of shredded fur and feather.

Once prised from the surrounding conglomerate waste of the pellet, the bones are clean and white, all trace of flesh and blood consumed with antiseptic thoroughness by the owl's digestive juices. After dissecting two or three, the windowsill in my bedroom resembled some miniature ossuary, the bones so light that shutting the door too vigorously would create sufficient air-currents to scatter them. I would sometimes rest a tiny femur, rib, or scapula in the palm of my hand, examining its design and marvelling at its smallness and perfection. Imagining the creature which had so recently hung its flesh upon this bony scaffolding led to frequent musings about its life and the manner in which one thing becomes another. Though the skulls held a predictably macabre appeal, it was the pelvises which most fascinated me. Usually they would be broken in half, though whether from the owl's beak or talons, or as a result of the digestive process, I was never sure. Occasionally, one would come out whole and, for whatever reason, these rarities were what constituted the real gold standard in my disreputable collection's black-market currency.

Why is it that some shapes make such a deep and immediate appeal, tugging at the sleeve of our attention with an insistence which demands that we take notice, whilst others cross and re-cross our line of sight repeatedly but are more or less unobserved? That question is close kin to the great mystery of attraction which, if solved, would explain so much about us. Why do some forms, faces, ideas move us to passion and others leave no trace of their existence? Is it possible that, deep in an unfathomable recess of the psyche, we have engraved upon us some secret hieroglyphics which delineate an arcane alphabet of symbols, so that when we encounter such shapes before us in the world we are simply bound to respond to them, prompted by their pre-existing inner echo? Are we dimly aware, prior to all sight of x-rays and anatomy textbooks, of the bony template we carry slung within us, according to whose blueprint our kind has trodden out its fantastic journey? Or does the pull of bones hark back to the campfire and that chapter in our history when slaughtering was done more openly, the blood and bone beneath the skin made common knowledge, instead of being kept so hidden that the perceived link between living animals and the meat we eat is frayed to breaking point? For whatever reason – archetype, collective unconsciousness, tribal memory or just personal idiosyncrasy – the pelvis shape has always struck me with particular force. It seems charged with meaning, totemic, something almost sacred.

Some people are disgusted by bones, because they see them as something dirty, unhygienic, fraught with the possibility of spreading the horrible contagion of decay. Or else they are so disturbed by such obvious and indissoluble reminders of their own inevitable fate that they wish to keep bones out of sight and mind. But, cleaned of their flesh, bleached white and naked, they have always struck me as objects of extraordinary beauty. Whether on the breathtakingly delicate scale of a mouse's vertebrae, or on the more massive measure of strength evidenced by the bony fortress of a horse's skull, they have about them such a sense of significance, destiny and history that one can understand the lure of relics, amulets and nostrums cast from their ore. It seems appropriate that the sacrum, the bone that forms the keystone of the pelvic arch, takes its name from the Latin for holy.

Bullfinches were a favourite prey of the nearest owls to us, easily recognisable in the pellets from the flat, thick-billed skulls. To cup a bullfinch's bones in your hand, to feel their almost nothingness and to know that woven into this desolate remnant was the brilliant colour of the plumage, the notes of a particular song, the shape and patterning of eggs, a whole life-cycle and history stretching right back to the dinosaurs, is to wonder at the terrible intricacies, the beauty and the savage violence of life's designs. The sheer scale of time, the complexity of relationships, the enormous energy required to arrive at the precise moment when owl killed finch, suggests a network of events at once so huge and subtle that it's hard to comprehend more than the tiniest fraction of it. To know that owl meat grows on such carnal ambrosia and that it draws from there its own incredible rapacious story is to feel some small measure of the massive voltage that surges through everything around us – though we do our best to earth it harmlessly through the trudging rubber soles of the mundane.

The earliest reliable fossil records of owls date from the Eocene, some forty to sixty million years ago, and they clearly evolved some millions of years before that. What does the ancient shape traced out by their presence on the earth suggest about the nature of the planet that has borne us, that has been host to both our species' blood and breath? Even now, the fugitive bones of generations of owls settle and decay where they fell, leaving their own unnoticed fingerprint upon the multi-creatured humus which sustains us all, their little cache of proteins broken down, recycled, eventually re-entering (through some other species' portals) the dazzling fabric of life. Even now, the whole pavan of hatching, hunting, killing, breeding, is being danced by Barn Owls, Elf Owls, Hawk Owls, Snowy Owls, Scops Owls and the scores of other species which make up the family *Strigiformes*. Moment by moment they are incising one of millions of intricate existential embroideries upon the tapestry of time. How do such patterns relate to ours? What can they tell us about the nature of nature, the valency of time and space?

As well as the miniature pelvises quarried from dried owl pellets, my collection came in time to boast larger specimens as well – a sheep's, a rabbit's, a fox's. Indeed, after I had thoroughly steeped it in bleach and left it outside to dry in the sun, I wore the fox's pelvis for a while, passing a leather thong through the twin holes of the *obturator foramen* and hanging it around my neck, a kind of natural crucifix, a bony cross upon which life had once become incarnate. This was in my long-haired teenage days when such jewellery did not excite censure or surprise among my peers. We were all frustrated shamans then, earnest pilgrims engaged in that eternal neanic quest for points of access between this world and what Georgia O'Keefe has called the 'Faraway Nearby'. Sex, drugs, speed, and rock and roll supplied our major conduits. As we grew older, other channels appeared, or else we lost heart and entered that dispirited state of mind which comes to believe that there is only one mundane and bounded world to live in.

Given my indigenous fascination with the pelviform, Georgia O'Keefe's pelvis paintings were like a set trap waiting to spring as soon as I set eyes on them. They closed around me with the force of revelation when I first saw them, splendidly reproduced in Viking Press's large-format book of her work. The pelvis series are now widely recognised as among O'Keefe's most striking paintings from the 1940s. The series features various perspectives on a cow's pelvis, painted with deft and eye-catching accuracy. In *Pelvis with Moon*, the whole bone is shown, hugely, but delicately, dominating the canvas, an abstract white colossus around and through which can be seen blue sky, white cloud, the moon and the dwarfed silhouette of a distant mountain range. *Pelvis with Blue* and *Pelvis III* show only part of the bone, with an endless depth of blue sky framed by its white whorls and portholes. In *Pelvis Red with Yellow*, it seems as though the sun itself is framed by the bone. Writing in the catalogue for her exhibition 'An American Place', O'Keefe said: 'When I started painting the pelvis bones I was most interested in the holes in the bones – what I saw through them –

particularly the blue from holding them up against the sky. They were most wonderful against the blue – that blue that will always be there as it is now, after all man's destruction is finished.'

It is this sense of the elemental, of something eternal, of dealing with ultimates, with absolutes, which gives these paintings so much of their power. Looking at them one has a sense of looking into the heart of things. Not the blood-filled fleshy pump thumping in our breasts which drives us for a while until it tires, but beyond it to the more durable abstract processes and forms on which everything depends. The paintings have a sense of looking through a powerful microscope at the mysterious sepulchral structure of cells and nuclei, at atoms and their dizzying particles, at the very stuff, the hidden infrastructure, of life itself.

The pelvis series, like many of O'Keefe's paintings of flowers, achieve some of their impact simply through a choice of scale, which ambushes the eye with unexpected size and makes it see things afresh, as surely as a koan momentarily de-rails the mind and briefly nudges our thinking onto some wholly novel track. Of course, the painting is exquisite. Magnification without the artist's skill would merely issue in the garish overstatement of an advertising poster. Nor is the pelvis series surreal in the manner of, say, Dali or Magritte, where the bizarre alteration of ordinary objects (molten watches in Dali's *The Persistence of Memory*, for example) or their unusual location (the apple obscuring the face of Magritte's *The Son of Man*) prompts a sense of the weird. The paintings in O'Keefe's pelvis series are at once more simple and profound. Avoiding gimmickry and artifice they plainly state, with the authority of intense and reverent insight, that this is how things are.

Without O'Keefe's example, I might not have had the courage of my native beachcombing convictions when, years after encountering her amazing paintings, I found an enormous pelvis wedged among some rocks on the shore near Fifeness, where Scotland's

East Neuk juts furthest out into the icy waters of the North Sea. Swathed in a pellet of seaweed, driftwood and detritus, it was as if the ocean, like some terrible owl, had disgorged from its innards a single shard of bone from one of its victims. I searched the area but found no other skeletal remains. The pelvis was some twenty-one inches measured from tip to tip across the iliac blades (each blade itself being almost eleven inches at its widest point). Each *acetabulum*, the socket where the rounded head of the femur snuggles securely into place, was a deep ovoid hollow some two and a half inches across by three inches long. It was a gruesome find. Under the hair-like tangle of seaweed it was discoloured with mould and slime. Here and there small gobbets of flesh, pale, putrid and unidentifiable with anything alive, still clung firmly to the bony anchor to which a body had once been moored. They still gave off the foul stench of rotting flesh despite a long immersion in the sea. And yet, for all its foulness, with O'Keefe's vision of beauty to inspire me, I tugged it free and took it home. It took weeks to clean it properly, scraping off the mould and flesh, steeping it in bleach strong enough to whiten but not dissolve the bone, leaving it to dry between soakings in the infrequent winter sun. But at last it was scoured clean enough to bring inside, where it sat like some eerie abstract sculpture, drawing all eyes to it as soon as people entered the room.

Like some sort of faithful spectral hound, the pelvis from Fifeness sits on the floor beside my desk as I write this nocturne, as if to remind me of what Miroslav Holub calls 'the dimension of the present moment' (in his book of essays of that title). Like a frozen shape in white lava, cooled into solidity over aeons, it seems ancient, volcanic, chthonic, utterly of the earth. And yet the anatomist's detailed mapping of the pelvis resembles nothing so much as lunar cartography, a peppering of names – Sea of Clouds, Bay of Rainbows, Lake of Dreams – attempting to claim from the moon's cratered, alien surface some human scale and sense. Sometimes I run my fingers slowly over its surface and recite its place names inwardly, a litany of secret geography: ramus of ischium, iliac crest, iliopectineal eminence, greater sciatic notch, symphyseal surface, picturing how the ligaments and musculature fit together, reconstructing a body in my mind from this extinct bone planet, the dark side of the moon of being.

For a long while I simply assumed, because of its size and weight, that it was bovine or equine in provenance. Now I'm not so sure. A visiting archaeologist, well practised in identifying bones and with years of experience in building up a reference catalogue of specimens, thought that, although it had probably belonged to an ungulate, it was much bigger than any cow or horse she had encountered. Perhaps it came from some massive Clydesdale cart horse, or, since it was found in Scotland, from a highland cow. Maybe some passing ship, plying the waters of the North Sea, had some zoo specimen on board which sickened on the voyage, and the remains were thrown overboard when it died. In some ways the uncertainty in identifying which species it belongs to adds to its potency as a device for heightening consciousness beyond the merely commonplace. Any bone, of course, will do as a reminder of both flesh and finitude. But the pelvis seems particularly apt, given that it holds the generative organs cupped within its bony girdle. What dramas of genesis have been played out within the arena of the loins once slung around, within, this bony stage of sex and death?

Once this great hulk of bone was no more than a grain, a speck of life within some tiny embryo, slowly knitting together into viable form. It was carried for months at the warm living core of some creature's being, drawing sustenance from its mother's blood, until it hardened into independence and could hold together the vital fabric of another sentient, moving, suffering life. Are the centuries of movement, stretching from the primeval mud to whatever modern pasturage this unknown animal last trod in, somewhere recorded in the pelvis's bony sediment? Just as the undulation of the waves stipple the shore's compacted tons of sand with an imprint of their motion, so is this calcified strand, from which the tide of individual being has long gone out, stippled by the vibrations of hoofbeats and by the more distant memory of swimming? Just as it is smoothed and hollowed to a snug embrace of curves and arches by the shoal of organs and flesh it once netted safely in its protective basin, is it likewise moulded by the stations of more distant function along its ancient way? Touching its cold, clean whiteness, I imagine it vivified by that warmth and vibration of life which can sunder and quicken the inertness of stone, mud and bone into being. And often the mind turns to that troubling question which gnaws so persistently at the edges of any consciousness fluent in the idiom of finitude: is the individual creature, of which this is a remnant, now utterly extinguished, completely erased, or does some trace of it somehow, somewhere, impossibly, survive? The fleeting individuated existence of a single unique life has left behind this more durable substrate like a question mark, as if to make us ask questions about its own continuance and ours. When we are gone and only our bones remain upon the earth, is that all that is left of us? And when those bones are pulverised to dust or ash and wholly dispersed, are we then utterly absent from existence, gone without remainder? Or is our momentary sentience somehow saved or transformed? Ideas of the soul, karma and rebirth, saviours, deities, enlightened beings, heaven, nirvana and such like, provide a range of escape capsules to bear us beyond the apparent terminus of death. But when we jettison our flesh and bones, do we not also lose any possible continuity of identity with what we think of as ourselves?

Sometimes, looking at the pelvis, I am reminded of the story of Sirima. Sirima was a wealthy prostitute in India at the time of the Buddha. She was widely famed for her beauty and skill in the arts of love. Grown disillusioned with her trade, Sirima opted for celibacy and became a valued lay supporter of the newly

WORDS OF THE GREY WIND

emergent order of monks. Inevitably, a young monk fell hope-lessly, completely in love with her. Before his love could be con-summated or rebuffed, however, Sirima fell victim to a deadly illness that was sweeping the country. The Buddha ordered that her naked body should be left exposed at the burning ground and that the lovesick monk should witness its decay. (To some West-ern perspectives the story is shocking and offensive. We need to remember that it wasn't an uncommon exercise in India to medi-tate on a corpse.) Faced so inexorably with the dissolution of the object of his love, the monk came to see the truth of the Buddha's teaching on impermanence and understood the logic behind his warnings against attachment.

The power of the story, beyond the dark drama of the merely gruesome, lies in the way in which it illustrates how the Buddha's *dharma*, the universal spiritual truth which he was concerned to communicate, is not just some abstract doctrine. It is, rather, something deeply inscribed on the very fundaments of our exis-tence. A problem with much religious thinking is that it seems de-pendent on a complicated superstructure of words, whose connection with the world of life and death is tenuous and ob-scure. Yet surely if it is only words which shore up its sense, if it can't be deduced from the irreducible elements of our being, if it is not written in the alphabet of bones and breath, a religious teaching cannot spell out anything of more than passing interest. Unless we can look at Sirima's nubile loveliness *and* at her de-composing corpse, at an owl's beautiful plumage and at the mess of bones from which its life is kindled, and see there the face of God, or *anicca*, or the *Tao*, then such purported ultimates have no sound claim to mould our vision of the way things are.

The first time I saw a human pelvis I was twelve years old. It was in a stone vault in the tiny graveyard at Loughinisland, a village in County Down known then only for its excellent trout fishing and ancient church ruins (the place has since become associated with one of Ulster's most brutal massacres). The graveyard was on the opposite side of the lough from where we parked. I, and a small tribe of cousins, rowed across to it one summer afternoon when our fathers were engrossed in fishing, standing like herons in their thigh-waders, silent, watchful, predatory, gracefully casting their lines. Overgrown and neglected, the vault's rusty metal door was, incredibly, unlocked, so we ventured in. There, laid out full length on two low, concrete platforms were the first human remains I had encountered, yellowed, dank and fascinating. The skulls and pelvises were what drew the eye. The rest of the bones had collapsed into a conglomerate mass of less easily identifiable splinters. We experienced that strange blend of trespass, reverence, disgust and curiosity which the remains of our kind can engender in us. We touched nothing, left the place as we had found it and told no grown-ups about our discovery.

Like the faces staring at us from old photographs, bones impose their own mute anonymity. Even where graves and vaults have names and dates inscribed upon them, this does not succeed in attaching any sense of person to the bones that they contain. Bones link us to the human swarm, the hive, the mass, the tribe. In our bones we have no name or age or standing, beyond that of our common species; we become just 'human remains'. And in such levelling there lurks the terror that, individually, we have no meaning either. What of the people lying in that lonely Loughinisland vault? Is the timbre of their individual voices still sounding somewhere in the incredible symphony of existence? Or, once their notes were uttered in whatever span of years the score allowed, did they disappear forever into silence, their uniqueness rendered altogether extinct and unrecoverable?

It's rare now for most of us to encounter the epiphany of bones. Cities shield from the sight of their citizens nearly all of the elemental organic processes – birth, illness, death, decay. Despite television's endless fare of disaster and violence, our finitude has been so hushed up, so cosmeticised, that it can sometimes almost be forgotten. Which – beyond its immediate aesthetic appeal – is why I keep the pelvis of a large unknown animal in my living space, an un-ignorable *memento mori*, and why I hang Georgia O'Keefe's paintings on my walls. They help remind me of that sometimes savage sense of the numinous which pervades so much of life's substance and, as such, provide useful touchstones against which to assess religious ideas. Bones are an excellent acid test for the adequacy of any world-view. They provide an earthing ballast which prevents thought from soaring off into those far reaches of the intellectual stratosphere beloved by theologians, where the oxygen of intelligibility becomes perilously thin.

O'Keefe's pelvis paintings, and many of her flower paintings too, are, I believe, authentic, non-partisan religious art of a sort that is badly needed. It is art which does not belong to any particular faith or denomination, but which speaks eloquently and with insight to a level of spirituality so fundamental that it's easy to overlook. Amidst all the swirling religious currents of our perplexing postmodern world, where our diversity of belief is still so often a source of conflict and confusion rather than of creativity, it is surely worth remembering the common icons and altars which we all carry within us. Compared to the shared sacramental bonds that they affirm, the differences between us seem almost laughably superficial.

The oldest bones so far discovered from our earliest known ancestor, *Australopithecus ramidus*, are only some 4.4 million years old (found at Aramis in Ethiopia). For almost all of its 4,600,000,000 years, the earth – itself a mere dust-speck in the universe – has been without us. The immensity of time, and the multiplicity of creatures that went before us, is at once humbling and inspiring. Against such a scale, do our current preoccupations and priorities really measure up a way of living that, on reflection, we would wish to countenance?

* * *

Owls' wing feathers are finely fringed or serrated along the leading edge, and their surface is covered with a downy pile. These adaptations deaden the noise as the bird beats through the air, allowing it (at least to human ears) entirely silent flight. If you hold an owl's wing feather in one hand and a comparably sized wing feather from, for example, a rook in the other, and move both hands up and down to simulate wing-beats, you can hear the rook's 'flight' but not the owl's. In a more innocent age than ours such adaptation might have been threaded into some naïve version of the argument from design, to try to prove the existence of God as creator, a deity whose omniscience attends even to such little details. Mindful of the kind of creator which the terrifying dynamics of nature might now spell out (think how many species are predatory or parasitic), contemporary theologians are more wary of such devices. But listening to the way in which the two feathers move through the air does suggest a way of characterising two important modes of thought, one of which has become so dominant that our flying has become lop-sided and we are at risk of flapping round and round in circles.

On the one hand there is the noisy clamour of our everyday discourse. Our ordinary diurnal intellection by which we plot our way ahead, moment by moment, investigate the things around us, communicate with our fellows, celebrate our delight and despair. This is the flight that gives voice to our thoughts and feelings and, refined into the objectivity of specialist discourse, allows science and technology to soar. It facilitates all the aerobatics which historians, psychologists, archaeologists, geographers and others delight in. On the other hand, there is a more subjective, less direct and logical mode, a silent gliding deep into the heart of things, hunting for that pulse of the elemental which they carry within them. O'Keefe's pelvis paintings fall into this category, as does the work of many other artists, poets and mystics. Such thinking (or is it seeing, dreaming, imagining?) has become increasingly out of favour in a world where matter-of-factness operates at such a level of superficiality that it denudes experience and information of all but its most obvious cladding. It may be more difficult, and less obviously useful, to see things from the perspectives afforded to our flight by such a meditative camber, but it may be essential to do so if, as a species, we are to remain airborne and able to continue our astonishing life-flight into the future.

LINEN

From the faded photographs, which are all we have left of her, you would never guess what colour her eyes were, and so one of the most striking things about her is already lost. For, according to those few who can still remember her, my great-grandmother's eyes were a quite startlingly brilliant blue. A family myth has it that this feature is what captured my great-grandfather's heart and made him marry her but, since we have come to believe that theirs was an age not given to letting the spontaneity of feeling override social and financial considerations, such romantic information is now taken with a pinch of salt. Turning through the family album, one photograph always strikes me with particular force. It shows her sitting in a straight-backed chair, a large square of linen spread across her knees. She has stopped working on it for the photograph, and is looking directly at the camera, but she seems to be focusing on something much further away. Her hands are relaxed on her lap but still hold the needle and crochet hook with which she has been picking out and embroidering her design. Something about her poise and expression arrests the eye. Even at this remove of years you can tell that the photograph has caught something of the person beyond the artificiality of any pose. The face invites inquiry, announcing eloquently in that wordless language of certain images that there is a life here as real as our own, with its own complex currents of desire, anxiety, contentment. To look at it is to feel oneself drawn into another world. But for all its interest and unexpected intimacy, the photograph is one of those sepia prints that gives a sepulchral solemnity to everything it frames. Even the piece of linen she is working on looks brown, as if time had reversed the bleaching process and returned it to the raw unfinished colour with which it left the loom. Its whiteness has completely vanished, just as the blue of flax flowers disappears before the cloth is wrested from the plant; just as the colour of my great-grandmother's eyes was lost in the process of fixing her image in a photograph. If we are ever to understand history we must attempt to put back into what happened the colours and textures which are so easily lost in time's transmission.

Although it is impossible to tell for sure, I like to think that the linen carver spread out on the desk on which I am writing is the same one that my great-grandmother is holding in the photograph. A carver is a small square or rectangle of linen designed to be put on top of a tablecloth at the head of the table, where the meat is carved, so that any spillage will necessitate only the washing of the carver rather than the whole cloth. Carvers are often intricately patterned with drawn thread work and embroidery, the first process relying on absence, the second on presence for its effect. Used together, their little acts of subtraction and addition, space and substance, can meld together into a harmony of balanced patterns, rather like the rhythms of speech, where sense relies on the symbiosis of sound and silence. This particular carver has at its centre an embroidered urn motif, overflowing with beautifully realised flowers. All around the border, meticulous drawn thread work has created a narrow strip of lace-like netting, the threads gathered and knotted into delicate diamond shapes.

Embellishing plain squares of linen into carvers or supper cloths (small tablecloths) was the kind of semi-recreational activity thought fitting for a genteel farmer's wife in nineteenth-century Ireland. No doubt my great-grandmother made scores of the things and I have no way of knowing if this one on my desk is the one pictured – the photograph doesn't catch enough detail to be certain. But it is, without doubt, a piece she worked on, and a harmless conceit to imagine that it's the one shown spread across her knees. It serves no real function on my desk beyond providing a ready sense of history, reminding me of all the hands that laboured to produce it before it reached my great-grandmother's lap, and all the things that have happened between her working on it and its current use. I said that it was spread out on the desk on which I am writing. That is not strictly accurate and does not do justice to the conceptual space between her time and mine. It is, rather, on the desk on which my computer sits. My use of keyboard and screen is radically unlike what she would have understood by writing. And the machinery whose weight now leaves its imprint on the linen is light years removed from the technology of the water-powered beetling mills which would have crushed its fabric into the close-weave mesh it still shows today.

To unravel the warp and woof of history, unpicking the fabric of the present and feeling back along each thread across the years, is as difficult a skill as drawing threads from a carver into line, where the slightest carelessness, a cut or tie in the wrong place, will result in unsightly tatters. There are many possible endings and beginnings. A thousand different stories clamour for our attention once we begin to listen. It is often difficult to see what led to a particular knot of circumstances, tempting simply to hack through rather than untangle, to rest content with some drastically attenuated sense of the past, all its complex interwoven threads and patterns merely amputated by some convenient cut-off point, which imposes its own simplistic pattern on events and only allows us to see things from a single blinkered perspective.

Linen is full of history, a fact I have only recently realised. For years I scarcely noticed the stuff, beyond dimly acknowledging that it constituted a respected currency for wedding presents. Although I was born and brought up in Ireland's principal area of linen production, the details of its manufacture and the weight of metaphor that each stage in the process carries with it almost wholly passed me by. For years it was simply something which held no interest for me. I was blind to the fact that the threads in my great-grandmother's carver provide a gateway into the endless fabric of time. Passing through affords all manner of glimpses into others' vanished lives, that source of endless fascination, mystery, tragedy, and fuels speculation about the lives held far off, as yet unborn, in the ever unfolding tapestry of the future.

Now, the carver sometimes seems more like a kind of fantastic kaleidoscope than a piece of linen, for turned in one direction it shows one thing, turned in another quite something else. It holds such a hoard of stories that I often think of its threads as nerves running through time, rather than as bits of dead vegetable matter teased laboriously from flax stems. Touch one nerve and my great-grandmother's story twitches momentarily back to life. There she is on a vanished summer's day, a pretty girl in a long skirt and starched white linen blouse. She is sitting on a garden swing, her hair in ribbons, her sister behind her gently pushing. They are maybe thirteen and eleven, growing up on a fertile County Antrim farm, dreamily preoccupied with all those speculations which so richly people the boundary between childhood and adulthood. The world is dominated by the British Empire. There are no such things as televisions, telephones, nuclear bombs. Gender roles are as inflexible as granite. People believe in God and go to church.

Tug sharply on the thread to ten years later and you can imagine my great-grandfather's steely Victorian stare soften into affection and glaze in ecstasy as he gazes into the flax-blue eyes of his new wife on their wedding night, their bodies warming the cool linen sheets and weaving a new fabric between them. Ten years after that, their son plays some timeless boyish game of swords, guns, adventure, running around the yard and getting in the way of the men bringing in the cows for milking. Before another decade passes he will be lying dead in the mud in France, dirtied linen bandages swathed uselessly around his head.

Look hard and you can see his mother at home working by lamplight on a carver (perhaps this carver) the evening before the telegram arrives. Every now and then there is the dull thud of moths hitting against the window, drawn by the light. Otherwise, the room is silent. She is thinking about her daughter's fast approaching marriage, still uncertain if the match is sound. That worry has temporarily eclipsed the other dreadful anxiety that began when her son shipped out to France. In only twelve hours she will discover that her worst fears have come to pass and that the person she loves most in all the world has gone. The mother of the German boy who shot him is another farmer's wife who, miles distant, has also spent each evening with her sewing, trying to still her worry through close-work. Taking just these four threads, two unmet mothers and their sons, if we were able to follow them through all of their intricate entwinings and relationships, we could reconstruct the tragedy of a vanished era.

My great-grandmother never recovered from her bereavement and went into such swift decline that another family myth has it that she died of a broken heart. As if mirroring her dissolution, the farm soon fell into disuse and was sold. Before long the linen industry, which had been so much a part of her surroundings, plummeted towards near extinction, superseded by synthetics.

Marooned in our own time, it's impossible to offer any succour to the past – and perhaps mere sentimentality to think of doing so. But even the hardest heart must sometimes be touched by the plight of those lost in its vanished years. History comes to us with such a peculiar mixture of closeness and distance. My great-grandmother's hands, alive and dexterous, worked on these same fibres that I can momentarily warm with the touch of my own fingers. Her hands, which held the coarse rope of the swing, which clenched in the pain of childbirth, which held the telegram announcing her son's death, once rested here, on this carver, where

I can trace out their imagined presence. Yet for all the apparent proximity it bears upon its fabric, I can't reach out to hold her hand in mine and offer any comfort. Although we are fixed on the same small strand of history, and stand cheek by jowl in comparison to the distances which time can place between two beings, there still remains an unbridgeable gulf between us. We can feel along the braille of linen to far distant destinations, past and future, interpret the ganglia knotted into its fibre, feel the store of human experience closely woven into its threads, but no matter how expert and sensitive our touch may be, little by little the tangible disappears and we are left with our own solitary imaginings.

Touch another thread with imagination's electricity and a completely different story will jump back into life, like a puppet whose strings have been pulled. This time it might be about lives of crushing poverty and hardship. How many Irish women destroyed their eyesight doing hours of endless linen piece-work for whatever meagre cash it could earn them? With husbands maimed in mill accidents, children working twelve or more hours a day, linen was for thousands a treadmill of deadening labour.

The stink of rotting flax, the choking dust in the mills, the deafening racket of mechanical processes, at nearly every stage after it was harvested linen mounted a terrible assault upon the senses. For all its virginal whiteness, the gross stain of hardship, invisible but indelible, mars the finished product. Instead of pitying my great-grandmother's individual sadness, why not bring back to mind the scores of ordinary, unknown souls who, without her cushioning of comparative wealth, led lives of near perpetual struggle and exhaustion? Why not think of those who planted and harvested the flax for this carver, those who milled it, spun it, wove it, rather than of someone who merely added decorations to the fruit of their sweated labour?

Run the fabric through your fingers until, like a poisonous

node, a cancer on the nerve of time, you can feel the starvation of thousands and the massive wrenching exodus of forced emigration. For somewhere on this linen's teased-out thread we would be led back to the terrible period of the potato famine. Or, edging forward into imagined futures, gaze with the mind's eye far along time's unfolding threads. What awaits us there? How will the land that bore these fibres look in five, in ten, or in a hundred years? And considering our own lives among so many others, considering our own infinitesimal individual presence upon whatever thread of years bears us towards extinction, we must surely ask if anything, beyond mere accident, links us together. Is there any design to the human fabric, of which we are all a part, or is it something woven only by impersonal processes which are as indifferent to our craving for some sense of meaning as a stone is indifferent to what befalls it? Do all the different stories in the human saga have any more connection with each other than the fact that they have happened, are happening, will happen? Do the threads of our brief lives lead anywhere beyond the alignments into which the vicissitudes of circumstance have led them?

Following another thread might lead us miles away from the lush green fields on which the flax for this particular carver was grown. Perhaps the seeds came from Riga, a much-used source at one time when it was believed that home-grown seeds yielded an inferior crop. In the process of their growing and harvest on Latvian farms, their transportation, the buying and selling which took place between exporter and importer, a whole store of human experience is contained. Trade routes, alliances, marriages, disputes, pay-offs, deals, profits, politics, all interwoven to make up the cloth of human history. Look how Belfast's growth as a city is linked to the blossoming of the linen industry. If some unknown, long-lost human mind had not discovered how to extract the unlikely treasure of linen from flax, would Belfast ever have grown into the place it has become? A single pound of flax can be spun into a thread that is sixty- or seventy-thousand yards long. Ireland must have produced and exported enough linen thread to loop the planet many times over, a skein of sinew pulling scores of unlikely people and incidents and possibilities together. If it had never been there, if we could tug on all the miles of linen yarn and remove them from history, how much that now enjoys the solidity of fact would collapse into non-being or wholly new alignments?

The threads of religion run all through the story of Irish linen, an inevitable leavening given the country's history. Huguenots, Quakers, Catholics and Presbyterians all made their particular contributions to its manufacture. And at a more profound level of spirituality, away from the mere divisiveness of Christian denominations, there are the bodies that have been reverently clad in fine linen for the grave, from the Pharaohs to Christ. Some mummies were wrapped in as much as 1,000 yards of linen. Think of the vestments, altar cloths and christening gowns woven from the thread; the delicate handkerchiefs to absorb the tears of joy and pain shed at our rites of passage. The ancient Egyptians believed that the gods themselves were clothed in linen before they made their first appearance on the earth. The gods have long since been stripped naked and exposed to the annihilating stare of modern scepticism. But although its sacrality may likewise have diminished, linen still retains an important sacramental function.

A linen thread can be followed back for centuries. Linen was first used in prehistoric times and we can find traces of it in Neolithic remains as far apart as Egypt and Switzerland. What anonymous Newton first saw its possibilities? By what stages did it spread across the globe? We have ample evidence of its use in ancient Egypt. Its culture was already considered ancient by those living at the time of the Pharaohs. It is supposed that Phoenician traders brought linen from the Mediterranean to Europe and we know that the Romans introduced linen manufacture throughout their colossal empire, but much of the genesis and development of our long association with this strongest of vegetable fibres can only be imagined. It is thought that cultivated strains of flax were first used about 5,000 years BC (there is evidence for this from both China and India), but we don't know for how long before that the wild variety was used.

To appreciate either the weight of history or the richness of metaphor borne on its fabric, you need to understand something of how linen is made. The simplicity of the finished product belies the complexity of the process that is required to produce it. One could as little guess the stages behind even the plainest linen handkerchief as one unacquainted with the rudiments of entomology could guess that egg, caterpillar and chrysalis precedes every butterfly.

Where does the thread of the story begin? In a sense, as with every genesis, we begin from apparent nothingness, a fact worth bearing in mind before we become preoccupied with more visible causes and effects. In a famous section of the *Chandogya Upanishad*, that epochal text of Hindu spirituality, the sage Uddalaka instructs his son Svetaketu about the nature of reality. In an attempt to illustrate the way in which things eventually recede into the mysteriously intangible when we inquire into their origin, Uddalaka has Svetaketu bring him the seed from a Banyan tree. He then instructs his son to split it open and describe what he sees. 'Nothing at all,' is Svetaketu's reply. Uddalaka then argues that it is precisely from such a subtle, invisible essence that the towering Banyan tree comes. (Whilst we might not contest this point, his claim that *everything* stems from such a source, that an invisible essence is the essence of the universe and that, ultimately, we are identical with it, is a view less easily agreed to.)

Imagine some Irish Uddalaka instructing his offspring about the origin of linen in all its vast industrial, commercial, domestic and cultural presence in the land. He might point to its earliest usage, far from Ireland, circa 7000 BC as a beginning, but given a more metaphysical turn of mind he might well start with a single flax seed and the emptiness within it, rather than with the mere weight of years. (Which is just another way of saying that we can trace things back so far and no further.) For all our understanding of things, there remains a sense, beneath all the chains of cause and effect which we can forge from the ore of history, that the way things are, the fact of there being anything at all, is ultimately unknown and mysterious. We may embroider all sorts of complex explanatory patterns on to the linen of history, but in the end it is more in the absence of drawn thread work, rather than in any embellishment, that we must look for answers.

Properly acknowledging the impossibility of establishing absolute beginnings, allowing in that sense of mystery, seems the best place to start unravelling those long inviting threads which linen trails so temptingly across our path. Is there a line stretching from the blossoming of the very first blue flax flower to the as yet unborn person looking at linen in a museum in 3000 AD? Are the threads of history that long? Is our place upon them secure? Can we ever move beyond the simplistic level of understanding carver and thread, little cut-out squares of proximate cause and effect, to understanding the fibres of time itself, the superstrings of ultimate substance? Answers recede into wondering and uncertainty and the kind of invisibility that seeds bear within them.

In Ireland, flax seed was sown in the spring, scattered on the earth by hand. Sowing was a male preserve, women being left to do the weeding which ensured the plants could flourish. It is a three-month crop, so by August or thereabouts, when the blue flowers had withered, the seed had formed but not yet ripened, and the stalk had yellowed, the flax (at this stage about three feet high) was harvested. Harvesting involved everyone, male and female, in a huge amount of work. The flax plants were uprooted by hand (to have cut them would have lost too much of the stem which, contains the precious fibres). As it was pulled, the flax was gathered into small bundles called beets, which were left to dry in stooks (little stacks of beets). If the seed was to be saved (it yields linseed oil and can be used as cattle feed) the beets were rippled – a process which involved pulling the head of the plants through a coarse metal comb mounted on a trestle, under which a sheet was spread to collect the falling seeds. The next stage was a process of controlled decay known as retting. The beets were submerged in specially dug ponds (called lint dams) which held three or four feet of stagnant water. The beets were submerged vertically, roots downwards, and were not supposed to touch the bottom. Placing them thus, and weighting them with stones, was a skilled and difficult task.

The retting process was designed to break down the flax stems, making it easier to extract their long fibres. It lasted ten days or a fortnight and created a foul and pungent stench of rotting vegetation. (Water retting is a bacterial process; in some other flax-growing areas of the world dew retting, which relies on fungal action, is used.) Once completed, the retted beets were lifted out of the lint dams by hand, a heavy and unsavoury task which required workers to stand waist deep in the stinking water. After being stacked on the banks to drain, the beets were moved to grassy fields and spread out to dry. Retting was done by men, grassing by women. Once dried (which took about three weeks), the flax was scutched and hackled. Scutching involved beating the stems with a wooden mallet to break them open and then striking the broken stems with a broad wooden blade to separate the fibres from the rest of the plant. Hackling involved combing the tangle of fibres left by scutching through metal combs of different thicknesses to straighten and soften the fibres in readiness for spinning. When scutched flax had passed through the finest hackle comb it was remarkably like hair, only incomparably stronger. Prior to the mid-eighteenth century, scutching and hackling, like the rest of the process, were carried out by hand. Thereafter mechanisation, first water and then steam power, slowly began to make an impact.

Hackled flax is spun into yarn. The individual fibres are between twelve and thirty inches long. Spun together to make a continuous yarn, they provide the raw material from which a weaver can make cloth. As it comes off the loom, though, the linen is still not instantly recognisable as the material we associate with that name. For that, two final processes are necessary: bleaching and beetling. Bleaching, involving both chemical processes and spreading the lengths of linen on bleaching greens exposed to the sun, leaves the cloth white. Beetling (beating the bleached linen with blunt, heavy pieces of wood) gives it a smooth hard finish with a more tightly closed weave than that of unbeetled cloth.

Fine grades of flax fibre are used to make lace, damask, clothes, soft furnishings and bed linen. Coarser grades end up as canvas, twines, fire hoses, bagging, fishing nets and industrial thread. Linen's strength, lustre, durability, absorbency and coolness (it carries heat away from the body) combine to multiply its usefulness. World flax production in 1989 was 769,000 metric tons. The former Soviet Union, China and Egypt are by far the biggest producers today, but the crop is grown on a smaller scale in a range of other countries, from Argentina to Japan. In Ireland the linen industry still survives, though on a much reduced scale compared to its past commercial dominance.

What a weight of human fortune has been forged by the blue-flowered flax! That we are sutured to the land and the plants upon it as securely as an embroidered design on a carver is something easily forgotten in an age of city dwelling and distancing technology. Think how much of history is the story of our relationship with plants. At the most fundamental level, without the crops that feed us and our livestock, there would *be* no history. The first cultivation of wheat and other cereals, which took place around seven or eight thousand years before Christ, was almost as great a revolution as the discovery of fire.

Without trees, without wood for the fires, wood for the tools which raised us above the other animals, would we ever have achieved our unlikely eminence? If the unnoticed ore of our un-acknowledged Wood Age had not been there, could we have forged the future into the mould that shapes us now? Without wood for our ships, our distribution, commerce, sense of place would all be radically different. Without wood for scaffolding, could we have learned to shore up stone into structure? Without firewood, all the metal ores we have exploited to such advantage might still lie undiscovered in their stony wombs. The course we follow is as much determined by the secret life of plants as by anything we choose to do. We are caught on the unseen webs of their roots as surely as any spider-ambushed fly. This massive underground net had already trawled through our options long before we appeared on the scene, allowing some futures to get away, holding others firmly in the mesh as possibilities. And without photosynthesis, life's crucial daily ritual, the easy alchemy by which plants harness and transmute the energy of light, how many of those possibilities could ever have been realised? At a more specialised level, tobacco, cocoa, cotton, spices, jute and many others have drawn the threads of our story into patterns that would never have happened without them. Think how differently things might have unfolded at the dawn of civilisation if papyrus had not been available to cradle and develop writing, that unlikely engine of social revolution. Think how differently Ireland's history would read if two plants had never been grown on Irish soil. Flax and potato are the warp and woof upon which the story of millions of individuals on the island have been acted out.

In a sense, we start below the ground with plants (and will re-turn there again). We are as dependent on them as we are on our mother's milk. As we sit in our cars or at our computers, apes far removed from the trees that gave them sanctuary, lost in illusions of power and independence, it's worth reflecting that for all the might of our industry, for all the sophistication of our technology, we are still in thrall to plants. If, one year, the movement of pollen should somehow be embargoed, if the wind didn't blow or the insects didn't come or the plants withheld their bounty, the outlook for us would be bleak.

The way in which linen is made offers a whole set of metaphors for our versions of history. Most obviously, perhaps, for an age grown suspicious of deception, bleaching and beetling offer potent images for those kinds of partisan perspectives which twist the facts to their own devices and put a favourable gloss on their own activities. How many histories of Ireland and other contested territories (and what place on earth can now genuinely claim to be wholly uncontested) have battered flat the fibres of what happened with retellings that have bleached out, with the lye of bias, everything that might cast a shadow over one side's, or another's, interpretation?

Scutching, hackling and spinning too can act as such obvious symbols of the way in which we tell our stories that, had they been invented by a novelist, rather than existing for a purpose quite independent of such artifice, we might make accusations of literary heavy-handedness. As if caricatured in the labour of the very ancestors about whom we weave our myths, we can see in the stages of the linen process the way in which we build up our sense of self and past. When we break open the stems of history, extract those fibres which suit our purposes, hackle and spin them into the requisite lengths, are we not likewise engaged in a process of extraction, selection, refinement, as deliberate as that which leads to linen?

And beyond all our partisan weightings, at a more fundamental level of omission, we often bleach out the role of plants (and animals), forgetting how closely our story is linked to theirs. Just as in the present we often contrive to forget the fact of our own finitude, so when we look at the past we tend to see it only in terms of our own kind, filtering out other lives, other stories, other points of view. Might we not learn from linen that it takes more than one thread to make a yarn and be more mindful of all the different strands that go to make up the fabric of what happens? In this of all centuries, when the incredible diversity of life is rendered ever more apparent, when an awareness of pluralism daily impacts upon our political, religious and aesthetic senses, it is surely time to adopt a deliberately multi-threaded understanding of Irish history, more sensitive to the reality of what happened than the picking out of any single thread can ever be.

It is easy to think of linen solely in terms of its obvious effects on us. When assessing its significance we tend to think of the many uses to which it can be put – clothing, canvas, paper, burial shrouds, thread and so on. We consider such uses in terms of how industry develops them and the ways in which such developments in their turn can mould a society's contours. Such things are, of course, important. (We cannot, for example, understand nineteenth-century Ireland without some idea of the ways in which flax fibre bound the affairs of our ancestors into particular arrangements.) But they do not exhaust flax's significance. The way in which the plant has woven important concepts into our vocabulary has also had a profound impact on us.

Apart from 'spinster' and 'distaff' and all the technical vocabulary which the production of linen demands – 'retting', 'scutching', 'rippling', 'hackling' and so on – linen gives us 'line' and all its cognates. Would our notions of straightness and seriality have gelled in the ways they have if it had not been for our relationship with this plant? Linearity is central to our outlook now; it is quite fundamental to the operations of the mind.

If evolution had yielded up no fibrous plants, no flax or jute or hemp, no ramie, sunn, kenaf or nettle, if there had been nothing from which to spin our thread, would we have understood lines in the way that we do now? Much of our vocabulary has its roots sunk deep in nature; in cultivating language out of the raw seeds of exclamation, we have drawn heavily on now forgotten natural metaphors like those provided by flax fibres. Sometimes it is good to recall such origins and remember how much we are of the earth. Despite our new-found alienation from it, our etymology betrays an ancient and abiding kinship. Words have provided us with a store of fibre even more fantastic than that secreted in flax stems. From them we have woven the astonishing material of language, with which whole cultures have been clad. And, though you could scarcely guess it from the finished product, the processes involved in making words make sense are quite as complex as those behind my great-grandmother's linen carver.

A TINCHEL ROUND MY FATHER

Though they are, naturally, doomed to failure, attempts to freeze time are nonetheless fascinating. Indeed, it is perhaps the sheer impossibility of what they attempt that gives them at least some of their interest. Time's customary fluidity, the unnoticed, ineluctable stream by which the future pours out incrementally before us, its endless nanoseconds pooling into minutes, lifetimes, centuries, is so liquid and invisible a medium that to see it stopped, momentarily solidified and open to examination is bound to arrest the eye.

From Joyce's massive dissection of a single day to a child's holiday postcard, writing affords a range of possibilities for performing such temporal stasis. In the self-conscious depiction of real moments undertaken by historians, diarists and autobiographers, there are whole galleries of snapshots where time is framed into an array of frozen poses. The way in which certain objects from the past carry with them an indelible sense of their period also offers an opportunity to gaze at stilled time and wonder at it. Such things seem like splinters sheered off the vanished iceberg of the past, bearing with them into our waters something of its temperature and texture. Art, too, can chill a face or landscape with the abstracting fixative of portraiture, so that it remains frozen for our scrutiny, taken out of time's perpetual flow and held up, stationary, for examination. But photography is the means *par excellence* by which we stop time in its tracks and net its passing moments.

Angling provides a good source of metaphor for the seeming alchemy involved. A photographic image is like a catch of fish hooked without their notice, with no injury or struggle, whisked out of their darting shoals and immobilised in some instant anaesthetic that freezes them just as they were at the moment the shutter clicked, perfect and undamaged. As soon as the camera's invisible rod tautened with their weight, they were rendered immune to any of the changes time will inflict upon their uncaught living templates. The fish that constitute the mutable organic moulds out of which the image of the photograph was poured, swim away from it, innocent of having left behind this visual echo of themselves, ghostly, exact and motionless. Photography is like temporal taxidermy, a two-dimensional pickling of what was. The glass cases of museums display the preserved bodies of creatures in all the similitude of life, long after the individuals that lived the lives in question have ceased to be. Photography provides a nonlethal version of this art. Its fixing of time doesn't require that it be pinned like a butterfly, or shot, or skinned. Instead, the visual layer is painlessly peeled off a moment, so that whatever was there can be gazed at repeatedly, long after the moment itself has vanished, long after the dissolution of whatever creatures inhabited it, briefly interrupting the light with the unique particularity of their contours. The shapes they leave imprinted on the fine clay of the film create perfect reflections of their little landscapes, conferring seeming immortality upon the fleeting present.

It is all, of course, an illusion. Neither words nor objects, neither art nor photographs, can stop time at all, still less catch and display it. They only offer us glimpses of its footprints, the consequences of its passing, what it bears upon its invisible waters. Time itself is as ungraspable as the wind. We can only apprehend it in the equivalent of rustling leaves, water whipped into waves, its touch upon our flesh as it blows rain, or warmth, or some sweet haunting scent against our soft receptive surfaces. Books disintegrate, paintings crack and fade, photos curl and yellow, we age and die. Life goes on, carried on time's unbroken back. All our tuggings on the various apparent reins are ineffectual. In the end they leave no impression on it and become just further time-borne particles that serve to make its passing visible. Most particles we scarcely notice. They constitute no more than the gentle dust of day-to-day happenstance, to whose soft, punctuating fall we've grown accustomed. Some, though, blow into our eyes like sand cut into jagged lenses and leave us reeling with perspectives not glimpsed before their smarting intrusion. Who'd have suspected the refractive power of a single black-and-white photo of my father, taken over sixty years ago? It has pulled the light of the past into new alignments, shifting the patterns of shadow and illumination that are thrown from it into the present.

Seeing what our parents looked like before we appeared on the scene to observe them directly is a kind of knowledge only a few generations have enjoyed. Family photographs have become such a commonplace of life that their recentness tends now to be forgotten. We've grown so used to seeing them that it requires a deliberate effort of the imagination to grasp something of the weight of consequence these seemingly most inconsequential of things carry with them. For the vast bulk of human history, from a visual perspective, the past carried away irretrievably all that happened in it. What was past was invisible beyond the recollection of portraiture and the more abstract, intimate canvases of remembrance. My father only had a few photographs of his parents. His parents had even fewer of theirs. Step back only two or three generations and the eye's territory is drastically circumscribed compared to that in which it now routinely roams. Until comparatively recently, no one could look at the likeness of people, places, or objects beyond the range of immediate sight. The distant and the dead couldn't appear before the eye in all the precision of their presence that the camera crafts so effortlessly.

Beyond the family album's visual cold storage of the past – which, in itself, must have revolutionised our encounter with time – photography has engineered a host of other changes. Time is not the only element of our experience transformed by lens and shutter and what they write upon the film. Looking at the perspectives opened up by slow-motion photography, time-lapse photography, photographs of the planets, of microscopic creatures, undersea photography, photographs of our own internal physiology as it conducts its once invisible processes within us, Thomas Martin has concluded, in his book *Images and the Imageless*, that 'human consciousness cannot be the same today as it was prior to the extension of its vision through film'. Undoubtedly, the range of vision open to us now is vastly wider than it was even a few decades ago. But it's less easy to be sure just what impact this expansion may have upon us. Consciousness is at once new and ancient, resilient and fragile. Its complexities make one wary of pronouncing change. And the effect of images remains to be mapped beyond the crudities of raw assumption. We're unsure if the heavy rain of pictures that now falls upon us daily, so often violent in what they show, creates inclement weather in which the psyche may sicken, or if such inundation of the eye is of no more matter than gazing at the stars. It may never be possible to quantify precisely the equivalents of rainfall, hours of sunshine, humidity and wind speed on either side of the divide, but it does seem certain that the worlds of pre- and post-photographic humanity lie on different sides of a range of visual Himalayas whose impact on our cognitive and emotional microclimates is profound.

How much is the sense I have of my father shaped by photographs? To what extent has my consciousness of him been determined by the camera, to what extent by encountering the man himself? Would my image of him be the same if I'd never leafed through the photos in his meticulously ordered albums? What would my memory of him be today if it had to rely entirely on its own recall, unaided by the visual prompts left whispering behind on film? In what ways are the person remembered and the person photographed related? Quite as miraculous to uncameraed generations as being able to look at an image of the surface of Mars, or at photographs of the unborn embryo's beating heart, the fact that by opening these black-paged volumes I can look at the face of my father, exactly as it was, decades before I was born. Here he is as a babe-in-arms, tiny, gown-clad, held by his mother just before he was christened. Here he is as a boy, with brothers and sisters, caught in a playful, carefree pose on some long-ago family holiday at the same seaside village in North Antrim where, half a lifetime later, he would take his own children. Here he is with other members of a school rugby team in Londonderry, here as a soldier in Egypt during World War II, wearing the same khaki shorts he later used to sunbathe in, miles removed from the pyramids, long after the noise of battle had subsided, silenced by the muffling remove of miles and years. A fishing trip to Lough Melvin, his honeymoon at Glendalough, later shots of him with his children, retired, as an old man, with grandchildren – the albums contain a whole spectrum of pictures of him from cradle more or less to grave.

There is no ciné film of him, though, no home videos, but this is an absence I don't lament. I agree with Tim Page here that 'human frailty is rarely portrayed with moving imagery – it remains the domain of the still photograph'. These still photographs seem like spyholes that allow a look back at the accumulated frailties of one life in its vulnerable, heroic, mundane progression through the years. They facilitate a kind of temporal voyeurism in which one can observe my father's intercourse with time, a series of embraces-with-moments held up frozen for scrutiny. Looking at them occasions in me a mingled sense of fascination and trespass. It's as if they afford forbidden knowledge, allowing the eye to light on times and places where it could never be, although its very possibility, the fact of its existence, is dependent on what happened there having happened just the way it did. Who knows how small a change in history would have nudged the past into an altogether different unfolding? One, perhaps, in which my gaze might never have awakened into being.

The most ambitious photographic attempt I've come across to freeze time on the grand scale and hold it up for scrutiny was in a book called something like, *A Day in the Life of the World*. I flicked through it years ago in a second-hand bookshop in Belfast and have forgotten editor, publisher, commentary – almost everything about it, except for some of the images it brought together and the guiding concept behind them. The book was an attempt to catch a single global moment in pictures. It assembled together a collection of photographs, taken by different photographers, both amateur and professional, from a whole range of countries. The photos were all taken at exactly the same time on the same day, synchronised exposures to make the point that all the scenes were happening together, that this was what was going on *now*. So, from Patagonia to Patmos, from Iceland to Korea, from New York City to the Australian outback, from Ontario to Otago, the New Guinea rainforest to the streets of Naples, from the urban wastes of Detroit to the Sahara, from the deck of a North Atlantic trawler to a Tokyo schoolroom, as the hands of the clock drew towards the appointed time, scores of photographers all around the globe raised their cameras, clicked the shutters, caught the moment.

Even though, inevitably, the photos only showed a minute fraction of what was happening within the moment they tried to picture, leafing through the book gave some idea of the crowding diversity of human lives that are perpetually unravelling, side-by-side, from their hugely different spools of circumstance. Yet, despite the pictured differences in the busy theatre of this single blink of time, there were enough similarities to kindle a sense of kinship. Beyond all the rifts of inequality, unfairness, the seeming chasms separating old and young, rich and poor, hungry and well fed, readers could still see in each frame a possible fate which they might have experienced at first hand had things been only slightly otherwise. Like a ghost trying out bodies, the imagination recognised in these assembled lives of strangers how easily things could have been different, how instead of this life we might have lived some other one. Cheek-by-jowl with the history in whose iron grip we're firmly caught, there's a powerful sense of alternative, of how close to accident and other possibilities the actual always treads.

I can still remember some of the array of images that met the eye, two by two on adjacent pages, the cargo of this paper ark seemingly arranged to emphasise the fact of difference, with jarring contrasts often deliberately juxtaposed:

A geisha pouring tea in Japan as British dock workers unload crates of oranges. A welder in New York working on some high gantry overlooking the city, as children in Mongolia race each other across the empty steppes on rough-haired ponies. A scene from a spartan hospice in Calcutta, a young woman with enormous, dark, dying eyes as centrepiece, a haunting, ravaged Madonna, beside a Hollywood starlet caught unposed, unprepared, eating an enormous hamburger. An old couple sitting outside their thatched cottage in remote rural Ireland, faces towards the camera, uncomfortable at its intrusion, and soldiers in Africa firing at some unseen adversaries. Crowds in a Chinese city opposite a lone Bedouin in the desert. A businessman asleep on a jet thirty-thousand feet above the Pacific, next to him a street urchin begging in Bogotá. German car workers on an assembly line and Thai villagers planting rice. Royal pomp in London as the Queen inspects a guard of honour, beside starving people queuing for food in Ethiopia. A patient and surgeons in an operating theatre opposite oil workers on a North Sea rig. An exhausted fire crew at a burnt-out building and a woman giving birth.

Looking at this now long-vanished moment, glimpsing a few of the lives that had occupied it with their various presences, raises a question that haunts our species. Are there sense-giving links between all the different moments we inhabit, are all our muddled, desperate, individual stories subsumed into some overarching, sense-bestowing narrative, or are we just the dust of accident, caught up in a mindless blizzard of circumstance, our sentience no more than a by-product of the brute fact of being, the way things are unstructured by any design beyond biological, chemical and physical imperatives? If we freeze time, use the camera to try to stop its flow, can we spot the glint of interconnecting threads that are normally invisible and that might serve to weave things together into the warming fabric of a more than material meaning? Sometimes, something seems to catch the light when I look at the photos in my father's album. But I'm unsure if it's a linking thread or just the shiny blade of repeated discontinuity, the flash of accidental happening, chopping time into a kaleidoscope of finally meaningless pieces.

I suppose that in a rough-hewn, amateurish sort of way, my father's albums were attempting, on an individual scale, something similar to *A Day in the Life of the World*. Whereas the book's quarry was a single moment caught as it dawned across the globe, encompassing scores and scores of lives, the albums attempted to net some pieces from one man's occupation of that chain of moments that links into a lifetime. The book's focus was horizontal, sweeping, taking the broad view. The albums were more vertical in emphasis, piling image after image of a single experience of time upon their pages. Naturally, both were incomplete. One can no more fully document an individual life than catch a global moment. But both offered a perspective on time that held it in a different manner from the ordinary tempo of its passing, making more measured consideration possible.

Being a methodical man, my father had arranged the 'snaps' (his favoured word for photos) chronologically, labelling each one carefully with date, place and names. They provide a scaffolding for my efforts to reconstruct something of those long years before he became my father, before our immediate family burgeoned into the little island from which we came to draw so much of our sense of identity and meaning. Who was he before that island rose up out of the environing sea of possibility, allowing us to stake our brief claims on time? How did his life link to ours, ours to those

lives that stretched out before his? What patterns can be deci-
phered from the trail that, together, we've left, snaking through
the centuries?

Of course, it would be extraordinarily naïve to suppose that
there's only one edifice that could be supported by this sporadic
scaffolding of images. Only the most innocent of observers fails
to appreciate that a photograph is replete with meanings.
Depending on how it is captioned, depending on the angle at
which it's held up to the light of interpretation, depending on the
weight of information and assumption we bring to our looking, so
it can function as an illustration for different stories altogether.
Photographs are posed, deliberate, periodic, and to that extent
they select, impose and manufacture meaning, create a mythology,
rather than neutrally reflect what happens just the way it was. Yet,
even allowing for the editing, authoring, omitting eye, they do still
offer direct insight into the way in which this individual life was
lived. They may seek, unconsciously, to mould what happened into
shapes dictated by convention rather than by actual circumstance
(a smile, for instance, is more often a requirement of the medium
than a natural fact of the moment), but they still show something
of the clay out of which my father's life was cast. Photography is
very far from being phenomenology. Nonetheless, it hands us
back time with a verisimilitude that escapes all our other arts.
Despite the dismemberment visited on the past by all the little
butcherings of individual photographs, the abstractions that they
frame provide more of a sense of mapping than of mutilation.

Writing about putting together a museum display, Barbara
Kirshenblatt-Gimblett poses a question relevant to anyone interested in freezing time, in understanding how its moments are embedded in a dense nexus of relationship, in teasing out some of the
interconnections that run between past and present. She asks,
'where does the object begin and where does it end?' (Her question can be found in Ivan Karp & Steven D. Lavine [eds.], *The
Poetics and Politics of Museum Display*). In the mundane world of myr-
iads of discrete objects, through which, around which, between

which we navigate without difficulty, it may seem obvious where one thing stops and another begins. We encounter no problems, after all, in mapping the separate and separable territories of telephone, desk, piano, computer and so on. It's not as if such objects are fluid or ill defined. No matter how intimate their juxtaposition and contiguity, they retain their own isolable, identifiable, photographable identities. Kirshenblatt-Gimblett's question may, therefore, seem more than slightly odd. She continues:

> This I see as an essentially surgical issue. Shall we exhibit the cup with the saucer, the tea, the cream and sugar, the spoon, the napkin and place mat, the table and chair, the rug? Where do we stop, where do we make the cut?

The little museum of my father that's constituted by his albums raised this 'essentially surgical' issue for me as forcefully as if I'd been curator of some more public and politically contentious display. Where should I stop? Where should I make the cut? My answers became increasingly uncertain as I looked at my father's photos, used their harvest of images to try to plot out the links between what had been and what is. In attempting to understand our relationships and ourselves, where should we begin? Where should we end? In exploring the boundaries of the moments we all occupy, should we concentrate on what's happening beside us, simultaneously, or should we excavate beneath the surface of the present to tap its roots in what came before? Should I stop with my father or go back further? Should I take just a handful of images or try to include them all? What about his parents, the generation before that, or before them again? What about siblings, friends? Or should I abandon such easy cuts completely and try to travel much further down time's meandering bloodline, the elemental artery that links us, now, these fleeting moments, to incomprehensible ancientness and futurity, following it into unphotographed regions accessible only to the imagination?

Obviously we can't hope to have 'the whole picture' of anyone or anything. To imagine this is possible would be to mistake simplistic abstraction for the stupendous fabric of the real. But how far towards such unattainable completeness can we go? To what extent can we see things in a fuller context than that provided by our everyday perspectives? William James once suggested that mysticism consists of 'very sudden and incomprehensible enlargements of the consciousness field'. Perhaps in this sense of a more inclusive awareness, we need to cultivate an element of mysticism to help season our customary looking and prevent it snagging on those blinkers that custom has a tendency to impose. How much, though, can consciousness take in? How far can vision be enlarged? When I step back, try to see the wider picture, intuit significance beyond the boundaries of the frames, once stable meanings shimmer into the uncertainty of mirage rather than the clear-cut light of some more encompassing, better-informed lucidity.

An ancient technique of deer hunting used long ago in Ireland was for a group of hunters to ring their prey at an unthreatening distance and then, slowly, to approach closer and closer, drawing in the circle until escape was impossible. The circle was called a tinchel. The photographs in *A Day in the Life of the World* were attempting to throw a tinchel round a single moment, closing in on it, cutting it off from the flow of time, isolating it, then catching it in a myriad of pictures. And of course they failed, the moment got away. All the shutter-clicking hunters caught were a few stray hairs of their quarry. Because even the most minutely specified moment in one individual's life stretches its boundaries towards infinity. What hope, then, of catching a *global* moment in all its astonishing richness? But although this attempted tinchel couldn't work, it was a useful reminder of a moment's scale and complexity and of how shallowly our usual pictures of the present are rooted in the soil of our immediate surroundings.

It's a technique that relies on co-operation and teamwork. I know that it could never be successfully accomplished single-handedly. But, for all that, it often feels when I'm looking through his albums as if, however ineptly, I'm trying to throw a tinchel round my father. My stealthy looking is trying to close in on the images generated by the range of poses, see who he is beyond the limited sense defined by my immediate knowledge of him. To what extent is it possible to see, in the strange fragmentary mirror of time's reflective surface, a known yet fugitive face, unravel some of its mysterious otherness? How far can the links between that face and my own be teased out beyond the mundane cradle of truncated meanings in which we're customarily enfolded? Can we ever see past the surface simplicities to the embeddedness of lives within lives?

The photos in my father's albums could be ordered in all sorts of different ways – black and white versus colour, shots of people or of places, family or non-family, Ireland and abroad, or (as my father arranged them) chronologically. When I look at them, though, I become the marker between which they fall into two categories. Those taken before I was born, and those taken after my father fathered me. It is, no doubt, an egocentric division, but do we not all measure things according to the scales we constitute ourselves? It's the first category, those taken before I was born, that interests me most, since they give access to what I can't see without them.

As with every album, the pictures tell only a small part of the story. There are shots of my father trout-fishing on Lough Corrib and Lough Mask, embarking on the ferry at Larne to visit friends in Galloway, enjoying seaside days at Castlerock, walking in the Mourne Mountains, swimming in Lough Swilly, at family gatherings in Derry, visiting the Giant's Causeway. Of Belfast, though, the city where he worked from leaving school until his retirement – barring the interruption of the war – there's almost nothing. Instead, the camera selects views from holidays, visits to relatives and friends. And so, ironically, there's much more evidence of a tiny fraction of how he spent these years than there is of the bulk of the passing of his days. We tend to focus on the unusual, forgetting that the everyday carries just as much that's extraordinary in it. It was only after his death that I realised how very little we knew of a period that amounted to so large a part of his life. He married late, so there's a long space in which he lived a solitary and, looking back at it, a seemingly enigmatic life – unphotographed and unremembered now that he is dead. It's possible to reconstruct a score of hypothetical lives for this unwitnessed period, hard to decide which, if any, reflects the one brought into actuality by his blood and breath and being.

Before my father stepped into that role, before I was born, before he married, before he met my mother, he travelled widely. He favoured cruises, so there are pictures of him in Palma, Lisbon, Ceuta, Tetuan ('Cruising on RMS *Lancastria*, 1935'), Madeira, Funchal, Lide, Casablanca, Rabat ('Cruising on TSS *Vandyck* 1938'). Shipboard photos, as well as those ashore, show a young man evidently having fun. One set in particular repeatedly features a very pretty girl. No name is given, just an initial: 'M' (Marianne? Michelle? Margaret?). Often she's photographed alone, but there are also shots of them together, taken by an unknown hand: 'On deck with M', 'At the Grand Mosque with M', 'With M and others dining at the Captain's table'. Was she Irish? French? Italian? There's a Mediterranean quality to her looks. One wonders how far their obvious attraction to each other went. Was it just a flirtatious holiday romance that lasted no longer than the cruise, or did something more serious blossom out of the potent chemistry that's so visible, even at this remove, even in just a handful of black-and-white images? Strange to think that, whatever may have happened between them, both these tanned and youthful bodies looking pertly from the pages are now no more than dust, and that M's story, like that of so many millions, is lost. Her moments, in all their incredible variety, have been reduced to the whirling atoms that constitute our common endings and beginnings. Perhaps, when I glimpse a face in a crowded street in Marseilles or Lisbon or Cairo, feel that strange jolt of almost-recognition which seems so out of place in the anonymity of these jostling foreign places where I'm just a passing stranger, it's blood calling out to blood the secret of its unacknowledged, illicit relationship. Or, more likely, it's just that sense of universal commonality, a mutual recognition, nicely described by Edward Hoagland as stemming from the knowledge that, finally, we all have an appointment with death.

Many of the photos of my father before I appeared on his horizon are from the war, which he spent mostly in Egypt. There are pictures of him and fellow officers at the Temple of the Sphinx, the pyramids of Gizeh, in Cairo, Aboukir and Alexandria. There he is with some unknown companion scaling one of the pyramids, another shows him riding a camel. He also visited what to him really was The Holy Land – Jericho, Jerusalem, Bethlehem. There are photos of him swimming in the Dead Sea, crossing the Allenby Bridge, in the Garden of Gethsemane. Then, after bomb shrapnel shattered his leg, the pictures show hospitals and hospital ships as he made the long journey home via a convalescent stay in South Africa – an unknown, exotic life into which these are now the only glimpses.

One photo in particular, though, came to haunt me. It's very ordinary compared to many of the others, particularly those showing the war in the desert. Yet it's this one that most regularly ruptures any tinchel I attempt to close on my father as I look through his albums, try to imagine the life pictured there and how mine is related to it. It's a small black-and-white print that shows a street scene. My father's standing face to camera, cigarette in hand, smiling slightly, a row of obviously Scottish tenement houses behind him. Written underneath, in white ink on the album's black pages, in my father's neat hand: 'Warrender Park Road, Edinburgh, 1932.'

I don't know why he was there, for how long, or who was with him. I don't know who took the photograph or why my father thought it worth keeping. He would have been twenty-seven then. As he walked down this road, still cobbled today as it was then, the tenements, at least externally, unchanged, he was, as we all are, unaware of what waited in time's wings – the war, his injury, marriage, a family. He walks towards me along that Scottish street as I never saw him, a young man without a limp, unmarried, no children, his hair unstreaked by any hint of grey.

Theodore Zeldin remarks, in his *Intimate History of Humanity*, that 'if the past is replayed too fast life seems futile and humanity resembles water flowing from a tap straight down the drain'. If you flick through a book like *A Day in the Life of the World*, the images cascade one on top of the other. The crowding diversities of fortune with their glaring inequalities, the way in which every state of being is capped at the instant of its happening by its opposite, seems to nullify any possible sense of purpose. Individual existence seems arbitrary, pushed and jostled by a billion other lives into futile randomness. With my father's albums, too, leafing through them quickly can reduce the images to history's drain-bound water. How easily we can move from embodying the warm uniqueness of our individuality to representing something nameless, almost iconic. Photographs, for all their promise of intimacy pictured and preserved, can also effortlessly slide us towards anonymity. Viewed too fast, images of a father cascade into a blur and cease to be of him at all. They become instead something more like general statements of the human condition: 'Man on board ship', 'Soldier with unholstered sidearm in desert', 'Man in hospital'. In trying to close a tinchel round my father, I sometimes find the ballast of familiarity slips. As I reach out to touch his recognised features, they liquefy into little more than the impersonal images of vanished strangers. We need to close our tinchels slowly, gently, step by careful step, otherwise we'll find nothing much remains at the centre. Given the elusiveness of our quarry, though, is it possible to summon the stealth and skill required?

In his short meditation on photography, *Camera Lucida*, Roland Barthes includes a photograph by A. Kertesz simply entitled

'Ernest, Paris, 1931'. It's an unremarkable picture showing a simple and now to our eyes old-fashioned schoolroom. Ernest is a boy of five or maybe six. He's standing facing the camera with his elbow resting on a wooden desk. Behind him, slightly out of focus, is a girl of the same age sitting at another desk. Behind her is a row of coats hanging from pegs on the wall. Looking at the date, which allows him 'to compute life, death, the inexorable extinction of the generations', Barthes, writing in 1980, comments, 'It is *possible* that Ernest is still alive today, but where? how? What a novel!'

Barthes' exclamation reminds us that if we use the imagination to carefully thaw out this simple black-and-white image of an unknown boy, frozen at that vanished moment when he faced the camera in Paris in 1931, there lies behind it all the incredible complexity of someone's existence, all the threads of inter-relationship that weave it into the fabric of time, suturing it to history. His hopes, fears, aspirations; his relationships with others; his first encounters with love, anger, death; his sense, if any, of the presence of God; his impressions as he first entered the world, naked and helpless, the last thought that crossed – or that has yet to cross – his mind before death fell/falls upon him. The places he lived, the possessions he held dear. What he looked forward to, what he dreaded, what made him smile, what caused him hurt. His *life* before us, open to our gaze.

Where shall we make the cut? Where does Ernest begin and end? At what speed should we replay the film in order to see what's written on it? The photo wrenches him away from the wider canvas, obscures the connections between him and us, between humanity and other species, between us and our hominid precursors, between them and the dinosaurs. But, if we look closely, we can still see the torn filaments of endless connection trailing off into vertiginous distances.

Barthes' exclamation can be attached to a photograph of anyone. I certainly came to see how whole novels seemed to be implicit in even the most ordinary images of my father, ream after ream of inter-linking narratives swirling their currents just below the surface. Looking at the photos as I turned the pages of the albums, I recognised that we're both – that we're all – implicated in a story of momentous scale and complexity. And yet this involvement so often goes unnoticed. Instead, the tiny contributory plot-lines of routine, quarried like gravel from the massive dimensions of each moment, catch us in their limiting perspectives, obscuring the connections that link them to the wider canvas, the unseeable complete picture towards which we can only go so far.

The Warrender Park Road photo sparked a particular sense of the density of meanings and interconnections that one associates with novels. Perhaps I'd seen it when leafing through the album as a child and it had lodged secretly in the subconscious, to exert a later unremembered influence. I'm only aware of noticing it some while after my father's death, so I'm unable to ask him about it. Now it makes me wonder about coincidence and accident, about the extent to which our lives are undergirded by invisible imperatives forged in some inner smithy, which we can't see, but that beats the shapeless stuff of experience into familiar shapes, shoeing us with symbols that weight our footsteps and make us follow pre-set routes. Was it just coincidence that one of his sons would leave Ireland and come to live in this same street, unaware at the time (unaware until long afterwards) that his father had been there some four decades earlier? What drew us both in this direction? It's a residential area, not a focus for tourists, not somewhere like Princes Street or the Castle that anyone going to Edinburgh might automatically visit. And yet we'd both stood there, breathed in the air amidst the same surroundings, taken in the same views, our eyes registering the same set of the land as it held the weather cupped in its particular topography. Our feet had fallen on the same hard surfaces, we had, more than likely, gone to sleep lulled by much the same noises as the Scottish wind hurled its invisible tonnage against the turreted roofs and rattled the casement windows. Why should it feel so strange to have been in one of the places where he'd been years before I was born? Perhaps because I knew how that long-gone day depicted in the photo was part of the process that knitted me into possibility. His standing there, gazing straight at the camera, was a step in the long dance on whose every pirouette my existence was dependent. From such crucibles we all come into being. Is it any wonder that looking into them sometimes sparks an unnerving sense of improbability and something close to reverence?

In *Image and Word*, his study of the interaction of photographs and text, Jefferson Hunter draws attention to the potent pairing of these two media that's evident in the pictures of Iron Age corpses in P.V. Glob's book *The Bog People* and in the poems of Seamus Heaney that were inspired by them. Many would agree with Hunter's assessment that Heaney's so-called 'bog poems' are 'the best poems ever written thanks to, if not actually about, photographs'. It's interesting, though, that the power of the photographs *as photographs* is not addressed by either archaeologist or poet, bearing out Roland Barthes' observation that 'whatever it grants to vision and whatever its manner, a photograph is always invisible: it is not it that we see'. Hunter deftly puts his finger on the nature of photography's power when he points out that it's 'a medium of preservation itself, with powers as uncanny as the bog's, and with an analogous relation to time'. My father's photo albums, their black pages accentuating the comparison, are like peat, soft earth into which moments of his life have fallen, to lie there perfectly preserved until retrieved by my excavating eye. Looking at one of the Iron Age bodies, Heaney wrote:

> I am the artful voyeur
> of your brain's exposed
> and darkened combs,
> your muscles' webbing
> and all your numbered bones.

I, too, looking at the remains of a less distant past, have a similar sense of exposure, curiosity, voyeurism, an unearthing of the dead.

We seem at once to be embedded in a wealth of possible narratives, yet locked into the iron of time's actual unfolding, as helplessly as sacrificial victims in a bog.

'Warrender Park Road, Edinburgh, 1932.' This was the place to which, fifteen years later, quite unbeknownst to my father, a young, pale-faced, dark-haired Polish woman came, following a very different route than his. Hers was a story of exile and slaughter. Her parents, sisters and brother perished, caught up in the Nazi contagion that had infected so much of Europe. And her husband was driven mad by the same war in which my father's leg was shattered. Captain Kratowlska's injuries were less visible, but far more deadly. They seeped a slow-acting poison into the psyche that ate away at his sanity, fuelling a remembrance of horror. He was plagued by nightmares, waking from them numbed and trembling. What icy terrors had he endured that same winter in Poland that a bomb exploded beneath the warm Egyptian sun, its shrapnel tearing into my father's flesh, scarring it forever? There are only a few photos of him. Most are in Edinburgh and show a heavily moustached thickset man, looking alien and ill at ease. Few survived from what Mrs Kratowlska always referred to as 'home'. The one I remember best, from just before the war, shows him in immaculate uniform, a parade-ground neatness far removed from the bloodiness of battle. Even as he fathered Marysia, his only child, safe in Scotland, the fighting over, the seed of his own destruction was ticking away inexorably within him. She always believed, from what her mother said, that he carried some terrible secret from the war. Perhaps he'd witnessed, or committed, an unhinging act of ghastly atrocity. Her only picture of him was from photographs and what her mother told her. She'd no direct memories of him. He shot himself when she was two months old.

There's a picture of Marysia and her pale-faced, dark-haired mother, standing outside the tenement in Warrender Park Road that had become their home. (They stayed on there despite the suicide, something I found hard to understand.) They're standing, or so it seems, very near to where my father stood as he took the cigarette from his mouth and turned to face the camera twenty-six years earlier, but the individual tenements are hard to tell apart, so it's difficult to be certain. So many routes to the same destination; so many destinations in one place; so much behind the simplicity of one small photograph. Looking at it, there's a recognition of 'the rather terrible thing' that Barthes saw in every photograph: 'the return of the dead'. Upstream in time and unheard as my father stood there, the muffled shot that broke the silence one winter morning in 1955. Also unheard, unimagined, his then unborn son's voice, my voice, this voice, in that same street, or the crying at another death that happened two further decades on. A node of overlaps, intersections, lives enmeshed in lives.

Should I stop here? Make the cut; leave these disjointed images occupying the mind? Or should I edge things forward frame-by-frame, tighten the tinchel, further document the tangle of intersections clumped so unexpectedly in this Edinburgh street? What's the best speed of recall to ensure that those I love don't just disappear down history's drain? What's the best scale on which to view them? Can slowing things down create more than a mirage of meaning that will only evaporate as soon as we reset things to their normal tempo? How much is the significance of time dependent on the speed at which we view it? We each leave behind a trail of images. Mostly invisible, unfixed, they evaporate with each passing moment. Photos are like plaster casts that catch the imprints of these visual footsteps. They allow us to retrace our steps, shadow others' journeys, see how the ground of human experience is hard-packed as we tread and re-tread our route beneath the stars, from Australopithecus to us, from us to whoever/whatever is being born from our moments.

Leaf forward in time's album from my father standing there in 1932, beyond three-year-old Marysia and her aproned mother standing on the same pavement holding hands in 1958, to a cluster of casual colour prints showing student life there in the 1970s. So many occupancies of this single place, so many deaths and births and destinies down this ordinary, unremarkable road. Though there's no photo of a baby to put beside my dark-suited father's twenty-seven-year-old self, this was where his first grandchild was conceived, Ireland and Poland, tears and love, the water-films of our intermingling rushing from ecstasy towards the oblivion of history's drain. Marysia's lithe and lovely muscles' webbing, all her unnumbered bones, our youthful, careless, passionate embraces. A life just started, a name not even given, beginnings, unravellings, and endings all clustering together in this place – as in every place. His breath, her breath, our breath, desire and death. A soft knosp of budding interconnections that baffles my attempted untangling into sense.

When Joseph Brodsky left Russia, he planned to embark on two circumnavigations of the globe, following the latitude and longitude on which his home in Leningrad was sited. Such journeys would help to underline the richness of every moment, the fact that scores of places plug into the same oxygen of time so that invisible isobars of simultaneous occurrence are always crisscrossing the globe. *A Day in the Life of the World* happening at every moment. Held in a dense network of latitudes and longitudes, our lives are oriented, parsed, defined by whatever grid reference of time locates us, locking us into being. I suppose in looking through my father's photos I was attempting to follow a familial longitude, to travel back, trying to see the way in which, ultimately, our presents root in common origins and how their interconnections and overlaps proliferate and crowd history with a tangle of meetings. We're all caught on the grid of time, woven to it by those isobars of simultaneous happening that bead us into unacknowledged brotherhood with all those unmet, unseen temporal siblings who secretly share our moments. The book *A Day in the Life of the World* and my father's photo albums represent the two axes of time, the latitude and longitude by which everything is pincered into the pose of what happens. Somewhere on the intricate network of this gridiron, one of its endlessly criss-crossing squares glimpsed in that small black-and-white photograph, my father's trip to Edinburgh, Marysia's father's death, our love, her terrible self-destructive guilt at what we did. And each of these framings is really an illusion. Beyond the tiny enclosures that they momentarily construct, the lines run unbroken through the aeons, uninterrupted by any of the cuts we make, drawing out a scale that leaves us wondering and dumbstruck.

The great photographer Henri-Cartier Bresson spoke of 'the decisive moment' when all the right elements seem to be in place for a photograph, when the messy confusions of the everyday surrender to an ordered composition, when things seem to fall into their proper place. This is similar to that sense of a 'haiku moment' – sometimes referred to as a moment of 'ah-ness' – that has inspired writers of this genre of verbal snapshot from Bashō to the present. However I frame it, though, however much I slow it down or speed it up, no matter how far back I step to try to put it into some kind of wider sense-giving context, I can see only the most shadowy and muddled composition appearing from 'Warrender Park Road, Edinburgh, 1932'. In the end, I'm left confronting the raw wonder and horror of what passes.

'Indra's net' – sometimes called the Net of Gems, or the Jewelled Net of Indra – is a powerful and beautiful Buddhist image that can be used to offer a metaphorical picture of the way in which any moment is embedded in the fabric of reality. The image stresses how everything interconnects, how reality is profoundly interrelated, how events, however independent they may seem, are in fact inter-dependent. There are other ways to try to visualise the intricate links between things, Jung's and Wolfgang Pauli's notion of the 'pleroma', for example, and David Bohm's ideas about 'the implicate order' explore similar territory. But as a way of seeing some of the detail behind Barthes' exclamation 'What a novel!', as a way of picturing the diverse, simultaneous experiences of *A Day in the Life of the World*, as a means of cupping in my hands the lives and deaths that intersected on Warrender Park Road, I prefer the poetry of Indra's Net to the efforts of psychologists and physicists.

Imagine a vast, cosmically encompassing, net. Each of the billions of intersections of its threads is marked by a jewel. There are an infinite number of these multi-faceted gems, perfectly reflecting each other. In each everything is reflected, in everything each. Each is lucidly transparent, so that any movement, any change in light, ripples visibly through the entire structure. A change in any of these jewels (variously interpreted as individual sentience, conscious moments, the irreducible atoms of being) affects all the others, however slightly. Any occurrence – the deliberate extinction of a life just started, a refugee mother and daughter holding hands far from home, a son looking at his father's photograph, a gunshot echoing against the stone of tenements – shimmers its happening across the whole reach of this subtle and delicate structure and contributes to the intricately seamless tapestry that we divide into what was, what is and what will be.

Indra's Net makes me think of cobwebs. It's doubtless an inappropriate association for such a great image and would be unlikely to meet with favour from the Hwa-Yen Masters in Tang Dynasty China who developed it to such sophisticated intellectual heights. But we must try to ground such things in our own experience, however modest it may be, if they're to be rooted in any workable scheme of sense. Bring to mind a crisp, cold winter's morning in a quiet County Antrim garden and the way in which a combination of hoarfrost and dew droplets render visible what must always be there, but are usually unseen, a whole network of spiders' webs misting the trees, the hedges and the grass with a gossamer draping of moisture-laden strands. The links, the interconnections are suddenly made visible. A moment is one tiny droplet, a breath condensed. The strand on which it hangs, sparkling and reflecting the light, is an individual life, interconnected with countless others. And all are tributaries to the same great river of time that bears everything upon its waters. Each glittering droplet is a portal into the mysterious currents that have washed over the planet, touched all our faces, for 4,500 million years.

Thrown over the shapes of the world like cobwebs draped over trees and hedges on a frosty morning, our human network spells out one view of things, though split into a mosaic of mind-boggling complexity made up of billions of individual stories. The networks of other species doubtless offer other views, for the world is draped in countless life-webs; ours is only one. Who knows what contours, invisible to us, are fingered by the gossamer of other constellations of feeling and perception? This flux of becoming, being, ending is played out not just on the single string of humanity's familiar resonance but on the strings of other species too, from microscopic mites to the shambling heaviness of crocodiles and rhinos. Time is colonised, lived in, experienced not just by us but by a wealth of creatures. Life's multi-stringed instrument plays veritable symphonies in the notes of what happens in each and every moment. And if we think beyond this planet's confines to how a moment ripples out into space, recognise that every 'now' also happens on each of the stars and planets around us, then even the most fractional nanosecond of being takes on a depth that's truly dwarfing. Though it may take light ten thousand years to reach a distant star, the imagination can reach out and touch it instantly as it imagines this moment, any moment, extending its awesome amplitude far out into the encompassing vastness of space. Dew-laden cobwebs become superstrings, threaded with the building blocks of matter.

Is everything interconnected, species with species, planet with planet, person with person, photograph with photograph? Is there one story, of which our multiple individual lives are but tiny parts, or are there countless different stories, essentially unrelated despite their dense intermingling? Are our little temporary webs of significance, woven from family and immediate relationships, of only momentary, minutely local significance, unattached to anything of wider sense or permanence? Are our moments more accurately seen as billions of independent pinpricks in the icy magnitudes of space-time, flickering on and off as we come into existence and go out of it again, a random peppering of sentience whose dots can't be joined up to make any kind of cobweb pattern we could recognise? Or, are they part of some linked fantastic fabric, everything cradled in its threads, a mesh of latitude and longitude that slings an unfailing safety net beneath us and cushions even the most brutal fall into apparent futility? The problem is that consciousness is an inherently pattern-finding faculty. We tirelessly weave the shape of meaning from the raw material around us. Is it possible to tell the difference between meaning imposed on experience, and meaning intrinsic to experience itself? Is Indra's Net just one of the mind's many dreams, or does its metaphorical finesse catch some glimpse of how things might, in fact, really be?

Will the photos that now remind us of so much, that carry such a cargo of the real with them, soon be viewed quite differently? As the digital technologies begin to erode distinctions between fantasy and documentary, will the link we've grown so used to between image and reality finally be sundered? In years to come, will such photos as that of my father in Warrender Park Road in 1932 incline more to the invented than the actual, carry with them the indices of imagination rather than of history? Will we soon be able to forge the imaginary into visual traces indistinguishable from the imprints left by what really happened? Are we, in other words, standing on the brink of another visual revolution? We're still reeling from the last one, trying to assess its impact. As Susan Sontag observed, 'the omnipresence of photographs has an incalculable effect on our ethical sensibility'. Who knows what the

effect of generated images will be? Will we soon be able to manufacture photographs of Indra's Net, map whole segments within
it, tease out the thread of a road, a life, a moment, and people it
with the images of all that happened there? Maybe even our
metaphors will become concretely pictureable. All I know is that
the moments frozen in my father's albums thaw when I look at
them and soon overspill the camera's framings. As they do, I can
feel gossamer threads catching on my face. The droplets that they
hold fall on my hands as I feel time's cobwebs link his infant self,
to my infant self, to that short, aborted life, and all of us to dwarfing distances, past and future, crowded with faces. Feeling the
momentary coolness of dew against my fleeting warmth, I recognise that where we are and who we are is beyond the grasp of any
photograph, any imagining, any combination of the two. Whether
we do our hunting with images or with words, metaphorically or
literally, in the end our tinchels fail us. We catch only a few shards
of emptiness, glittering with the incredible, uncatchable mystery
of being.

TABLE MANNERS

W hen age and infirmity finally made living on their farm too difficult to continue, my father's last two surviving aunts moved to the nearby village of Portnablagh (the name means 'Port of the Milk', or 'Harbour of the Buttermilk'). The house they bought there was simply called 'The Tower'. It was an old coast-guard station, converted to domestic use, which overlooked Sheephaven Bay and Horn Head, that bleakly beautiful headland that juts out into the Atlantic on Ireland's northwest flank, a massive natural breakwater whose cliffs provide sanctuary for thousands of seabirds. The views from the large picture windows of The Tower were so arresting that to use that word, at least so far as occasional visitors were concerned, is no exaggeration. En-tering one of the front rooms, you did tend just to stop and stare out at the sea and sky and headland held cupped in the giant panorama the place afforded. 'It's better than television,' my great-Aunt Mabel once said tersely, one of the few remarks she ever addressed to me directly. She was a self-contained, often seem-ingly severe individual with a reputation for sharpness and acts of unexpected kindness. I suspect she was uneasy in the company of children.

In the positioning of their chairs, as in so much else about them, Mabel and her sister, Bella, demonstrated two very differ-ent outlooks on the world. Mabel's faced the sea and was drawn right up to the window. She spent hours sitting there, just looking out. Bella's was turned towards the fireplace and had a small table ready to hand beside it, cluttered with her book, glasses, knitting or embroidery. She was always reading or making something with wool or linen. Only occasionally did she take her eyes off whatever close work engaged her and glance out across the bay. I often wondered if Bella had been susceptible to the stopping power of the view when they'd first moved to The Tower and if it had merely lessened with familiarity, or if she'd always had an immunity or aversion to it. Sometimes it almost seemed as if she was afraid of what she saw, or resented it in some way, as if her glances out revealed an old enemy still patiently waiting, the wrong it had done her still not brought to book.

Their contrasting attitude to The Tower's wonderful sea views was not the most obvious of the differences between them. A visitor would first notice Mabel's reticence, the silence she seemed to carry with her, her withdrawal from conversation, compared to Bella's smiling friendliness and readiness to talk. Mabel had an air of authority about her and despite her physical slightness was an almost intimidating figure; Bella was warm and welcoming, her quietly jovial softness made more evident by her sister's apparent sternness. Small children are reliable barometers of someone's approachability, so it came as no surprise on one visit to watch a cousin's three-year-old, there for the first time, make unhesitatingly for Bella's knee. For the whole afternoon the child was there, she gave Mabel a wide and wary berth.

But the most potent statement of sisterly dissimilarity lay neither in their contrasting attitudes to the view, nor in their readiness to socialise, nor in their approachability to children, but in their very different attitudes to a tall, narrow table that stood in one corner of the room. When the farm was sold, most of their furniture had been included in the price. There was no space for it in The Tower and they'd not wanted either the inconvenience of private sale, or what they saw as the indignity of public auction with the spectre of their things being exposed to the scrutiny and comment of everyone for miles around. My father's sister, May, keen on antiques, had been given some choice pieces, but the table was what she wanted most of all. Much to her annoyance, Mabel and Bella decided to keep it and take it with them to The Tower. Or, rather, Mabel had decided to keep it. Had the fate of the table been in Bella's hands, it would have been given gladly to her niece (or indeed to anyone who wanted it), or sold, or just left on the farm. It was the only thing I knew that seemed to vex Bella's gentle good humour. 'Mabel's dreadful table', I once heard her call it.

It was considerably higher than an ordinary dining table, its surface nearly chest-high to a standing man of average height. Some six feet long by two feet wide, it was made of Irish yew, its highly polished top inlaid with an elegantly simple pattern in a slightly darker timber. The legs were long and graceful, but sturdy, designed to bear a weight. My aunt valued it as a rare piece, worth a considerable sum; my great-Aunt Mabel valued it for its practical use and for the sense of tradition it evidently held for her; my great-Aunt Bella hated it. I was intrigued by it, never before having seen a table designed for this one's very particular purpose.

It was a coffin table, made to set a coffin on when the body lay in the house the night before a funeral. Its height meant that pallbearers could lift and lower a coffin with comparative ease. On one occasion, ignoring Bella's chidings – 'Not in front of the boy, Mabel', (an attempt to exclude me from the adult world that, at thirteen, I deeply resented) – Mabel explained something of the table's history and function to my mother, who was unfamiliar with such a, to her eyes macabre, piece of furniture. I could see that my mother, a respectable farmer's daughter from County Antrim, viewed the funerary practices of these wild Donegal in-laws as something alien and distasteful, further evidence of their alarming eccentricity.

At the farm, the table had seen use for my great-aunts' two brothers and two elder sisters. Before that, it had briefly borne the weight of their parents' remains. Mabel always remembered it being in the house and thought that her father had inherited it from his. Thinking about it now, the table seems like a compact occasional platform, easily cleared of the pot-plants it normally bore, on which family members made their last bow, surrounded by mourners, before being taken for burial in the churchyard in Letterkenny. Suggestive of tragedy and drama, it was like a portable stage, always ready to bear upon it those actors whose mute stillness commands attention in the end-role we all get to play sooner or later.

Its present rarity and value made my Aunt May repeatedly chide Mabel and Bella about proper insurance, about taking better care of it, making sure the top was protected from the sun and that water from the plants that stood on it was never allowed to spill onto the wood and stain it. Eventually, tired of her niece's repeated reminders of how much an antique dealer would give for it and that she'd like to have it for herself, Mabel, an unsentimental woman with more than a hint of ruthlessness about her, arranged for a local handyman to saw off one of the table's corners. This was purportedly to make it fit better into its particular niche in The Tower. But the real reason, as everyone knew, was to destroy its monetary value and silence her niece's unwanted badgering.

It's easy to foist simplistic interpretations onto people's actions, to be dazzled by appearances into accepting explanations that do little more than join up the dots of the obvious into neat pictures that offer very little likeness of what's going on beneath them. Following the more complex line of what underlies them is a much harder business. Motivation, interest, likes and dislikes, memories, passions, experience, all the currents and confluences that together animate a personality, are as difficult to map as water and their visible dots join up into patterns that are often as hard to decipher as hieroglyphics. I say this as a reminder, a self-rebuke, a counterweight to stand before the bifurcation drawn here. Mabel and Bella should not just be reduced to totems of opposing outlooks. Their story, like everyone's, is much more complicated, much less amenable to caricature than the essayist's pen might suggest. But though I know there's much, much more to them than this picture might suggest, it's in terms of representing two attitudes to death (and so to life) that they've lodged in my memory.

Indeed, rather like the china firedogs that sat on either side of their hearth, I came in time to view them as frozen into particular poses. Unlike the identical dogs, though, they looked in opposite directions and bore different expressions, reading the cues of existence in very different ways.

Is it better to live with a moment-by-moment awareness of our finitude, to keep the fact of death in clear view all the while, or to lose oneself in whatever immediate preoccupations and diversions the days bring and try not to think about our mortality except when it intrudes its inevitable extinction so brutally into our little routines that we can no longer just ignore it? Is it better to carry an awareness of our end along with us, part of our familiar baggage, or to try to forget about it until the last possible moment? Is it better, to put it in terms of the local vocabulary evident in the daily domestic symbolism of The Tower, to keep the coffin table in full view, ready to hand, a daily *memento mori* always ready for use, its presence beside us a reminder of loved ones lying cold upon it, their journey ended, and of our own eventual destination, or to hide it away, or sell it, to get rid of the stage on which this grim part of our human drama is acted out and concentrate instead on other less terrifying aspects of our role? Either option can be championed or derided. It's easy to ridicule Bella as a soft, unrealistic woman given to comforting illusions, and to lionise Mabel as someone with the courage to stare death in the eye. Equally, the interpretation can be spun in the other direction such that Mabel appears as morbidly preoccupied and Bella as happily adjusted. Perhaps it's less a case of there being a better or worse way to do things, a definite right or wrong, and more a case of finding the strategy that fits the contours of one's personality with as little sense of grating as possible. And, no doubt, there's some elusive middle way harmoniously balanced between the excesses of either extreme position.

Because, I suppose, it offered the best view in the house, my great-aunts (or, most likely it was Mabel) chose to have their sitting room upstairs. This was a novelty to visiting grand-nephews like my brother and myself, so accustomed to the invariable rule of guests being entertained downstairs that to be invited to 'come up' held an appealing aura of foreignness and the flouting of convention. As they grew older, though, and their differences grew more pronounced, Bella increasingly sat alone downstairs in a small back room they called the parlour, with the radio or TV on, a book open, the fire blazing, leaving Mabel to keep her solitary, silent vigil by the window in the frequently icy room upstairs, where she seemed not to feel, or not to mind, the cold. It was as if the passing years had eroded the surface niceties of manners and what was expected, leaving increasingly exposed the bedrock of true feeling. The two sisters were perfectly amicable, though. Their differences caused increasing separation, but no loss of mutual affection.

Although the only ticking was in the hall, where a battered grandfather clock from the farm stood just inside the door, its face so worn you could scarcely make out the faded roman numerals, it was the silent upstairs sitting room that made me think of time. One wall was almost entirely taken up with window, and it is the outlook, the sense of light and space, rather than the room itself, that sticks in my mind now, years after I last set foot in the place. Being there was almost like being inside some giant eye. As the light poured into it, bearing on its brightness the panorama of sea and headland, you almost felt that you'd become part of the scene, absorbed into it, held motionless in the crow's nest of the room, as visual wave after wave surged together seamlessly, broke upon the giant retina, transfixed you with a lucid sense of immediacy and presence, and made it seem somehow as if, for a moment, time had stalled, stood still and then moved on again, allowing every moment to be scrutinised. Being in the room, you felt moved by the same rhythm as the waves, endlessly forming and breaking in the bay outside. It was at once a lulling and exhilarating place in which to sit and watch the effulgent interplay of sea and sky.

It's hard to convey to anyone who's never looked out on the

view from that upstairs window, never heard the clock ticking downstairs, never witnessed Mabel's stare or Bella's smile, the extraordinarily potent sense of a house split between two highly dissimilar outlooks on life and death. Sometimes it felt as though The Tower was divided into two time zones. Within Bella's downstairs orbit, the minutes moved at the pace of routine things: TV and radio schedules, mealtimes, how long a fire would burn without tending, the duration of a visitor's stay. Then, some sort of metaphysical dateline was crossed when you ventured upstairs to Mabel's eyrie. There, time seemed to have shaken off its quotidian moorings to reveal something of its true scale and unnerving nature. It seemed appropriate that the glass-fronted cabinet standing against the back wall of this upstairs room should contain fossils, geological specimens and flint arrowheads collected by one of Mabel's brothers, my Great-Uncle Willie. These talismans of ancientness seemed well-placed in this light-filled ocular space that somehow registered the aeons in its view, allowing the observer to look past the hours and seasons that entrap us and catch a glimpse of the slow shift of a more gargantuan stratum of time's passing, hear echoes of the metronome according to whose rhythms the sea is daily beckoned by the moon's invisible pull, its water slowly moulding the massif of Horn Head into new shapes, making sand out of the rock of the planet's very beginnings.

I wonder now how much of Mabel's life was spent sitting in that upstairs room just gazing out at the view. You sometimes hear statistics quoted about how many years, cumulatively, we spend watching television (one estimate suggests eight years for an average life-time). Moving to The Tower late in life, and living there for only a dozen years or so before she died, I don't suppose Mabel would have clocked up such a score. But if, as I suspect, she spent most of her days sitting there, it would together amount to a considerable span. 'Doesn't she get bored just sitting there? What a waste of time!' I remember my brother's exasperated exclamation after one of our periodic visits. But how do we assess the worth of a life, the values that should be attached to the different ways in which people spend their days? An old woman sitting on her own, staring out to sea; is it a wasted life, an empty life? I would be loath to pass judgement. Perhaps my brother's condemnation was justified. Or, equally possible, perhaps Mabel's contemplative stare, her hours of sitting in the giant iris of The Tower's upstairs eye, her thoughts playing over the waves like spectral seabirds of the mind gliding endlessly on imperceptible currents of imagination, was a better way to spend her days than anything we ever did. Do we really know what constitutes a life well spent, or how best we should approach that moment when the coffin table is dusted down and pulled out from the wall to bear the deadweight of our mortal remains?

Some old people just doze away their days, overtaken by the hypnotism of sleep, a kind of psychic coasting down time's final gradients. Not Mabel. Her posture in the chair by the window was more zazen than gaga – inclining to the pole of Zen-sharp meditation rather than to that of senility's dull and misted outlook. Sometimes, such was the intensity of her gaze, she seemed like some sort of fierce raptor, stationary yet soaring above the waves of her panoramic outlook, searching for prey. What it was she sought with such concentration, though, no one seemed to know, and she was not a person who invited inquiry or intimacy. I heard several adult family members say they'd love to know what Mabel thought about all day, but then follow their remark immediately with the qualification that perhaps it was better not to know. They'd certainly never have dared to ask. Sometimes, when we were walking round Horn Head, or looking with trepidation into the Poldooths, those two great boulder-encrusted holes in the land behind Portnablagh's tiny harbour where the captive sea swills about with terrifying, crashing power, it felt that Mabel was watching, as if The Tower's great eye was tracking us, silently monitoring our progress.

When, years after my visits to The Tower, I read stories about Bodhidharma, the first Zen Patriarch, I was instantly reminded of Mabel. Something in her mien suggested the same radical independence of mind, a kindred fierceness and concentration.

And the alarming abruptness of her occasional remarks seemed similar to some of his reported dialogues. One story in particular seemed to fit her. Tradition has it that once when Bodhidharma was meditating he started to get drowsy. Determined to stay alert and wakeful, he cut his eyelids off and threw them on the ground in disgust. From those pieces of discarded lazy flesh, the first tea plants grew and, ever since, tea has played an important ritual role in Zen. Mabel never inflicted injury on herself (though sawing off the corner of the coffin table would surely have delighted Bodhidharma), but she used tea to fend off drowsiness with a deliberation and discipline worthy of any meditation master.

Once, during a storm, when the waves drew our gaze with an even stronger magnetism than the sea usually exerts upon us, there was something in the manner of Mabel's own scrutiny of the view that had sufficient power about it to make me look at her for a while, surreptitiously, warily, instead of at the drama of the massive breakers repeatedly forming and exploding in spray on the rocks. She carried an aura of quiet with her that was almost tangible, making words seem trite. It felt as if her silence had pooled into an invisible reservoir in that room, pellucid, alert, rawly numinous.

Does it matter what one old woman thinks? Does it matter what any of us thinks? Every life, in the end, whether it's spent in frenetic activity, or staring out to sea in reasoned contemplation, or cowering superstition, or idle daydreams, comes to the coffin table. Whether we carry an awareness of death with us, or live as if we might go on forever, whether we're rich or poor, violent or peaceful, the same quietus awaits us all. Beyond the crude measures of 'good' or 'bad' that can be applied to lives devoted to one or other extreme, do we really have any way of measuring the worth of an individual's existence? What was happening in the world as she sat there in The Tower? What slabs of history were being laid down, carved with the crudities that, in years to come, would be taken to be 'what happened'? Wars, famine, plague, poverty, violence were no doubt inflicting their woes. And, oblivious to them, millions of unmet others were just passing their lives in ways as unremarkable as the quiet routines of my great-aunts. Like a gull or, more aptly, a sea-eagle, soaring over an immensity of outlook, Mabel would no doubt read out of the view only what the complex wiring of her personality predisposed her to see. What shape did her search-image take, what was she looking for? Did she imagine the enormous complication of things beneath the surface of the simple land- and seascape that met her eye, catch any glimpse of history-in-the-making beyond the bobbing motions of the local fishing boats? Think of all the people, at any time, who are gazing out to sea. Do their gazes collide, invisibly intersect and tangle? Or are gazes hard and insoluble so that their collisions would be more a jangle of steel rods, rather than any commingling? What is the half-life of a gaze? Does it die at a blink or a change of thought, or only when the eye that looked it lies cold and closed upon the coffin table? Or do the horizon-probing gazes, whether of sea-farers or old women, continue on into space, reach distant galaxies long after the eyes they issued from have vanished?

Three lines from Seamus Heaney's poem 'Elegy' (from his collection *Fieldwork*) tend to come to mind whenever I think of The Tower and its view, my great-aunts and their coffin table:

> The way we are living,
> timorous or bold,
> will have been our life.

Perhaps what matters is that we recognise this obvious but easily forgotten truth, and do not come to the yew table (to coin yet another euphemism for death) cargoed with regrets about time ill-spent, things left undone, places unvisited.

Prisoners – like all of us – of circumstance, Mabel and Bella spent their years in The Tower quietly, unremarkably. Did they feel fulfilled, or let down, haunted by the thought that life had passed them by, that theirs had been wasted existences? There was no sense of discontentment or disappointment evident in Mabel's apparently empty life, only a very small measure in Bella's. Bit-players with tiny incidental parts in the great dramas of history, their lives would have provided scant material for a novelist. The quiet day-by-day filling of the hours contained nothing around which the drama of a story might be structured. What they did offered none of those hand- and footholds of precarious ascent that constitute the precipice of excitement we love to inch along via narrative towards some point of resolution. They offered none of the raw material for the kind of dizzying ups and downs that are the storyteller's lifeblood. Particularly in an age dominated by the facile, obvious action of TV, lives that give the appearance of nothing happening are hard to chronicle effectively or value properly. Even for an essayist's more modest climb, Mabel's and Bella's quiet lives sometimes present a sheer wall of ice on which it's more or less impossible for words to get a grip. Yet they seemed impressively at one with themselves. Indeed, they displayed a contentment that has long eluded me and that I don't see evidenced among my friends. With Bella there was occasionally a sense of self-conscious hiding, a deliberate taking shelter in her books and knitting, evading uncomfortable realities she knew were there but chose to encircle and temporarily eclipse with the curtains of TV, radio, popular novels and such like devices. But Mabel seemed so self-contained, self-assured, almost serene in her outlook (for all her spiky awkwardness in company) that I wonder if her window-gazing had taken her to some high viewpoint of the spirit from which all sorts of things that are otherwise bothersome, muddled, terrifying come into focus.

'The world of the happy man,' says Wittgenstein, 'is different from that of the unhappy man'. Of course he's right (a point brilliantly substantiated in William James's delineation of two psychological types, the sick-souled and the healthy-minded, with sharply contrasting worldviews). But there are also many varieties of happiness. In their different ways, my Great-Aunt Mabel and my Great-Aunt Bella were happy. And yet they lived in very different worlds. They may have seemed, to the casual onlooker, to have lived lives of near identical quietness and seclusion in The Tower, but here, as everywhere, different personalities, though they flowed in the same temporal direction, cut very different tracks into the sand of the days they were allotted.

'I want to live in the real world', is a common assertion among the more naïve and immature of the students I've taught over as many years now as Mabel and Bella occupied The Tower. Such students, trying to grasp experience with clumsy deliberation, do not seem to realise that reality is unavoidable, encounter with it inevitable and independent of anything we choose to do. To them, my great-aunts' lives would have seemed insulated, insular, unexciting, occupying a territory miles distant from the 'real world' they so earnestly want to find. They were old, untravelled, alone. Their days were passed in a routine that didn't take them far beyond Portnablagh and Dunfanaghy, the next village along the coast. Mostly they sat inside. Yet in their unhurried, repeated daily encounters with time and space, in their consciousness of finitude, in their different styles of swimming through the days, Mabel and Bella were in much closer contact with the pulse of being than these impatient adolescents are likely to appreciate for years.

Once, after Mabel and Bella had died and The Tower was briefly uninhabited, its ownership and future temporarily uncertain, I stayed there for a few days with a friend. I was keen to make a final visit before a place I held in such regard passed out of the family's hands and into those of strangers. On our first night, I couldn't sleep, my mind full and frantic with a race of memories brought back just by being there again. I got up and went to the uncurtained upstairs lounge where, harbouring an uneasy sense of mingled kinship and trespass, I sat in the chair that had been Mabel's and gazed out at the darkness. It was a clear night, with the moon close to full. Its silvery light streaked the sea's cold surface as it filled Sheephaven Bay with the enormity of its huge, wind-rippled presence. The same mingled moon-glow and starlight that streaked the sea shone through the window and fell palely on the coffin table. Its polished top reflected the weak, spectral light back out into the hunched immensity of the gathered dark. I went over and touched its cold surface, wondering about where the tree had grown that had supplied the timber for it. How old had it been when it was felled? (Yews have a reputation for living longer than any other tree in Ireland. Some are well over a thousand years old.) I thought of fish and other creatures moving silently beneath the waters of the bay, bearing with them, as we each bear with us, a history of aeons, as evolution unfolds its slow progression towards the fleeting present. I thought of the stupendous distances light travels across space, of the unpeopled, icy stars long dead by the time we see their sparkle in our sky. I thought of my friend sleeping upstairs, oblivious to my wakefulness. I thought of Mabel as a baby, a young girl, a grown woman sitting in this room, then lying cold upon the table, and I marvelled at how we can perform the routine miracle by which the incomprehensible space between us, the distances we travel, the distances we've come from and vanish into, the differences in our outlook and opinion, the different ways our lives are spent, can be bridged, allowing us to reach out and, however icy the shadow cast by the yew table, feel, like a sun-warm glow, a sense of human-scale companionship.

SWAN SONG

I've often tried to write about Boll, but every time abandoned the attempt soon after starting, leaving a litter of scored-out sentences, pages quarter filled, paper crumpled up and thrown away in frustration. Each time I come round to him I shy away at the last moment, like a nervous horse faced with the prospect of clearing an impossibly high fence. In that inner circuit of the mind and heart around which consciousness flows in the invisible daily dressage of identity, I keep on coming back to Boll of course, and the knowledge of repeated failure has made the prospect of writing about him increasingly daunting. Now, at last, an image has come to hand that seems proof against the sense of inadequacy and trespass that made me abort so many beginnings embarked on before this one. Who would have guessed that the ritually eloquent gesture of strangers dead three thousand years would at last provide me with a talisman to steel my nerve, take up my pen and leap?

Writing about the difficulty of writing about Boll could become just another fudging of the jump. Let me say about it only this: where the subject lies close-quartered with the heart, getting words to work is hard. Such proximity makes them prey to so many meltdowns – into cliché, melodrama, exaggeration, pathos, sentimentality – that it's tempting to lapse into silence and say nothing, or rest content with the roughest of approximations. By contrast, in those more outlying orbits, occupied by topics remote from what moves us, prose can be cool, precise, rock-steady, durable. Go far enough from the bright sun of our feelings and there is so little emotional gravity that the weightlessness of objectivity can take over and allow all sorts of verbal acrobatics to be performed with ease. Boll occupies my planet's core, so any words I use about him have to be cast to withstand the temperatures and pressures that govern there. I'm not sure if this is possible. They may end up being warped and twisted into shapes that can no longer carry the cargo I so much want them to bear.

Apart from the general difficulties that attend the chronicling of any intimacy, I have held off writing about Boll for two additional reasons. First, the knowledge that anything I write will, inevitably, seem like my memorial to him. Since any memorial is necessarily inadequate, efforts to erect one are rendered futile from the start. Secondly, there is a sense that, if anything is said, it should be said in a key in which I find it hard to pitch my voice. Boll's life seems to call for the delicacy of touch of a poem rather than an essay's weight of words. The clumsiness of gathered sentences seems almost an affront, risking something close to desecration.

These difficulties notwithstanding, I find myself back in the same ancient Scottish town where he died five years ago, watching the seagulls wheel and cry like lost and dissonant pieces of some urgent, broken utterance, as the dawn breaks into morning, slowly splitting the dark with its unstoppable wedges of light. I sit at a desk by a high window and search for words that might hold some sense of the preciousness of Boll's being and the loss his passing caused. Armed with my new, unbidden talisman, discovered quite by accident, I feel able, as I have not felt able before, to attempt the jump of writing about my son's brief existence and its impact on my own.

Like any talisman, the potency of this one is not self-evident. In revealing it I'm aware of how easily what is sacred in one context can appear mundane, even ridiculous, in another. I'm reminded of the anthropologist Colin Turnbull's experiences with the Ituri Pygmies. In his book *The Forest People*, Turnbull describes the key role played in the Pygmies' religious life by the *molimo*, or sacred trumpet. It is used by the tribe's elders to 'waken the forest', on whose complex webs of life the Pygmies are utterly dependent. Eventually, having gained their trust, Turnbull is shown the *molimo*, which is treated with great reverence and secrecy. To his surprise, the Pygmies' most sacred object turns out to be a length of metal drainpipe.

The image that has allowed me to write about Boll acts like a kind of *molimo*, allowing me to waken the past and summon back from there the delicate web of a life that's gone. But I know that, to other eyes, my *molimo* may appear as ill-fitted to its task as a length of metal drainpipe does for anything sacramental.

Where the Ituri Pygmies found their *molimo*, I don't know. Mine was discovered in the Ulster Museum in Belfast, when I was looking round the *Early Ireland* exhibition. On a display board headed 'Ideas and Beliefs', I read that no evidence survives of the ideas, feelings and customs of Ireland's Mesolithic people. Then, in the same section, showing how such inner invisibilities may be inferred, even though they leave behind no direct residue of their nature, there was a simple black-and-white drawing of a burial. The caption beside it said:

> In a grave at Vedbaek, Denmark, archaeologists discovered the remains of a young woman buried alongside an infant lying on a swan's wing.

I had no swan's wing for Boll. Compared to the wordless eloquence with which these ancient Danes laid their treasured infant to rest, what I did for mine seemed clumsy and inarticulate. But though I admire the elegant simplicity of their gesture – its assured and accurate statement of feeling, the high level of symbolic competence it showed, the fact they knew exactly what to do

– I know I should not envy it. Such fluency with loss could only come with practice. We are not used to infant death.

In his Wilde lectures on comparative religion, delivered at the University of Oxford in 1972, John Bowker pictures religion as an attempt to plot a meaningful way through the impenetrable and frightening limitations with which our lives are hedged. The unforeseeable nature of the future, the unreachable presence of the past, always at our heels, forever unalterable, no matter how much we might ache with regret and want to change what happened, the randomness of suffering, the fact of death – such things Bowker presents as limitations which threaten to circumscribe our existence and rob it of any sense of sense. The most threatening and intransigent of all limitations, says Bowker, is that of death. Religions attempt to forge a way through it by means of rituals that are sufficiently rich in symbolic associations that meaning seems assured. So, for example, burying a body 'gains suggestive confirmation from the burial of a seed and the growth of a new plant'. Or, tapping into a different key of association, burning a body 'gains suggestive confirmation from the observation that burning anything releases something into the air, and leaves only a changed and much smaller part of whatever was there in the ashes'. In the same way, floating a body out to sea 'gains confirmation from the observation that salt dissolves in water'. Bowker proposes that religions should be thought of as 'route-finding activities, mapping the paths along which human beings can trace their way from birth to death and through death'.

I have considerable doubt about the extent to which religions can offer any kind of reliable route through life, still less that they can somehow liberate us from the 'limitations' Bowker identifies. Indeed such limitations might better be seen simply as conditions of life rather than constraints; they are things that define as much as threaten us. Does it make any more sense to say that we need to find a 'way through' the 'limitation' of oxygen dependency than it does to say that we need to find a way through death? Breathing and mortality are fundamental characteristics of our existence, not unnatural hurdles that stand in the way of its fulfilment and have somehow to be overcome. This (serious) criticism apart, I think Bowker does put his finger accurately on an important part of the consolation religions offer in the face of things that are hard to bear, via their recourse to well-chosen symbols.

Certainly the resonance suggested by my unexpected Ulster Museum talisman is consoling. The silent symbolic notes that are sounded in the heart by the gesture of laying a dead infant on a swan's wing and placing it thus cushioned in the grave, play gently over a range of comforting tones with unobtrusive virtuosity. The whiteness and purity of a swan's virginally regal plumage deftly catches something of the unsullied nature of the small life borne upon it and of the fact that its newness and fleetingness made it all the more valuable, as priceless as a prince or princess of the rarest and most royal blood. The softness of feathers makes them a fitting cradle for unhardened bones. The strength and vigour suggested by the fact that they came from a swan-sized and swan-natured bird is a reminder of iron-in-the-softness; the fact that we would defend our children to the death. At home in water and in air, elements that boast a freedom not so obviously manifested in the earth, a swan's wing suggests the possibility of movement and escape. And, above all else, the wing suggests *flight*, an arising into the sky, a shaking off of heavy corporeal shackles, an unfettered soaring of the spirit. Freedom. Life.

What I'm presenting here as ritual competence may seem no more than superstition, ignorance, wishful thinking. I know (and have no doubt that the grieving adults of Vedbaek knew this too) that no swan's wing has the power to raise even the tiniest, lightest corpse from the irreversible gravity of death. The burial at Vedbaek displays symbolic eloquence, not failed magic. It became my talisman not because it offered some incredible 'way through' the fact of death by escaping from or denying it, but because it chose to frame that fact in a particular way. It is a way that uses the razor's edge of our mortality to incise a boundary of high value around the life of a child, rather than sever the jugular of sense with the knowledge of our common annihilation.

Effective though it has been in facing a sense of loss, which at times felt as though it might overwhelm me completely, I'm glad only to have discovered my talisman years after Boll's death. If I'd realised at the time how fitting a gesture it was, I'd have been faced with the awkward issue of where to find a swan and how to kill it. Indeed this would have been a legal as well as a practical conundrum, since swans are considered 'royal birds' in the UK and it's an offence to kill one. As it was, shocked by his death and inarticulate with grief, I fell back on more recent and socially sanctioned traditions of coping with the 'limitation' of death – a small white coffin, black hearse, prayers offered to a god I don't believe in by a minister of a church to which I don't belong.

'Boll' was the name chosen by Lucy, my then three-year-old daughter. She was keen to find something that would fit a boy or girl since we didn't know, and didn't wish to discover until the moment of birth, what gender our second child would be. I don't know whether she'd heard 'Boll' somewhere, or made it up, or if it was a variation on 'ball' (though the pronunciation was subtly different). Leaning her head against Jane's swelling belly as the pregnancy progressed, she would sometimes talk to Boll, tell him/her what the world was like and that she too had once occupied 'mummy's tummy'. When Boll started to kick, she was delighted at this sign of an imminent playmate and patted where she thought his hand might be. Boll was included in her bedtime ritual and bidden 'night, night' along with us. Things progressed without any indication of the imminence of tragedy. Everything seemed 'normal'. All the usual checks yielded all the usual results. We went to some antenatal classes, though without the same earnestness as first time round. As full term approached, we visited the labour suite of the hospital so that it would be familiar territory on the day. Jane bloomed and swelled. Boll's movements grew more vigorous. You could see the live pulse of soon-to-be independent life in a growing repertoire of movements that momentarily – magically – dented and rippled his mother's flesh.

One afternoon only two weeks before his due date, Jane felt an unaccustomed stillness and the absence of anyone inside her. It was as if his familiar presence had suddenly and inexplicably gone away. The local doctor failed to find a heartbeat. He tried to offer comfort, assuring us that this sometimes happens and doesn't necessarily indicate anything more than that the baby's position means the heart is temporarily inaudible. But at the hospital he was soon pronounced dead. Jane was induced. We went through the long hours of labour still hoping against hope. After all, doctors can be wrong. On this occasion, though, they'd made no mistake. When at last he was born, Boll turned out to be a beautiful, but lifeless, boy.

I don't want to say much more about the birth itself. It's not that I've forgotten – in fact I remember its unfolding with complete clarity – it's just that some things seem improper to disclose, seem to warrant discretion, not description. They demand privacy with the same silent authority by which the dead bid us shut their eyes and draw some veil across their face. Later, the hospital told us that it used to be the custom in cases of stillbirth for the infant's body to be spirited away immediately, as if the whole thing had never happened. No one was allowed to see, still less touch or hold it. We were at least fortunate to suffer our loss at a period of medical thinking that saw the wisdom in letting parents nurse the warm body of their child in an unhurried manner, only surrendering it when they felt ready to do so. So, obeying the deep-rooted instinct to rock a child in your arms, on your knee, we rocked our beautiful Boll, and his terrible unresponsive stillness and silence, his eventual unwarmable coldness, led to a surer acceptance of what had happened than if he'd been taken from us and hidden away.

No one was ever able to tell us, then or later, why he died. He was perfect in every respect save that he came into the world with a heart that had stopped beating and with lungs that would never take a breath. There were tests; there was an autopsy. We met with all the specialists. But his death remained a mystery. It would not yield up the secret of its untimely occurrence to any expertise. There seemed to be no reason for it. It was just one of those hard facts of life that hurts a lot and never goes away. It demands endurance; it does not admit of any cure.

A key question for many people was whether Boll had been born alive and then died, or been born dead. This (to me Jesuitical) distinction seemed to demarcate two quite different categories of response. According to which applied, our loss was viewed as serious or merely unfortunate. For those who asked this question, a stillbirth was seen as far less traumatic, almost as if it didn't count. In their view it meant that Boll had never really been. As such, we'd not lost anyone and so it simply didn't matter much, certainly not on the same scale as it would have done if, say, he'd drawn breath and lived for – well, I'm not sure how long would have been needed for him to have qualified for membership of the other constituency of loss: a few minutes, an hour, days, weeks, years?

This view, never expressed in so many words but clearly evident from some people's attitude, saw Boll as an incipient person only, someone (in fact not quite someone) who had never managed to arrive in the company of other people. He was seen as not quite human, so not deserving of full-scale grief. Since the earth had never borne the independent weight of his tread, since he had not made any noises audible beyond the womb, since he had never drawn breath, or felt the sun fall directly on his face, they reasoned that he had never really been here properly; in fact, that he had never really *been* at all and that, as such, his not-being too was suspect, different, inferior, second class; something that could not cause bereavement in the same way as someone born alive. To those who reasoned thus, our loss of Boll belonged in the same grey area of pain, rarely spoken of, almost illicit, that accompanies miscarriage and termination.

I know how difficult it is to determine when a person begins and when they end and so adjudge the rights and wrongs of abortion or euthanasia. These are areas of contention into which I have no wish to enter here. But I know I held a person in my arms, a someone, not a something, albeit snuffed out before we could ever look into each other's eyes. I'm as certain that Boll didn't cease to be a person simply because his fingers never tightened in a grip around my thumb as I'm sure that my father ceased to be himself long before he died. To my surprise, I shed many more tears for Boll than for my father. Dad's death came after a long, full life and when illness had so eroded his health that continuance in the end was cruel; Boll's death was in every way the opposite of opportune or welcome. Physically, Boll was perfect, complete, fully formed, no different in appearance from any other new-born infant – except that his heartbeat and movement, so vigorous behind his mother's curtaining of flesh, had slipped secretly into stillness in the sepulchre of the womb.

In his poem 'In Memory of Angelica', Jorge Luis Borges talks about 'How many possible lives must have gone out in this so modest and diminutive death'. Contrasting it with his own eventual extinction, when 'a certain past would die', when this six-year-old niece drowned in a swimming pool it was as if 'a yet-to-be' had died. This catches something of the desolation felt at Boll's death; a desolation that had a different, more desperate, flavour to it than anything my father's dying caused. Partly, I think this had to do with the sense of lost potential, of something struck down, taken away before it could unfold; a story left unfinished just as it was starting. In part it also had to do with an absence of those tokens of familiar presence by which, with most deaths, we can pace our sense of loss and bereavement. For years after his death I wore my father's shirts, sat in the chairs he used to sit in, read the books that still bore his name signed strongly on the flyleaf. With Boll there was nothing to ease his going, no traces that might have gentled the sense of annihilation, made it more acceptable through the illusion of seeming to be gradual. He was gone with a suddenness and finality that was hard to bear. His was, to use Borges' words again, 'a white future blindly obliterated by the stars'. The nothingness he left was, is, stunning.

I'm not sure if it's another ripple of symbolism emanating from my swan's-wing talisman, or if it's something I would have done anyway, but when I visit my son's grave now I often take a feather and leave it there, quill pushed into the earth as if it's a flower-stalk. I know the wind will blow it away before long, and I know it can do nothing in any practical sense. It cannot effect any change in what has happened, it can offer Boll no comfort since, however much I may wish to comfort him, I know he is not there. He is lost even to the most extravagant expression of longing, let alone to this bringing of flotsam. This is another gesture of the heart, not the head. Feathers, like seashells (I bring them too), seem almost like tokens of long life because of their close association with the creatures that bore them and their continuance in a semblance powerfully reminiscent of the appearance of the living body. I do not set out to look for things to bring, but bring things come across by chance as I've been walking, whether by the sea or in the mountains or the woods. Offering such everyday souvenirs is the closest I can come to sharing walks with Boll. And for the same reason of impossible companionship I sometimes take a stone from his grave and carry it in my pocket for a while, where it warms with my body's heat and then cools as soon as I put it down again. At one level I know such actions make no sense, or that what little sense they do make is of an unwelcome variety, skirting, if not entering, realms of which I would rather not claim citizenship – the superstitious, the sentimental, the mawkish. Is it possible to find consolation without conning oneself into making almost sacramental a loss whose true index of value admits of nothing positive, whose raw unpalatable taste is that of an open grave and a small cold body and the knowledge that no communion of meaning can summon back what has gone forever?

Thinking about death and feathers brings to mind the ancient Egyptian belief that the judgement we face after death involves weighing the deceased's heart against *Maat*. *Maat*, sometimes pictured as a goddess, though more often thought of in abstract terms, as a concept rather than a deity, has to do with truth, order, justice, regularity, the maintenance of things according to their accepted patterns. The earthly duty of the pharaohs was to uphold *Maat*, indeed to be its embodiment and representative, royal bastions against chaos. The Egyptians believed that when we die, our hearts are placed on one side of a set of scales and *Maat*'s symbol, a feather, is placed on the other. We are brought to account according to how well we fitted in with life's essential pattern; how much we challenged the natural order, the way things ought to be. Looking at the various pictures of this scene, as it is depicted in the *Egyptian Book of the Dead*, prompts a mix of emotions. Aesthetically, I've always found myself drawn to the ancient Egyptian style. There's a simplicity of line and colour I find pleasing, a clarity and straightforwardness, almost boldness, in the ready celebration of sensuality and beauty. At some other level, the animal-headed deities address a less explicable attraction. The Ibis-headed Thoth, Anubis's chilling jackal features, Horus's hawk's head, seem to people dramas with whose intricate and complex unfoldings I have long been familiar, but not at any level over which consciousness can claim suzerainty. Are they the stuff of dreams, perhaps, so that seeing them depicted prompts memories of the forgotten script of sleep? Or do they touch that potent human nerve which snakes its way mysteriously throughout our history, making us raise up symbols to put faces on our terrors and desires?

As with death's removal of anyone loved, I often wonder if there is any part of Boll that might have survived his seeming annihilation. The picture-book eschatology of the Egyptian papyri suggests a richly imagined post-mortem existence. For example, looking at one of the illustrations in the *Papyrus of Hunefer* (which dates from around 1370 BC), Anubis is shown leading the deceased Hunefer by the hand into the hall of *Maat*, where his heart is being weighed on a gigantic pair of scales. Thoth watches and records the result, while a maned, green-headed creature midway between dog and lion, mouth slightly open to reveal its fangs, sits and watches. This is Ammit, 'Eater of the Dead'. Part of the ritual of weighing the essence of the person, their heart, their conscience, the sum total of their earthly deeds distilled into a soul or spirit, involved the 'Protestation of Innocence'. This is where the deceased addresses each of the gods in turn. Each deity is assured that the person standing before them did not commit a particular sin, that they cannot be arraigned for disturbing the balance of *Maat*, for disrupting the order of things, for muddying truth or thwarting justice.

It strikes me that it is only the unborn or the very young who could offer up a Protestation of Innocence that would be truly credible. This sense of being wholly blameless increases the feeling of injustice at Boll's death, the sense that *Maat* was flouted by so premature an end. It also provides some slight measure of fugitive reassurance. For, if there were any judgement of the dead, there would, surely, be no grounds on which he could be sentenced. The grim figure of Ammit is a parent's nightmare. A child dying passes forever beyond their protection; they can only hope there are no monsters in any world beyond as there are in this one. Or, if there are, that there might also be guardians who would be moved by the lonely innocence of a child's vulnerable spirit and stand guard beside its unaccompanied presence, protecting it from harm. I'm reminded, often, of Louis MacNeice's poem, 'Prayer Before Birth', which surely expresses the hopes and fears not of the unborn who apparently speaks the verses but of their parents. MacNeice lists 'the bloodsucking bat', 'the club-footed ghoul', 'the man who is beast or who thinks he is God' among those that might threaten to harm this imagined imminent life, who asks for

> ... water to dandle me, grass to grow for me, trees to talk
> to me, sky to sing to me, birds and a white light
> in the back of my mind to guide me.

I wished all this and more for my son. But the white light in the back of his mind was only the endless tundra of extinction, which I hope at least extends the mercy of being unpeopled by any of the demons MacNeice imagines.

Mostly, though, I put all imaginings of continuance from my mind. Except for odd moments, they are eclipsed by a surety that death unravels us completely. Our thread may be re-spun into other forms at the level of the atoms and elements that for a time constitute our flesh, bones, feathers, shells; but our sense of self, what makes us who we are, that daily dressage of consciousness, is gone forever. Perhaps, in recognition of that fell fact, we should have had Boll cremated, since there is nothing tangible left at all when one so young is committed to the flames. We were gently warned that they would have consumed him completely. So we opted for burial instead, the weight of the tiny coffin bearing the lie that there was something, someone still there. It was too difficult at the moment of bereavement to face parting from him completely, to contemplate vaporising the tiny corporeal residue that was all we had left. But though burial might mask such complete absence in the immediate painful present, the process of unravelling conducted in the dark, in what in Scotland they call a lair (as if, like animals, we finally return to some familiar fastness to lick our wound of mortality), is as sure as fire. The bacteria and worms and beetles, the tiny microbes, the crushing pressure of the earth tumbled in on top of that frail pod, will do annihilation's work as surely as any furnace, only more slowly.

At the end of December 2003, as I was drafting some ideas towards what would eventually become this essay, news was coming in of the earthquake that devastated the historic Iranian city of Bam. It left many thousands dead. I know that on any Richter scale of suffering, Boll's passing would scarcely register a tremor. What is a single, silent ceasing-to-be, one tiny life eclipsed within the gentle enclosure of its mother's body, compared to acres of visible devastation and entire families violently snuffed out? One of the images that has stayed in my mind from the scores of terrible photographs generated by this cataclysm, is of a father carrying his two sons to their grave. They are maybe four and six. The picture is a rear view, so we are spared looking at the face of someone visited by such grief. The father cradles a boy in each arm, held tightly against him, their bruised lifeless faces visible over his shoulders, their arms hanging loosely by his side. In the midst of so much death he was denied even the small comfort of laying them to rest in a chosen grave. Instead, the sheer scale of what happened meant communal burial, trenches full of bodies, the dead laid side-by-side in anonymous rows and earth hurriedly bulldozed over them.

Comparison of pain can quickly become grotesque, if not odious. There is no way we can accurately compute the weights that suffering's many guises variously lay upon us. Did the grieving parents of the child at Vedbaek or the father carrying his dead children at Bam feel more sorrow? Is the widow bereaved after fifty years of happy marriage more afflicted with grief than the mother who loses a baby before it draws its first breath? Does a deeper sense of anguish attend those lost to earthquake, flood, volcano, or those slaughtered in some genocidal frenzy? Should we delight more in the rescue from the rubble of Bam of a six-month-old baby or an eighty-year-old woman? To pose such questions with any expectation that they can be answered would be obtuse. What arithmetic of loss we can work out is simple, brutal, shocking in love's ruthless partiality. I have no doubt that the father at Bam, the parents at Vedbaek, the parents of Boll would have sacrificed each other's children if that could have saved their own; that they would have consigned untold numbers of strangers to the grave as readily as any Nero if it could have kept their own flesh and blood cradled in life's swan's wing for just a little longer, cushioned against the dark of death.

History's holocaust threatens to dwarf any individual extinction into insignificance. Of what importance is any particular loss when set beside the fact that everything that has ever been alive, that is alive, that will ever be alive will also perish? Boll's momentary being, the secret hidden intimacies of his conception and development, the silent moment of his death, these are such very little things when put against the backdrop of what there is. They can seem reduced to complete unimportance simply by placing the weight of comparison alongside them. All those huddled corpses in the snow at Stalingrad, the thousands killed in the Battle of the Somme, the ash-covered corpses at Pompeii, mass graves at Treblinka, rivers flowing with bloated, butchered bodies in Rwanda, such things can make my tears for Boll seem ridiculous, self-indulgent, out of all proportion to the enormity of loss that others suffer. In *Escape from the Anthill*, Hubert Butler notes the way in which we are now assailed by intrusive information about the experiences of strangers in places remote from us. Facts 'settle like butterflies on the brain till every cell is clogged with the larvae from their unwanted eggs'. Butler asks how we can protect ourselves 'from the ravages of secondhand experience'. Such ravages can easily end up pulverising individual anguish into irrelevance by making it seem grotesquely disproportionate. Yet, for all the terrible dwarfing that history's dire colossi of pain can effect, throwing their huge shadows across our lives and eclipsing anything Boll-scaled, the only power such colossi have in the end is that they too are rooted in individual anguish.

Those who attended Boll's birth were beyond reproach in their conduct. The midwives in particular (whose tears enhanced rather than dented their professionalism) handled what was a difficult situation for everyone with enormous competence and care. Some while afterwards, though, an anonymous 'health care professional', of whose role I am uncertain, advised – in answer to a question about how Boll's death might affect his three-year-old sister – that at that age 'they' are very resilient and that she'd forget all about it in two or three weeks. With the assessment of resilience I concur; as for forgetting, this was entirely wide of the mark. We have been careful neither to emphasise nor ignore what happened, but to treat it as honestly and openly as possible. In our judgement, it was inappropriate for a three-year-old to see her baby brother's body or to attend the funeral, though later she has accompanied us (as, more recently, has her younger sister) on our infrequent visits to the grave – infrequent not through any choice, but because we were living temporarily in Scotland when Boll died there and are domiciled hundreds of miles from where our son is laid to rest. Five years later Lucy still talks about the brother she almost had. And she wishes we had let her see him.

In part, I suspect that the experience of Boll's death was profoundly different for the three of us; in part, the same. For Jane, who had been so intimately conjoined to her son for nine months, who had each day felt his emergent life growing within her, his death honed the blade of loss to a keenness it is hard for my blunter male perspective to appreciate. I know it cut her more deeply than anything had done before. For Lucy, at three, struggling to make sense of the finality of death, her brother's disappearance posed a problem of an order of difficulty that adults schooled in loss can scarcely grasp. She moved from the ludicrous (why didn't we just put Boll in a glass case and fit him with batteries?) to the assured realisation of what loss really means with a speed that was impressive. All of us intermittently ask ourselves, and sometimes each other, what would have happened if he had lived, what Boll would be like now, what sort of person our unmet son or brother would have been. Often we feel his shadow when we see a child of comparable age. And with the birth of Laura, our second daughter, two years after Boll died, the slightness of the chance that any of us exist was emphasised. For, if he had lived, she would almost certainly never have come to be. Her existence is the unexpected blessing bestowed by his extinction. Though we could not have thought it at the time, seen in the light of this new life the desolation of our bereavement was not to be the wholly barren, bitter fruit it seemed.

Things that show what is no longer there exert a special fascination. For instance, there is a poignancy about tracks in sand or snow when no one is in sight. But photographs are perhaps our most potent and familiar amber, through which we can gaze at the denizens of the recent past, trapped in their smiling poses as surely as any prehistoric insect caught and preserved in pine resin. I have one photograph of Jane, heavily pregnant with Boll, standing in the tropical ravine in Belfast's Botanical Gardens, only a stone's throw from the museum with the then undiscovered talisman of the swan's-wing burial at Vedbaek. In the amber of that moment Boll was alive. We were animated with expectation. Now, whenever we pause and smile to camera, he is not there, and still he is not there and never will be with us. So every family photo now contains the invisible ghost of his absence. And I know we are forever diminished by his loss, no matter how softly I try to lay his memory upon a swan's wing of words.

For how long should we remember the dead? I have no answer. Sometimes I almost forget, then something happens to make it all come flooding back with a sharpness that makes me doubt the power of time to erode into bluntness the sharp edges of this particular death. Last summer robins nested in a shed in our garden.

Watching them gather moss and twigs to build the nest, I suggested to Lucy she might like to help. So we stripped the hair out of her hairbrush and left it in a flowerbed where the robins often hopped about. They bred successfully and raised a brood. For a time, before the territorial imperative made them disperse, we were able to watch the whole family, red-breasted adults energetically collecting food for their spotty, still clumsy juveniles. In the winter, we removed the nest (they build them new each season). In it, there was one unhatched egg and, wound about the shallow cup, clearly visible, strands of human hair. Boll left not even a single hair in the world that a robin might gather for its nest. There is nothing anywhere that is his. But we felt him, still feel him, in our midst, as certainly as a brooding bird must feel an egg beneath her.

Perhaps the Vedbaek burial on a swan's wing was the precursor of a trend that later characterised some of the contents of cremation urns found elsewhere in Denmark. Along with the ashes in these Bronze Age finds, archaeologists have found the wings of jackdaws, crows and rooks. As Hilda Davidson puts it (in *Pagan Scandinavia*), the presence of birds' wings emphasises 'the idea of a journeying spirit'. I often wonder where Boll's journey has led him, whether to the full stop of annihilation or, somehow, to another destination. But such speculations are, I fear, merely the stuff of desperation, wishful thinking rooted in the barren soil of impossibility. For where would there be room for all our wandering spirits, for all the deaths that have happened across time? Sometimes the planet itself seems not unlike a giant catafalque hurtling through space, densely laden with our remains – the anonymous ashes dusting jackdaws' wing-feathers, the pharaohs in their sarcophagi, the nameless slaves entombed with them, the cindered remains of the war-slaughtered, the bodies laid out in neat composure in well-ordered cemeteries, the pits for the plague-stricken, the bones that gently move to the rhythm of the tides as the sea erodes them back into their elements, the crushed and asphyxiated thousands of Bam. It is no wonder that as we weave our way among the remains we are soon fated to join, we, the temporarily living, grasp at straws, look for ways through death's defining limitation, seek out any swan's wing of comfort that might gentle our hard way for us.

Before I die and my ashes join Boll in his cold lair, I want to take a blackbird's feather from the County Antrim garden where so much of my childhood was spent. I will bear it carefully across the sea to Scotland and, at some quiet time when there will be no witnesses to such groundless shamanism, I will push it into the earth beside my son's headstone. I will quietly say some words, hope to feel the shiver of some sense of a presence I know cannot be there. Then I will go again, leaving the feather to conduct into the dark earth in which he lies a tiny ripple of vibration, as if from a wind-stirred tuning fork, a natural prayer flag, bearing with its movement the memory of flight and song chirruping out of a bright yellow beak to greet the morning as the light comes, gently illuminating the world from which he is long vanished, leaving us to try to cope as best we can – with words, with images, with imaginings and secret rituals stolen from other times and other places. Knowing all the while that what we have to cope with is as resistant to our wish that it were otherwise as granite is to the whisper of our pleading breath upon it.

TRAIN SOUNDS

The station was only half a mile or so from where we lived in Lisburn, so the sound of trains was something I grew up with. It was one of those constants of childhood, an important seam in the fabric of place whose threads, unnoticed until you leave, graft some small area of planet Earth upon the psyche, laying down layer after layer of little associations that, compacted together, assume the weight of familiarity and constitute our sense of home. But though the sound of trains was an important ingredient in the complex recipe of sensations that made up the inimitable flavour of belonging, it was a sound that ranged across a set of variations, rather than invariably playing in the same set monotone. My mother could reliably predict what the weather held in store from the precise timbre and volume of train noise heard from our garden on any given day. She'd lived in Lisburn all her life and possessed that folk wisdom of the native built on years of observation. When heavy rain was imminent, there was a particular quality to the sound that's difficult to describe. It made the trains seem closer, louder, but with an oddly abortive reverberation. It added a plangent element to their sound at the same moment as it imposed a definite muting. It was as if an echo just begun had suddenly been muffled. Why did the noises from the station alter according to the weather? I suppose this unlikely aural barometer depended on changes in wind speed and direction, humidity, cloud cover, pressure, and other subtle changes in the movable geography that plays over every Irish landscape, animating and refreshing it with repeated difference. For whatever reason, it was something that could be decoded. We learn to read our habitats as surely as any other animal.

The station itself was a place where the customary dominance of sight was challenged by a clamour of noises breaking on the ear. My picture of it (how much our language betrays our enslavement by the eye!) was more an aural than a visual one. As well as the sound of the trains themselves, there were the periodic tannoy announcements of arrival, departure, destination, platform, time, a resonant electronic litany that was probably of little use to anyone. Locals knew the arrangements without being told; visitors would find the strong Ulster accent, further accentuated by the loudspeaker, virtually incomprehensible. There was the clunk as signals were dropped or raised, the slamming of carriage doors, the Station Master's shrill staccato whistle, the sound of cardboard packages and canvas mail sacks sliding across concrete as porters loaded and unloaded the small amount of mail or freight carried in the guard's van of the passenger trains. The footbridge that ran over the line, and the steps leading up to and down from it, seemed to amplify the sound of passengers' footsteps. And, though this was drowned out by the volume of human traffic using it at busy times, when only one or two people were walking across it and no trains were sitting in the station, engines loudly thrumming, the footbridge gave out a silvery tambourine jingle of remarkable delicacy as the walker's weight vibrated its wooden planks and gently jostled the wired-in sides against the metal struts of the balustrades. It was a place of much whistling and shouting, the sounds echoing down the drafty platforms as uniformed staff attended to their business. The sound-signature of the station would have left a bold black flourish on the page, more finely ornamented, when closely examined, with the subtle whorls of unexpected embellishment. Of these, the most unexpected were the bird noises.

The Station Master's rooster could make itself heard above almost everything except The Enterprise – the Belfast to Dublin express train that sped through without stopping. The rooster could usually be seen strutting about on the grassy wasteland just beyond the platform, marshalling its harem, oblivious to passing trains. It was like a busy feathered engine endlessly shunting wayward, clucking carriages into place. At the other end of the scale from its brassy cock-a-doodle-dooing was the churring intricacy of skylark song that, come the summer, could be heard high overhead as you walked across the footbridge. The station was situated between a park and houses with large gardens on one side, and the town on the other. It was almost as if it was a transitional, liminal space, magically transforming the green of nature into the iron tones of the town as you walked through it, or vice versa depending on the direction you were headed. Looking one way, the birdsong didn't seem strange at all (you could hear blackbird, robin, wren, chaffinch, all the common species, as well as the summer skylarks and the year-round claxon of the rooster). Looking the other way, towards the bustle of the town, it seemed entirely out of place.

I can still remember when there were steam trains in use on the Belfast–Lisburn line, adding their hugely impressive cacophony to the station's voice. To stand on the footbridge right above the track as one went underneath was to be so engulfed in noise as to feel your sense of self momentarily dissolve, dispersed into nothingness by the potent acid of sheer volume. Like the vanished steam trains, some of the station's other noises were also lost or muted as I grew up. Electronic signalling replaced the wire and pulley system so that lights flicked silently on or off instead of signal heads clunking up and down. Automatic doors on the trains meant that the individual door-slamming of imminent departure was changed into an orchestrated whir, preceded by a high-pitched warning signal, as all the carriages sealed themselves at once. Surprisingly, the rooster, rather *a* rooster, was still there the last time I visited, even though the Station Master's house had been sold off into private hands. Perhaps some other member of station staff now tended the hencoop that still stood in the garden, or maybe the birds had become independent and lived a semi-wild existence on that rough littoral strip between tracks and fence. The skylarks, though, have long gone, another once common species edging from absence into rarity, if not extinction. I've not heard one for years, and feel the poorer for it. It's one of those small subtractions that stealthily, bird by bird and plant by plant, has built into the ominous scale of loss that takes so much away from us. The skylarks' sky-borne trilling song, high above the station, like some ethereal distillate of the crude sounds rumbling heavily below, exists now only as a ghostly revenant, playing silently, brokenly, in the imperfect recall of memories like mine. Soon, no one will even remember that they were once a part of the picture.

Perhaps because of its customary melange of sounds, whenever the station did fall briefly silent, this unaccustomed state had an almost eerie quality. It was as if the whole place was waiting for something to happen. Keyed up, tense, alert, infected by the waiting passengers' restless pacing and frequent glances up and down the line, the platforms took on an almost theatrical persona, self-conscious and posed. They seemed more like platforms in a film than platforms for real, so heavily did the plot's demand for action sit upon them. The aura of anticipation was almost palpable. When the silence was broken it came with the relief of desired resolution rather than regret at the intrusion of tranquillity-disrupting sound. It was as if some spell had been broken and you could breathe and start moving again, released from the dreamlike drifting in a momentary bubble of noiselessness back into the station's sharp reality, punctuated by its claxon rosary of sounds. Looking along the line could induce a sort of contemplative state of mind, as the rails led the gaze into distance and disappearance, nudging an awareness of arrival and departure, life's defining frames that stretch and cut our canvas into shape, emphasising the fact that each of us is only ever passing through. But it wasn't the sort of contemplation that needed silence. The station's sacrality, if so blunt and raw a place could be said to possess any, was primarily an aural one. It celebrated its sacraments in a litany of rough, ritual noises rather than in any kind of cloistered quiet.

Waiting for the train to Belfast, I used to think about the tendrils of sound emanating from the station and reaching out across the trees and houses to where we lived, only five minutes' walk away. Distance progressively filtered out most of the fine detail. On cold, clear winter mornings we could hear the echo of the tannoy as well as the trains themselves, and sometimes the amplified ring of the telephone mounted on a yellow case on one of the pillars supporting the platform's roof. And, once or twice, the slam of carriage doors was audible from the bottom of our garden. But the rest was confined within the smaller amphitheatre of proximity immediately around the station, at least so far as our ears were concerned. To the more highly attuned hearing of other animals, I suppose the station's book of hours chimed its divisions of the day from miles off, regular, predictable, but incomprehensible. As she lay dozing in the sun, perhaps our dog could pick out, with a delicacy beyond our senses, the skid of parcels across concrete platforms, the sound of hurrying passengers crossing the footbridge, even the whispered remnant of the skylarks' churring as its volume dimmed in the distance, and the very first breath-gentle rumbles of trains, approaching or departing, heard from the outermost boundaries of sensation tuned to such different modalities than ours.

As I lay in my pram in the shade of the weeping cherry tree that overhung our lawn, what imprint did the station's noises leave on my infant consciousness? Does sound wash over us neutral and inert as ozone, leaving no trace of its passage, or are we subtly weathered by all its resonances, its varied notes sculpting their signature on the coastline of the psyche as surely as a river's banks are moulded by the gentle, irresistible persistence of the water's snaking current? My early aural education, begun so gently with the sound of wind stirring the cherry tree's leaves, the voices of parents (not yet hatched into the sense of recognisable persons), the station's complex cocktail of noises suggesting the fact of distance, was a far cry from the schooling some have the misfortune to receive. What shapes are moulded in the infant psyche by shots, shouts, explosions? How different would my world have been if the gentle harmonies of home-garden-station had been replaced by other less benign sounds? As speech develops, is it eased into birth by the noises that surround our cradle, laying down upon the tendons of our budding talk a backdrop of pace, tempo and volume that they henceforth mimic and expect?

What happens to noises when they stop? All the hundreds of occasions on which the sound of trains warned us of the approaching rain, the billions of words we've spoken, a dog's early morning barking, everything we hear – it all soon lapses into silence. As I lay awake at night, looking out at the stars and listening to the inexplicably pleasing sound of trains in the dark (how is it that night-trains fill the mind with such a sonorous and haunting chord of pleasure?), I used to think of our house, silent except for the grandfather clock ticking on the landing, as a kind of sound-bubble, a mausoleum of our spoken words, trapping in the air pocket of each room our different voices and the music of their talk together. Is it not incredible to think of life being drawn out of the planets' silent elements into all the different filaments of individual being and, eventually, after aeons of unfolding, speaking to each other about the circumstances of its existence? It's as if the stones were raised and made to talk. But no sound-bubble, whether cave or house or cathedral, can do more than momentarily cup our utterances within it. They disappear like morning mist (and the advent of audio-recording, though wonderful, does little to change the essential evanescence of sound).

One of those mock-serious questions we used to pose to one another as children had to do with trying to assess and picture accumulations of things. Perhaps this was a playful precursor to the philosopher's more serious interrogations, for one of the marks of a good philosopher is retention of the child's ability to pose disarming, unexpected questions of lucid simplicity. Would all the bananas our family had eaten over a lifetime fit into the house, or overflow its confinement, their abundance oozing out of doors and roof and windows? How many miles would we walk if you added together all the footsteps of a lifetime? Would there be enough to go once, twice around the globe, to reach to the moon and back? And, the childish preoccupation with bodily function irrepressible as always, how much spit or urine, how great a tonnage of faeces, would we produce in total, altogether, in a span of seven or eight decades? Related to, though at a respectable remove from, such lavatorial speculations, I also wondered what all the sounds that had ever been made would sound like, taken together, in their awesome totality. I can't remember who remarked that 'God is God because he thinks all thoughts at once'. If God exists, and if he is a he – two propositions much in doubt – perhaps this would be a characteristic of omnipotence. But what would a single world-thought be like?

As a corollary to this hypothesis, presumably, if there were a God, a feature of omnipotence would be the ability to hear all sounds at once. Think how infinitesimal, within this Everest of noise, the sound of trains before rain in a County Antrim town is. Any meaning that I try to lash onto it is soon stripped away, dwarfed into inconsequentiality by the sheer scale of the wider context in which it's set. What, taking out of that immense cacophony only human speech, would a single world-voice sound like, from the first utterance of the earliest hominids that qualify as human, crossing that Rubicon that runs between mere noise and speech, to business calls over a mobile phone, from Hitler's whispered endearments to Eva Braun to the last desperate goodbyes of those in the death camps? Or, to subdivide this massive speculative totality, what would all the sounds sound like that had happened here in this one place – house, street, station – from the beginning of time until its end? Would their massed accumulation just amount to a raucous, unintelligible din, or might some sense of sense emerge beyond the clamour? If we could step back, listen in a more panoramic mode than we're normally capable of, what would Ireland's voice sound like? Would the keening or the laughter have the upper hand? Would reason or extremism be the stronger note in its accent?

It was in this territory of the ear, while thinking about skylarks, that I almost lost an eye. On a sunny afternoon one August, taking a short-cut through the station to the town, I noticed a small bird lying by the side of the footbridge. It was a skylark, dead for long enough that time and the summer sun had mummified it into something dry, fleshless, odourless and inoffensive. All the soft tissue had gone, the tiny abdomen had been ripped open and eviscerated. It was a dry husk of feather and bone. How it got there I don't know. Possibly the wind had picked it up and carried it from wherever it had fallen, but the feathers seemed too perfect for it to have been blown scudding like a leaf along the ground. Perhaps a cat had carried it to here and then abandoned it. Or maybe it was light enough for a seagull or crow to have lifted from wherever it had first fallen, letting it slip again so that it fell to earth on the footbridge. It was strange to see a creature that was so much of the air, so associated with altitude, lying grounded on the dusty planks of the footbridge. They sing from so high up that you sometimes need to scan the sky for several minutes before you spot the small quivering speck that generates the sound. I lifted the tiny mummified corpse, marvelling at its lightness, imagined the body, supple and vibrating, as it hovered, suspended in the sky, its song like elfin sonar fingering the heavy grounded shapes of trains and people in the station below. The skylark's song is so much a part of it that it almost felt I was holding a tuning-fork, keyed to a pitch that mocks our clambering, gravity-bound words. It seemed wrong for something that was so essentially of the air and out of reach to have been discarded here on this dusty footbridge, shaken by passing feet, at risk of being trampled by them. As I held it, dust-light on my palm, I wondered about the long taproot of its now silenced song, the way in which it must snake back to the age of reptiles and, before them, to that moment when life first fractured the water. I felt almost like a geologist of its flesh, knowing that the chalky stratum of bone that underlay the song was itself underlain by further immeasurable distances and that, even to contemplate them, means demolishing the tongue's walls, recognising that 'skylark' is just a name, a convenience, and that, beneath it, as beneath all the things we glibly label, there are unplumbed depths. The meanings we give things are utility's mirages. Catching a glimpse of what lies beyond them is both exhilarating and terrifying.

It's impossible to describe sudden impact. The unheralded intrusion of pain is not something that can be conveyed in words. Without any warning, a sharp blow on the side of my head made me reel. Dropping the dead skylark, I turned in time to see a small gang of boys at the other end of the footbridge. One was lowering a catapult. They were laughing excitedly. In retrospect, when the shock and pain and outrage had dimmed, cooling into only the memory of rage, I'm glad I didn't catch up with them, for I fear I would have meted out more violent retribution than their age would have warranted. At the time, though, I was furious they got away. I reached their end of the footbridge at a sprint, just in time to see them cycling away at a speed I knew I could never match on foot. It was lucky the velocity of the stone that hit me must almost have been spent, otherwise it would, I suppose, have knocked me out. As it was, my head was singing and I could feel blood trickling down my temple, catching in my hair, pooling and then overflowing. If I'd been turned towards them, even a degree or two, it would have hit me in the eye. No doubt the boys hadn't intended me any serious harm, they were simply possessed of that lethal combination of irresponsibility, lack of imagination, and inability to calculate likely outcomes, that has been the source of so much woe. It was, no doubt, boys like these, perhaps even these boys, who periodically threw window-breaking stones at the passing trains between Lisburn and Belfast, showering the passengers with glass, who put stones, bottles, branches on the line, who ran across the tracks, daring each other to linger as the trains approached. There seems to be some madness or malignancy, and sometimes both, rooted deeply in us – or is it only in males? The loud *'thuck!'* as the stone hit me, their raucous laughing jeers, my own incoherent shout of rage and thudding footsteps as I tried to reach them, these were all added to the station's reservoir of sound, an ugly little discord breaking into the usual tones and rhythms.

The way in which things intersect, coincide, collide, how one thing leads to another, has fascinated me for years. Every moment floats on a densely cross-hatched sea of cause and effect, waved with endless undulations that seem to embody in their continual movement and variety both the flux of possibility and the iron that every moment cools into, the shape of circumstance locking us into the way things are. The intricacy of the grid of inter-relationships on which each moment is mapped is hard to grasp beyond the simplification of a picture. Unravelling the history of any event leads us back, step by step, into the stupendous complexities of time. As the Buddha said of a teaching known as Interdependent Origination (*paticcasamuppada*), a causal theory which addresses the complexities of how one thing gives rise to another, 'deep indeed is this *paticcasamuppada* and deep does it appear'. Scholars have suggested that to penetrate this doctrine is to 'penetrate to the very core of existence'. They see understanding it as tantamount to enlightenment. Somewhere, lodged in the world-sound – itself a mere whisper in the planetary symphonies that echo through the cosmos – the Buddha's voice speaks his teachings. Within the totality of utterances, one voice is like a droplet in the ocean, but through the centuries this one has acquired the force of a tidal wave. To map the way in which his words fit somewhere into the same universe of sound as the station noises heard from our house, is to confront a jigsaw of awesome scale and complexity.

I suppose incidents that happen just this side of disaster have more of a propensity than the ordinary run of routine events to spark an awareness of chance and make us think about the chain-mail networks of cause and effect in which things are clad as soon as they emerge out of the sea of possibility. When the armoured actuality of what happens pushes us close to injury or death, it's easier to see what's always there – how close to the edge of alternative outcomes we always walk, how some other set of circumstances could have been forged from the ore of what might have been and frozen into the unassailable gridlock of history. A different grip on any of time's passing seconds could bring about a change of suit in all the implications that tune the torque of every moment. If I'd turned my head a fraction more so that the catapulter's missile had struck face on. If the boy who fired the catapult had been stronger, closer, his projectile more aerodynamic, sharper, almost everything might have been different for me, though I suppose the station and its noises would have continued unchanged, a constant backdrop for all the individual lives lived around it no matter whether they're paced with tragedy or joy. Perhaps it was because the station suggested a slowed-down model of events, pictured very simply a segment of what happens, that the catapult incident made so much of an impression and sparked many reveries about the way our lives unfold. Like heavy thoughts lumbering towards utterance, the trains entered and left the station. Or perhaps they were more like the fixing of sound in print, the shackling to the rails of script of the mercurial movements of the mind. Looking into the distant, parallel silver lines of the rails receding to a vanishing point, and watching the approaching and departing trains, was almost like being faced with some sort of model of the atoms and molecules of causation, held in their fateful trajectories and bearing out the Buddha's words, 'That arising, this becomes; this ceasing to be, that ceases to be.' The line taken by a stone, its short journey through time and space to that moment of impact, was governed by a billion prior factors. The nexus of surrounding events that determined precisely when, where and how hard it would hit as I knelt to look at the skylark's body, suggests a baffling complexity. The consequences following from this incident, the impossibility of going back and retrieving what's been done, of changing what's happened once it's happened, the hard fact of the way things are, much occupied my thoughts. Not long after the stone hit me, two gunmen boarded a train a few stops down the line from Lisburn. They selected their victim in the packed commuter carriage, shot him in the head, got off the train again, leaving a dark blizzard of consequences, the flakes, like shrapnel, blasting into everyone who witnessed the killing. Somewhere down the lines of familiarity and well-loved places, the horror of modern Ulster's burden has been branded into us with great brutality, making us fearful of our journeys' destinations.

As well as being the source of that rich medley of sounds that made me think of home, beyond the simple pleasure of just watching trains, I think much of the fascination that the station exerted on me came from the symbolic simplifications it offered in such abundance. The obvious theme of arrival and departure, knotted into us so tightly that it sometimes constricts the blood of remembrance, making us forget it, was played out here repeatedly, almost in slow motion, written in block letters so that even a child could not mistake the meaning. People come, people go. Our life-journeys are punctuated with greetings and goodbyes. Different fates, circumstances and inclinations bear us off in different directions. And our ultimate point of origin and end, pointed to in each direction along the track, a hazy vanishing point as the parallel lines converge into apparent nothingness, disappear into the distance and we hope for something beyond the termination they suggest. The way in which the noise of departing trains thinned and vanished, gradually receding into silence as, diluted by space, they became lost in the inaudible background hum of things, offered in sound the same leitmotif of transience that the trains offered to the eye. The symmetry of the rails, the way they gleamed in the sun, like lines ruled on the ground with iridescent silver, the predictability of the signals, when the station would be bustling and crowded, when it would be deserted, the orchestration of the timetable, the neat flowers on the platform, all this suggested order, a lulling sense of regulation. Things orchestrated into human scale and priority. And the litany of stops between Lisburn and Belfast: Hilden, Lambeg, Derriaghy, Dunmurry, Finaghy, Balmoral, Adelaide – a route travelled scores of times by me, my friends and family – were little beads in some reassuring rosary. It's amazing how much can be summoned to the mind when I say them now. Travelling by train on winter evenings when it got dark early, it sometimes felt as if the line from Lisburn to Belfast was like an incision drawn into Ulster and that travelling it, looking through uncurtained windows at the lives briefly illuminated within, was like seeing into an ants' nest, like taking a cross-section through a living landscape.

The station had its own semi-resident icon of disorder to remind travellers of how easy it is to go off the rails, how the order and regularity of things, the imperatives of timetable, all our planned excursions, are hedged about by the inevitabilities of disaster. Snowy seemed almost like an embodiment of the first three of the Four Passing Sights that had so profound an impact on the youthful Buddha: old age, illness and death. Snowy was old, ill and had been left the way he was by so unnerving an encounter with death that it had made him take up a wandering life. But unlike the Buddha, for whom a fourth sight inspired him into salvific action, Snowy seemed cruelly imprisoned, impaled on the barbs of his own madness and pain. The name had been given because of his white hair and beard, though they were usually as dirty as snow at the side of a busy road. No one knew his real name. He was probably in his late 60s or early 70s. He wore black rubber boots, a greasy grey raincoat tied with a cord, and carried a hessian sack slung over one shoulder. He had a lurching walk, often talked to himself, ignored other people and, every now and then, to the terror and delight of children, issued loud hooting noises. Heard in the quiet of the station, where he often sat for hours, they were almost like a child's imitation of a train. Local wisdom – or invention – held that Snowy had once been head waiter at an expensive London hotel and that during the blitz the dining room had suffered a direct hit. The sight of the carnage, shattered diners sprawled amongst the blasted food, had unhinged his mind. Station staff were kind to him, allowing him to sit in the waiting room when it was cold, providing the occasional sandwich and cup of tea, and ensuring that schoolchildren didn't bait him. His weird hooting sound cut through the skylarks and rooster, the tannoy and the door-slamming, a raw, wrenching noise that starkly reminded anyone who heard it of the derailment and destruction that can be visited on any of us.

I used to wonder about sound travelling in the *other* direction, from our house to the station. My father's piano playing, my laughter, the dog's howling, touching the skylarks' consciousness as they floated, seemingly stationary, high above the station, like sound buoys anchored in the depths of the sky. And perhaps a whisper of our sound would reach Snowy's hearing as he sat there, hour after hour on the platform, in whatever world it was he occupied, performing those strange repetitive Stations of the Cross that his madness demanded. Could he hear such things, or the talk of waiting passengers, or the Station Master's rooster, or had the massive discord that had derailed him, the huge catapult blow of the wartime bombs, ruptured his hearing, making him deaf to the pitch of ordinary noises?

Where do sounds go to when they've stopped? The air, sculpted momentarily into the vibration of Snowy's hooting or the churring of a skylark, no doubt straightens out again, becomes receptive and malleable to new possibilities. Can a place's air become sound-exhausted, just the way oxygen runs out, so that nothing new can be sounded there? Does somewhere like Auschwitz allow the possibility of a new overlay of sound after all that happened in it? Or has it become sound-encrusted with the terrible barnacles of particular noises that are wedded to it so tightly this will characterise the aural environment for centuries to come? Does the ghost of Snowy's hooting and the skylarks' singing still exist somewhere? If there are creatures that could hear across time – as, of course, we all can to a limited extent – could they, on their far-off planet, detect such sound-signatures long after they were made, in the same way as we can perceive light from planets dead by the time their illumination strikes our eyes? Could they hear the tendrils of sound that have stretched out from the Big Bang to the present moment, pick out from this web of noises our individual sound-signatures from the moment that we fill our lungs, draw breath for the first time and cry, to whatever words will turn out to be the last we ever say?

In his influential book, *The Idea of the Holy*, Rudolf Otto talks about 'original numinous sounds'. These occur when a sound fits so well into the contour of its meaning that object and utterance have an instantaneous relationship that bypasses thought and reflection. Otto had specifically in mind the kind of primal exclamation that might be forced from the mouth in the presence of a sense of deity. Perhaps Snowy's hooting was a kind of 'original despairing noise', something wrenched from him automatically, forged by the senseless slaughter he'd witnessed. His strange banshee wail was, arguably, more suitable as a response to the violence that was happening around him in Ulster's towns and villages than all the reasoned, strategic condemnations of the politicians and churchmen. Perhaps what's really needed to express our depth of anguish is a cry not unlike the one that Robert Graves imagines in *The Shout*. This disturbing story tells of a man learning from an aborigine shaman how to make a noise of such pure evil that it kills anyone who hears it. Maybe we need to learn a cry of pure lamentation, or of desperation, that will have a similarly profound impact on all who hear it.

The idea of a one-to-one correspondence between experience and utterance is appealing. To sense the presence of the sacred and, in a seamless, instantaneously concomitant cry, to give voice to that fact in a sound that fits it as snugly as an egg fits inside its shell, would this not be to reach that elusive expressive goal sought by writers throughout history, perfect description, where thoughts and feelings are translated into words without remainder or addition? The grail of an Edenic language, in which words and objects enjoy a paradisal intimacy, is something people have periodically searched for, hoping to retrieve that closeness of connection where sound and sense are fused together so closely that there's no space for inaccuracy or falsehood to enter. 'May my speech be one with my mind, and my mind be one with my speech.' So runs a plea in the Upanishads, Hinduism's great speculative treatises. And in the Abrahamic faiths there's a belief that in the beginning God did provide for such a unity, creating a single perfect language that offered a flawless fit between idea and utterance. There were correct and unambiguous names for everything, thus allowing the possibility of completely satisfactory communication. But that original tongue was fractured through human sin and folly into the shards of unsatisfactory pieces that confront us today. *The Search for a Perfect Language*, something that Umberto Eco has explored in his book of this same title, is an idea that's had a long and interesting history as people have striven to retrieve or reinvent this perfect fit between experience and utterance.

If language did mirror all the weathers of the psyche so faithfully that there was no perceived disjunction between what we felt, what we thought and what we said, would we feel relieved or constrained? Despite the appeal in the heart's finding a voice to cup and cradle its every beat, the prospect of such an intimate alignment is, finally, unappealing. It would, surely, involve losing the incredible diversity and unpredictability of language. It would move us back towards shrieks and cries that, however snugly they might contour things, couldn't offer the leverage to lift the weight of experience from us, allow us to probe and dissect it, rather than merely reflect its occurrence. We crave more than merely to *echo* the circumstances we find ourselves in.

The sound of trains from Lisburn station before the onset of heavy downpours constitutes only one trill of notes in the symphony of sounds sedimented in my memory over a lifetime. I've not heard it directly for some time now and, who knows, may never do so again. But I can summon it, pitch-perfect, from remembrance, even though it eludes the grasp of words. Caught in the delicate web of my neuronal pathways, it has metamorphosed from sound to that most shadowy and ghostly of things: the memory of sound. As I try to do some justice to it here, I think again, for the umpteenth time, of that most astonishing of all noises, language, and the miraculous transactions it allows us to perform. Even if it can't quite catch the train sounds of my childhood, its network of words allows us to embark on journeys whose distances and destinations dwarf anything that rails can measure.

WITNESS

Some things stress more forcefully than others the fact that any accounts we give of them are inadequate. It's not just those instances generally acknowledged to be difficult to put into words that have this potential. Everyone knows, for example, that explaining what it feels like to be in love, or describing the birth of a child, or summoning a dream back into waking diction, places such strains on language that we may come to doubt its ability to catch more than a fraction of what we want to say. Sometimes seemingly ordinary moments too can ambush us with their resistance to description. Such ambushes rob our words of substance and leave utterance eviscerated, so that underneath whatever's said you can almost hear the whispering of hollow husks, haunting the sentences with a ghostly sense of emptiness.

For me, it is these moments, not the classically difficult exemplars, that most seriously call into question whether the raw impress of what happens can be caught satisfactorily in language. On such occasions there seems to be so great a loss of meaning that the act of expression feels more like corruption than communication. Looking at the way seemingly unproblematic occurrences can sometimes trigger the imagination and spiral away from the mundane into proximate galaxies of complexity that are more than sufficient to bankrupt words, makes me wonder if there is a sense in which *everything* is ineffable, rather than just a few special, known circumstances when we expect to end up speechless.

I'm not sure why some things spark a kind of chain reaction

in the mind, almost nuclear in intensity, quickly exploding the dullness of a moment into the sort of uncatchable incandescence that ruptures words, reducing them to spectral remnants that only have the power of shadows. I do know, though, that this is a brightness I crave, despite all the perplexity it causes, and in whose absence (which can be frequent, prolonged and painful) I feel only half alive.

Far from being the kind of thing that might seem likely to explode into unexpected dimensions, defying the reins of language, the moment I want to look at here sounds reasonably straightforward on first hearing. It is, admittedly, unusual. But, rather than being something descriptively elusive, it seems more like another of those quotidian, yet weird, juxtapositions that Ulster's years of conflict have generated so regularly they've become commonplace. By 'quotidian, yet weird, juxtaposition' I don't mean the way bombs and bullets suddenly shatter people's lives – you never get used to that. But some of the consequences that ripple out from the proximity of such terrible acts to the ordinary *do* become so familiar that, after a while, for all their strangeness, they're just accepted as the norm. So, natives of the place have variously got used to things like accepting body searches before going into shops; meeting heavily armed security forces, bristling with firepower, patrolling countryside that seems utterly tranquil; seeing flags declaring allegiance to murderous paramilitary groups fluttering in abundance in quiet villages and market towns; coming across burnt-out buildings and graffiti alongside high-rise city office blocks whose architecture – plush, international, anonymous – seems to deny any proximity to local hatreds. Like these, the juxtaposition I stumbled across one July afternoon in Lisburn, the sprawling County Antrim town where I was raised, emphasised the unnerving contiguity of violence to everyday life. In this case, though, it came in the unexpected form of encountering a terrorist in a second-hand bookshop.

Stated bluntly, this probably sounds much more dramatic than it was. The terrorist in question was eighteen at most, slight, unarmed and not intent on causing harm. What struck me most about him were the pinched and pock-marked pallor of his face and the uneasy restlessness of his stance. He seemed intensely uncomfortable with himself, his movements jerky, unrelaxed, self-conscious. He was profoundly unstill. His eyes suggested a depth of wariness, aggression and hurt that at once made one nervous of, and sorry for, him. He was unshaven, and his cheap clothes so crumpled it seemed likely he'd slept in them. The mingled air of desperation, unpredictability and poverty that his whole mien suggested immediately made me think he was on drugs (a supposition that turned out to be accurate).

The door of the bookshop had some kind of cowbell fixed to it so that each entry and exit was marked by a resonant chime that made customers look up from whatever they were reading. Almost immediately the boy came in, another customer left, hurriedly, as if in response, giving his departure the air of flight. In his haste to leave, the customer didn't quite shut the door behind him and a few minutes later the wind caught it and the bell sounded again. Perhaps the proprietor, who was busy on the phone at the back of the shop, heard the chime and assumed I'd also left. Perhaps I'd been hunkered down out of sight in the Irish history section for so long that he'd forgotten I was there. Or, maybe I just seemed like a tourist (I was wearing a garish tee-shirt and carrying a camera), someone so far removed from local allegiances that it would be safe to display them in my hearing. For whatever reason, when he'd finished his call, the proprietor went over to where the boy was standing, just inside the door, flicking through a book he'd pulled at random from the nearest shelf, and greeted him by name.

Though it seemed like longer, they probably only talked for three or four minutes at most. Beyond a few phrases that stick in mind, I won't try to reproduce their actual words. It was a broken, uneasy dialogue, interspersed with uncomfortable silences, in which the boy, Tony, seemed to be asking the bookshop proprietor for help. The proprietor seemed sympathetic, though rather coldly so, and reluctant to get too involved. I couldn't work out their relationship at all. The boy seemed submissive, respectful, almost fearful, but with an undertow of truculence. He treated the proprietor as a cross between confessor and commander. It was clear from what was said that Tony had stolen from friends he'd been living with, in order to buy drugs. He'd moved to another flat 'over in Old Warren' (an area of the town about a mile from the bookshop) and was on his own now, but badly missing his friends. He felt sorry for what he'd done, and wanted to talk to them. But he said he 'couldn't face them', that he felt ashamed and wanted the bookshop proprietor to apologise on his behalf. Again, this puzzled me. The proprietor was middle aged and had a dishevelled air of respectability. What connection had he with Tony and his friends? The proprietor assured him that if they were real friends they'd understand without needing to be told. At which point, as if to emphasise why he needed an inter-mediary, Tony said, 'But I've done some terrible things, you know, terrible, I just couldn't face them now.' This was met with the re-sponse: 'You've got to get out of that stuff, Tony, it'll be the death of you,' to which Tony's reply, said with a depth of resignation far beyond his years, was: 'They'd not let me now, not after everything.'

At that point I still thought it was all to do with drugs. The 'terrible things' might have involved further thefts (there'd been some particularly nasty targeting of old folks in their homes around that time), or maybe Tony had even prostituted himself for funds. The 'they' who wouldn't let him out would be his suppliers. When the proprietor said: 'Why don't you get away, right away, across the water?' (local parlance for moving to the British main-land), that and Tony's 'Sure I'd only be having to look over my shoulder the whole time' again seemed likely to be drug-related. It was only when the boy left the shop that things fell into a different focus. The proprietor went quickly to the phone and dialled a number. Even hearing just one side of the conversation, it soon became clear that Tony's predicament wasn't only caused by drugs. I don't know who the proprietor was talking to, but what he said went something like this (the dots representing the unheard responses at the other end):

It's me ... Tony's back ... Don't panic ... Calm down. It's not a problem ... really ... OK ... yes ... I don't know ... He looks dreadful ... No ... Well ... I just thought I should warn you, you know ... That's OK ... It's very unlikely ... I don't know if he even *knows* your address ... But just in case ... No, I couldn't do that ... No, not at this stage anyway ... No, no that's out of the question ... It's not the drugs so much ... yes ... yes ... Oh he's still on them all right ... I know it's a problem ... He's doing stuff again for them ... What? ... No, you know, the paramilitaries ... Worse than before ... He's in far deeper ... Very serious stuff ... He didn't say, obviously ... Yes ... That recent thing ... Definitely ... there's no doubt at all ... yes ... I'm quite sure ... I knew about it already ... It's possible ... Yes, maybe that too ... It's quite possible ... And that other business, you know, what Davey was talking about? I know ... terrible ... No, not anymore ... He lives on his own now, some wee flat in Old Warren ... No ... He says he wants out ... Well that's what he says ... I know ... of course ... they'd never let him ... But he came into the shop, I couldn't just ... No you're right ... I agree ... OK, I'll have a word with him ... I'm not sure ... maybe ... Look I've got to go ... You've got Davey's number ... Well, just in case he calls ... I've got to go ... Yes, I know, I'll be careful, but I'm sure he doesn't know ... I'll see you later ... Call me if you're worried ... Bye.

A man had come into the shop with a box of books to sell. He put them on the counter, cutting the proprietor's call short. As soon as they were engaged in looking through the volumes and haggling about prices I left, uneasily aware that I'd witnessed something of Ulster's shadow-side – albeit partially, obliquely, momentarily. I'd caught a glimpse up close of the face of terror that, for decades, has run like a malign nerve through our history, causing intermittent contractions of agony. That it was pathetic rather than bestial emphasised the tragedy of Ulster's plight. Tony was clearly no godfather of violence masterminding a campaign behind the scenes. He wasn't even a hard-bitten lieutenant charged with marshalling personnel and munitions, putting strategy into bloody operation. He was the poorest of the poor foot-soldiers, at the sharp end, exploited, expendable, 'doing stuff' for the paramilitaries and obviously terrified. That's not to say he was blameless. He'd admitted to doing 'terrible things' which, measured on Ulster's scale of brutality, and against what I suspected 'that recent thing' referred to, strongly suggested his involvement in some truly monstrous deeds. Yet, for all that, he came across more as a pathetic boy than as someone guilty of heinous crimes.

Now, what's so difficult about describing my unexpected encounter with the miserable (and misery-causing) Tony? I can specify the time, the place, the date. I can make a reasonable enough stab at recording what happened at these co-ordinates. The paragraphs above offer an account whose accuracy would, I'm sure, have been endorsed supposing another person had been in the shop. Aldous Huxley once warned, 'facts are ventriloquists' dummies, sitting on a wise man's knee they may be made to utter words of wisdom, elsewhere they say nothing, or talk nonsense, or indulge in sheer diabolism'. For all that, though, and without adopting some kind of naïve objectivity that supposes there is only one version of events, I think independent witnesses would have agreed my account of the facts without significant alterations.

At one level there is no problem about describing what happened. Words work well enough, drawing the weight of meaning out like the reliable workhorses we expect them to be. Although the load they carry is a long way from constructing anything so lofty as wisdom, I'm confident they at least avoid nonsense and diabolism and can be used to make a serviceable shelter in which to house my memory of Tony and the bookshop proprietor. The difficulty only comes when, as happened in this case, another order of perception leans its weight on these everyday terms of reference, causing them to buckle and implode into a nexus of intertwining complexities that seem to defy sense (even as they hint at something sensible beyond it). Although 'seeing a terrorist in a second-hand bookshop' may be convenient shorthand, it does not remotely describe what 'really' happened that afternoon. It's a simplification of such massive proportions that offering it seems almost like bearing false witness. The truth is something ungainly, untidy and complicated. To even approach telling it necessitates an excursion into memory, history, accident.

It's not always clear where the weight comes from that nudges some moments into mystery but leaves others untouched, their bare descriptors fluttering like flags of seeming victory above them. But with my ill-met terrorist in the bookshop, the weight that split the atom of mundane recounting, revealing gargantuan hidden dimensions swirling beneath their simplistic terms of reference, came from two sources I *can* identify. To begin with, I'd been thinking about time and how its passing impacts upon our sense of place. This had been sparked by conversations with my mother and her friends about their memories of Lisburn from decades before I was born. Their temporal depth of vision, allowing them to see things through the frame of change afforded by remembered history, had already shaken my faith in the adequacy of those bland co-ordinates by which we customarily situate things purely in the immediacy of the present. Then there was the further disruptive influence of browsing in a second-hand bookshop when, given the direction in which my thoughts were already turning, I was particularly liable to fall through some of those many portals, disguised as books, that lead out of the common order of experience and into other modes of outlook altogether. It is these scattered portals that make second-hand bookshops such interesting, almost magical, places. Browsing there you can find yourself transported without warning to ancient Thebes, finding out about mummification, or looking at the structure of an atom, or considering the memoirs of some pious eighteenth-century cleric, or discovering the mating habits of gorillas, or admiring the delicacies of Chinese art. Bookshops that only sell new books offer something of the same, but their organisation, the lack of unpredictability, the rigid arrangement by section, minimises accidental discovery. It's less likely there that you'll pick up something unanticipated and suddenly find doors opening into other worlds. The bookshop in Lisburn was one where, despite apparent arrangement, a pleasing undertow of chaos could pull you down without warning. Here, Wilfred Thesiger's *The Marsh Arabs* had Stephen Hawking's *A Brief History of Time* as its nearest neighbour. Robert Burton's *Anatomy of Melancholy* was shelved under 'medical', flanked by a book on wine and some self-help volumes on hay-fever and migraines. Esler Crawford's wonderful book of aerial photographs of Northern Ireland, *The North from the Air*, was in between a volume of erotic bookplates and Augusta and Burian's *Prehistoric Man*.

One of the occupational hazards of an essayist is to let the implicit order of language leach out, so that – however confused and untidy the experiences one is attempting to describe may be – they acquire a measure of linearity and logic simply because of the verbal dressing put on them. Stealthy systematisation via sentences can edge a jumble of events and ideas towards a coherence they do not possess in the raw. It is as if words were stained with some unfast dye that colours everything they touch, marking it with whatever shade sense comes clad in. Words have already leaked their patterns into what I've said about Tony, providing a ghostly scaffolding to shore up the encounter, giving it a more stable form than it had at the moment of its passing. Then, it sprawled across a combination of perception, remembrance, knowledge and imagination. It was fluid, surprising, almost unnerving. To some extent this unstoppable oozing of colours from our verbal palette is unproblematic. Far from being an occupational hazard, it might be viewed as an inevitable feature of perception or, indeed, as the foundation of the writer's task of weaving graspable meaning out of the tangle of things life throws at us. It only becomes a kind of pitfall if we lose the ability to negotiate back and forth between the realms of experience and description, and come to assume too great a measure of exactness in our mapping of one with the other. This essay seeks to underscore what should be obvious but often isn't, namely that the simplifications of ordinary language shouldn't be taken too seriously; that, looked at closely, they are not reliable statements of record at all.

It might more accurately pinpoint what really happened when I saw Tony in the bookshop (and 'saw' already simplifies that complex confluence of perception, memory, imagination, desire, comparison – all the rivulets in our stream of consciousness that allow experience to happen) if I merely attached a string of words to the elements of the moment. Such a labelling might provide some ballast to act as counterweight against the supposition that my meeting with Tony was straightforward, neatly cut and dried, something that surrenders easily enough to description. This kind of strategy might issue in some such word-cluster as: *finches, birdsong, 'God', pet shop, dinosaur, universe, canal, barges, Buddha, neutron star, meditation, galaxy.* Let me fish from this unlikely shoal of seemingly unrelated verbal shards a few of its staccato components and attempt to explain how they framed my encounter with Tony and edged it towards mystery, rather than coralling it in the mundane. I hope this will illustrate how 'I saw a terrorist in a bookshop' is so severe a whittling down that the sequoia forest of sensation is reduced to a matchstick report in which the colossal plenitude of experience is lost.

While he stood fidgeting, waiting for the bookshop proprietor to finish his phone call, Tony had pulled a book from one of the shelves. If, reaching up for it, his hand had been placed there thirty years earlier, it would have caused a flurry of feathers. Would those brightly coloured Australian finches that used to occupy the same space as the rows of books on religion, have pecked his pale fingers with the nails bitten to their quicks? Or would they have perched their tiny quivering bodies there for a second, their lightness almost imperceptible as they trilled out the shrill rapidity of their scolding song, made at such a volume that it seemed incredible so small a frame could generate it? The space now occupied by the bookshop's religion section had once been a bank of cages. Budgies, finches and cockatiels used to fly there, through air now occupied by dense-packed pages heavily blacked with lines of print. Set beside the deft fluency of the birds' movements, even within the constraints imposed on them by wire and wood, words like 'God', 'heaven' and 'hell' have a heavy flightless quality to them. They seem as unlikely to get airborne as the kind of ridiculous contraptions that preceded aviation.

What was now a bookshop had, for many years, been a pet shop. I could remember visiting it often as a boy. I bought several tortoises there (they never survived a winter), budgies, a rabbit, goldfish, and made regular trips both to purchase supplies – fishfood, rabbit pellets, birdseed, millet, cuttlefish bone for beaks – and just to gaze at the livestock. The transition from pet shop to bookshop was not direct, a number of businesses had operated from these premises in between. But none of them had flourished and I have only indistinct and shadowy memories of a short-lived sewing shop, a cut-price jeweller and a charity clothes shop. For me, the transition may as well have been immediate. The bookshop was haunted by pet shop memories that were sufficiently potent to intrude their images into the present. Alongside the smell of books was the well-remembered dusty aroma of the hessian sacks of meal and seed that used to sit on the floor below the counter, each one with a small silver metal scoop planted in it, ready for measuring out a customer's requirement. This powerful background perfume clung to your clothes for an hour or more after you'd left the shop. Laced in with it, too, was the sharper reek of fur and feathers, pet food and excrement.

Where the history section was there used to be tanks of fish, a neat statement in miniature of our watery origins, the aquatic aeons underlying with enormous depth the tiny strip of human years we colonise. Rabbits, hamsters and mice were housed in cramped cages in the section now occupied by 'militaria' and sport. Occasionally, there were puppies, and often kittens, kept near where the bookshop proprietor now had a portable gas fire (on low, even in the summer, and adding to the already stuffy atmosphere). To my childhood eyes, the pet shop owner had seemed an ancient woman. She was red-faced, wrinkled and rotund, though whether her girth was due to flesh or clothing it was hard to tell, for she wore layer upon layer of greasy-looking cardigans. She breathed in a wheezy, laboured fashion and always complained if you paid entirely in copper coins. Her bedraggled-looking parrot – an African grey – sat on a perch that was thickly encrusted with droppings and which had pinned to it a faded cardboard label, nibbled at the edges, saying 'Not for Sale'. They made all sorts of noises to each other, keeping up a perpetual private dialogue that ranged from gentle intimacies to shrieks of exasperation. She lived above the shop, and near closing time the parrot would hop on her shoulder and scold any customers, impatient for them to leave so that they could shut up shop and retreat to whatever domestic arrangements they enjoyed.

The occupancy of this place across time took in myself, Tony, the bookshop proprietor, the pet shop owner and her parrot, and all the varied livestock that used to line the walls. The street in which the shop stood was nearly three centuries old, being one of the first in the town to be rebuilt after the great fire of 1707 that razed Lisburn to the ground. So, given the length of time there had been human habitation around and in these premises, quite a cluster of other unknown faces could no doubt be added to the list of life-forms that had passed some moments of their finitude here, at these particular co-ordinates, beneath the stars. Projecting back and forwards through the amplitude of time, using the shop as pivot, how many creatures, and of what nature, would join the little band of tenants who have sojourned (or will sojourn) in this locus? Were there any connections between them other than the accident of being in this place, oblivious to the lives that came crowding before and that would come after?

My imagining Tony reaching out his hand into space occupied thirty years ago by those brightly coloured Australian finches has, of course, an incoherence built into it. For clearly thirty years before our momentary encounter in the bookshop Tony did not exist, or at least not in any form recognisable as such. He was not yet conceived, his parents would probably still have been children, the meeting and mating that issued in him was still years away and had yet to negotiate all manner of alternatives and options before resulting in that particular outcome. But such incoherence is no bar to the imagination, which can see individuals not simply as they appear to the eye, standing before us in all their visual simplicity, but as entrances to time. Tony's life leads back (as all our lives do) through ancestors innumerable to a sense of the species, the form we're held in, crowded with our fellows, variations on a stupendous theme. This, in turn, leads back to the ungraspable scale of geological aeons, the beginning of life, the birth of our world, the genesis of the universe itself. Had his parents been patrons of the pet shop when they'd been children? Perhaps, for life seems filled with such connections, we had all three stood there together some Saturday morning all those years ago, looking with as yet unfocused childish desire at the fish, the mice, the rabbits, our pocket-money hot in our hands.

As I stood in the bookshop watching this youthful terrorist thumb through a book, I had a striking image – momentary but very vivid – of Tony's hand unspooling back towards its ultimate origin. I saw it speeded up, winding back through the aeons, through each of its progenitors, like some kind of crazy organic firework fizzling out the incredible story of its becoming. And, side by side with it, a parallel picture emerged of the tiny gem-like finches that had once been exactly where his hand reached up for the book. They also acted as tunnels stretching back to what had led to them, tiny vortexes that drew the mind's eye ever further downwards, back through the centuries. Two rushing series of bounded events, held cupped in bird-shaped and human-shaped containers, spiralling back from here and now to that event which spawned them, a genesis so far distant from our fleeting present that it seems to belong to some strange other-world, distant and alien to our familiar Irish earth. Seeing Tony and the finches anchored to inconceivable ancientness, to pre-hominids, to dinosaurs, to amoeba, made 'seeing a terrorist in a bookshop' seem an impoverished and ill-fitting locution for the moment.

Perhaps it was remembering the pet shop whilst surrounded by books that brought a comment of William James's back to mind. He once suggested that we may be in the universe in the same way as cats and dogs are in a library. Its meaning may be as far beyond the grasp of our intellect as reading Kant would be to canine or feline apprehension. Thinking of all the tortoises and budgies, rabbits and mice, budgies and kittens that had been sold from the pet shop, thinking of their origins and ends and how they had been briefly entangled with scores of families' lives in Lisburn and the surrounding area, thinking of my own boyhood self standing in this place and buying birdseed, innocent of the later incarnation who would look back at such a moment three decades later and wonder about a killer standing close by, quite oblivious to such speculations, I found myself wondering if James's remark might be true. Seeing Tony in the bookshop was framed, edged, tinted by all of this. It was as if I saw him through the ghosts of long-dead finches, heard the pet shop owner's slippers drag and shuffle on the same floor on which, half a lifetime on, Tony stood shifting uneasily from foot to foot in his dirty trainers.

Once described by Johnson's biographer James Boswell as 'one of the prettiest towns I ever saw', Lisburn, like so many places in Ireland, has undergone massive changes to its physical fabric over that span of years through which the memories of my generation and the one before it range and think of as their own. Such changes will not be apparent to someone just passing through, or to those who have only lived there briefly. For them, Lisburn will appear securely held in the present hand of roads and buildings it shows to the world. Here, as elsewhere, the past's invisibility helps to foster the illusion of fixity. Those innocent of time's endless shuffling and dealing will tend to think the town possesses the same apparent permanence as stone. Such outlooks anchor to their comforting bedrock the diction of name and place and number – those building blocks of commonsense report – and impart to their accounts a lithic certainty that, without any sense of history to erode it, seems unproblematic and free from doubt. According to such building blocks, saying something like 'I saw a terrorist in a bookshop' is sufficient to convey what I witnessed. For me, on this occasion, such a declaration seems tantamount to lying and serves more to point to and encircle something I don't understand at all, rather than explain any part of it.

Though Lisburn is not on the coast, at one time it boasted nine quays in a bustling harbour. Whoever lived in the house that became the pet shop and then bookshop was only a couple of minutes walk from the epicentre of the town's now lost identity as an inland port. At the bottom of the street where the pet shop owner and her parrot had conducted their daily dialogue over the years, just a stone's throw from where Tony had stood confessing to the 'terrible things' he'd done, was where the canal's waters touched the town. The river Lagan is still there today, flowing as it always has, oblivious to human affairs, but only a remnant is left of the Lagan Canal, which used to link Belfast to Lough Neagh (the Belfast–Lisburn stretch opened in 1763). For over one hundred and fifty years the canal was a crucial part of Ulster's commercial infrastructure. It snaked its way like a watery nerve through Edenderry, Ballyskeagh, Lambeg, Lisburn, Flatfield, Soldierstown, Aghalee, until it reached Lough Neagh, Ulster's giant inland sea (the largest freshwater lake in the British Isles). There's a rough poetry of vanished lives and untold stories in the names of the locks the waters passed through, all now derelict, forgotten: Molly Ward's, Mickey Taylor's, Rosie's, McQuiston's, Becky Hogg's, Dan Horner's, Goudy Lock, Turtle Dove Lock, and, oddest of all, the lock at Lough Neagh itself, Ellis's Gut. For over a century, lives were moulded by the canal. Lock-keepers, haulers (the men who led the horses which plodded along the towpaths pulling the barges), bank rangers (responsible for keeping the grass and weed from clogging the waterway), the lightermen and their families who lived on the barges, almost like water-borne gypsies, a close clannish community which held itself apart from those fixed to the land. A whole way of life now vanished, its rhythms almost entirely forgotten, only a few physical traces remaining, mostly unnoticed by, and irrelevant to, those whose way of life is now current in this place.

When I'd heard that Tony lived somewhere in Old Warren, I'd immediately wondered if he could see what remained of the canal from his window. Some of the houses in Old Warren overlook a stretch of the canal that, for all of my boyhood, had been in a state of enticing dereliction. It was a dangerous place, a sheer-sided channel dropping into deep water, with the remains of half-closed lock gates daring us to venture out and jump from one side to the other. I played there often with a friend whose family's farm bordered the river and canal. Old Warren was on the other side, smaller than it is today, ringed with woods, the land still safe for years from the town's expansion. If Tony's eyes had seen the glint of sun on water that morning when he first looked out, it would have been reflected off the same place where I used to play, which was the same place my mother and her best friend passed through frequently on barges when they hitched lifts along the canal, a favourite pastime when they were children. The thought of the triangulation of gazes rooted to this small stretch of glinting water, my mother's, mine and Tony's, surged like a tidal bore along the channel of the present, sweeping my perception of it out into non-navigable waters where I knew I was out of my depth and miles beyond any of the life-rafts of language. My mother – looking at the lush countryside go slowly by, listening to the clop and squelch of the horse's steady walking, smelling the bacon the lighterman's wife was frying in the tiny galley – might have swept her eyes innocently over the precise spot on the bank where, years further down the waterways her life was to follow, an unimagined son of an unmet husband would play, oblivious to her childhood passage. And she would certainly have seen the tree-clad rise of land where, when she was seventy, a boy called Tony would live in his lonely flat and lament the terrible things he had done.

According to William James:

> Our normal waking consciousness is but one special type of consciousness, whilst all about it, parted only by the filmiest of screens, there lie potential forms of consciousness entirely different.

Standing in the bookshop listening to Tony and the proprietor talk, I felt a parting of filmy screens as that present seemed to open into other vistas altogether, stretching out beyond the horizons of the ordinary.

Just as Lough Neagh used to be the watery heart for a whole network of canals – the Lagan Canal, the Ulster Canal, the Newry Canal, Ducart's Canal, Coalisland Canal, the Lower Bann Canal – consciousness seems like a kind of liquid hub from which and into which flow the channels of the senses. Ordinary waking awareness follows an ordered pattern, as if the sulci in the brain were governed by a whole series of lock gates that allow their

levels to rise or fall according to whatever cargo the mind is trans-
porting. But there are times, and the moment in the bookshop
was one of them, when the whole system seems to flood and one
is left dumbfounded and overwhelmed by the incredible circumstance of being.

I instantly recognised the book that Tony pulled from the religion
shelves as he waited for the proprietor to finish his phone call. It
was Edward Conze's *Buddhist Meditation* in the paperback edition
that has on its cover a picture of the famous granite Buddha, seated
in meditation, that can still be seen today in Sri Lanka's ancient capital. The sculpture is over a thousand years old and exudes such an
aura of strength and serenity that something of it is evident even
from the not very good black-and-white photograph on Conze's
book. Tony had pulled it down from the shelf so rapidly after stepping inside the shop and seeing the proprietor was busy, that it
seemed much more like the random, almost desperate, act of
someone who wanted to merge with the background and not be
noticed, rather than the deliberate choice of a reader genuinely
interested in the topic. He flicked through the pages, more in the
manner of someone shuffling cards than of someone actually reading. Whatever his choice of book had been, I doubt whether Tony
would have managed to merge into the background in a bookshop.
He was utterly out of his element in such surroundings.

It would have been symbolically more apt, providing a nice
cameo of Ulster's terrible psychosis, if Tony had found his way to
the local interest section and taken down one of the volumes that
attempt to chronicle or explain the violence he was part of. What
a gift for an essayist to have seen a terrorist leafing through, say,
Jonathan Bardon's *A History of Ulster*! But the religion section was
first inside the door and Tony's desire for the camouflage he evidently thought any book would bestow was strong enough to
make him stop there, rather than advance any further into such

alien territory. Although it lacked something of the ironic appro-
priateness that could have been brought into play had Tony chosen Bardon's admirable volume, the very fact that Conze's *Buddhist
Meditation* was on the shelves at all was part of a fascinating story,
and seeing it in Tony's hands sparked an interesting chain of reflections. Anyhow, if Tony had edged further into the shop to
where *A History of Ulster* was shelved, he would doubtless have
spotted me and I might then never have witnessed what happened.

The realisation that there are other faiths in the world beyond
the one you're familiar with is both an uneven and unpredictable
phenomenon, with different places and different people mani-
festing very different levels of it. Certainly in the Ulster I grew up
in, religion meant either Catholic or Protestant. Beyond the de-
nominational divisions of Christianity – Church of Ireland, Presbyterian, Methodist, Baptist, Catholic – there was, I suppose, a
muted, low-key recognition of the existence of Jews. From the
doorstepping of Jehovah's Witnesses and Mormons, these
churches, too, had some claim to inclusion in our map of people's
religious allegiances, though they were not considered 'respectable'. And, since there was a long-established Quaker school
in Lisburn, to which many non-Quakers went (myself included),
we knew about 'the Friends'. But of the fact that millions of people in the world followed Islam or Buddhism, that many times the
population of Ireland worshipped Shiva or Vishnu, we were entirely innocent. Some of the hymns we sang in school and church
referred to 'heathens', an indiscriminately dismissive catchall in
which we could lump together and forget about anyone beyond
Europe and North America.

When did such now incredible ignorance and self-centredness
start to change? Probably not until the 1960s. It is amazing to
think how recently our awareness has taken a quantum leap forward. I'd be surprised if, prior to 1960, any bookshop in Ireland
would have stocked books about non-Christian religions, with the
possible exception of Judaism and, perhaps, some missionary in-
vective directed at 'heathens'. The story behind the particular copy

of Conze's *Buddhist Meditation* that Tony took from the shelf of the Lisburn bookshop that July afternoon would be interesting to know. If we could tap into it we might be able to pick out one thread in the fabric of that revolutionary change in religious consciousness that has started to dawn in our time. Although encounters between westerners and Buddhists began as long ago as 326 BC with Alexander's invasion of India, it has only been in the last one hundred and fifty years that any *reliable* information about this great religion has been available to us. For most of Buddhism's long history, its very existence was barely known in the west. When did the *dharma*, the Buddha's teaching, first appear in Lisburn? Who heard it first and via what means? What impact did it have on them? What County Antrim hippy had bought Conze's study (a book that first appeared in 1956, with many reprints since then)? How many hands had this book passed through between its original owner and the moment Tony's hand took it from the bookshelf? What reception had the *dharma* encountered in an Ulster context? Perhaps it is just as well we cannot read much from the objects we encounter, were their stories perceptible to touch we would be overwhelmed with history.

Did Tony's attention focus on the book for long enough to glean anything at all about it? As he flicked through the pages did some of the section headings catch his eye – 'The Recollection of Death', 'Distaste for the Body', 'Mindfulness', 'The Practice of Introversion', 'Emptiness'? Did he know what Buddhism was? Had he heard the story of the Buddha's life? What did he believe about the origin of suffering, the nature of the self, what happens to us when we die? How would he face death, this edgy, awkward boy who had dealt out death to others? Seeing him holding Conze's volume, I thought in particular of the section on *pratitya-samutpada*, interdependent origination, the great Buddhist teaching on causation, and I wondered if Tony's predicament might be more accurately pictured by the idea of karma and rebirth than the delineation offered by more prosaic terms. Interdependent origination is pictured in simplified form in that striking Buddhist symbol, the Wheel of Life, the constituent parts of which encourage a deconstruction of individuals into the processes that give rise to their particular situations. I saw Tony caught in some hell realm, a terrible universe parallel to our everyday reality, doing evil, having evil done to him, thousands of lives away from salvation. His individual story fragmented into a whole history of consequences, outcomes, confluences, stretching across vast tundras of time, eroding the plausibility of seeing him on some simpler stage with a beginning and an ending, a clearly written role to play.

One of the books I'd looked at before getting lodged in the Irish history section of the shop was in a popular scientific series. It was simply entitled *The Universe* and provided a compendium of those stupendous facts of life that most of us are vaguely aware of but whose vertiginous perspectives make one wonder if the mind is really designed to hold them. Being in a bookshop with a terrorist is a paltry circumstance compared to recognising that we are on a 4,600-million-year-old planet, one of billions of heavenly bodies in a galaxy that measures 100,000 light years across. The universe, which may contain one thousand million galaxies, each with one hundred billion stars, is thought to have started 15 billion years ago with the Big Bang. During this event, all energy and matter that would exist was created in an instant, in an area probably no larger than a child's marble. The book contained wonderful graphics and seemed to make clear these dazzling imponderables. One of the facts that stuck in my mind was that after a supernova, when a massive star explodes, its remains may collapse into a so-called 'neutron star'. This is the densest type of star – a handful of its material would weigh billions of tons. The moment of my encounter with Tony in the bookshop seemed similarly dense. Trying to grasp it soon revealed an unexpected weight; a handful could plunge one through the ice of ordinary discourse and take one plummeting down and down into the unfathomable depths beneath its fragile surface.

To know that seconds after the Big Bang, when time, matter, energy, space – everything – was created, the universe was a buzz of particles happening in something not much bigger than the size of a pea, is also to feel a shadow of this kind of radical density fall upon our discourse and cause it to implode. Ever since the Big Bang, the universe has been expanding. Tony and I, the pet shop owner and her parrot, Lisburn, Ireland, all of us, are infinitesimal particles in the maelstrom, part of this expansion, brought together momentarily on the cusp of the billowing now. As William Blake famously put it, 'If the doors of perception were cleansed, everything would appear to man as it is, infinite.' Seeing Tony in the bookshop seemed to allow light from a tiny patch of such cleansing to flood through. Its brightness was too radiant for words and seemed to spark some kind of perceptual supernova that ravelled unmeasurable density out of the apparently familiar.

If the world could appear to us 'as it really is', how would we see it and each other? Arne Trankell's book, *Reliability of Evidence* (Stockholm, 1972), is one of many studies that helps to edge us towards a better understanding of the complexities of witnessing than the naïvely commonsensical outlook which supposes that simply being there confers authority on subsequent accounts of what happened. Quite apart from the fallibility of recall, the selectivity of what we see, the paucity of terms with which to catch something as elusive as, for example, someone's appearance – not to mention the impact of subjectivity on all our experiences – it's clear that in situations where we're startled, frightened, or apprehensive, conditions may simply not be conducive to the kind of attention to detail that description relies on. What colour was Tony's shirt? What height was he? I could only hazard guesses. Nor am I sure if I'd recognise him again supposing our paths crossed outside the bookshop. Certainly if he was clean-shaven, neatly dressed, matured beyond the terrible unease of that discomfiting youth who flicked through Conze's book, I'm quite sure I'd pass him by without a flicker of recognition. And yet I have a vivid image still in mind of that moment in the bookshop, of his standing there, of his face, his body language. But it is an image that quickly dissolves into uncertainties if I try to pin it down to easily itemised particulars. In this I suppose I am no better (though I hope no worse) than any eyewitness called to testify.

In a more profound sense than this, though, I have come to doubt my reliability as a witness. What are we witnesses to? What are we witnessing now, as the blood and breath run through us, as the sun warms our skin? What is happening, this moment, as the world passes before our eyes in all the complexity of its intermingling components, its processes threaded through an immensity of time? What meets the eye? What falls upon the mind? How should we describe it? Is it less misleading to say, 'I saw a terrorist in a bookshop', or to try to describe the interlocking mesh of factors that combined to channel that glimpse of Tony into something almost approaching an epiphany?

In an essay contributed to the superb Graywolf Forum collection, *The Business of Memory: the Art of Remembering in an Age of Forgetting* (edited by Charles Baxter, 1999), Lydia Davis comments:

> There are certain things I think I 'ought to' remember, if
> I am to be a responsible representative of my time and
> generation, but where there should be a memory there is
> often a blank.

I often wonder what *ought* to be remembered from Ulster's years of agony and turmoil, who did what to whom. For those bereaved, or maimed, or rendered homeless by the violent activities of Tony and his ilk, the weight of remembrance must often be hard to bear. For those, like myself, who have witnessed much, though our lives have not been directly affected beyond fear and inconvenience, should we remember those responsible for terrorising a community, should we recall the dates of dreadful crimes and what was done, the names of individuals slaughtered and those who did the slaughtering? Or would it be better to let a slow tide of forgetfulness accumulate and slowly buoy us towards healing, forgiveness and reconciliation?

On a wider scale, though, far beyond Ireland and its history, what should be remembered if we are to be responsible representatives not just of our time and generation, but of our situation seen against wider perspectives? What should we bear witness to? How should we describe what happens to us? These are impossible questions. Perhaps rather than answers we need to remember their interrogations and not let any witness statement set too hard into that cement of certainty to which the human mind seems so drawn. What happened that July afternoon in the bookshop? Did I see a terrorist? Or did I see a lost and miserable boy? Or was it a collection of processes involving the filaments of the universe, stretching through the aeons in patterns of astounding complexity? The moment (like every moment) could be described in an almost infinite number of ways. At one level, it's easy enough to deal with, we can skitter across the surface of things, fix them with the abbreviations and simplifications of language, deftly deal with complexities via commonsense. But such words do not contain more than a fraction of what passes, even in the most ordinary of happenstances. Nudge them just a fraction and they soon acquire dimensions of an altogether different order. Perhaps one of the tragedies of modern Ireland is our resolute staying at the surface; our preoccupation with the small scale, the local, the little perspectives in which bitterness can fester.

As Tony and I continue on our own brief individual trajectories through the immensities of space-time, two specks of sentience lost in the swarm of humanity, blown through our days by the irresistible forces of inheritance, accident, desire, I sometimes wonder about his progress. Perhaps he is a reformed character now, drug-free, in a job, maybe with a wife and child, his connection with the paramilitaries somehow safely severed. Or it may be he's already dead. Like all the individual mites of consciousness that pepper time's gargantuan vistas with their momentary presences, we were both raised from the muteness of stone through millions of years of complex processes, all shot out from the naked singularity that spawned everything, some 15 billion years ago. Maybe the temporary assemblage of matter known for a flash of time as 'Tony' has been unspun back into the constituent elements from which it was forged, the ancient building blocks fired in the inconceivable heat of that initial incomprehensible event. If so, I hope the unspinning was neither brutal nor prolonged. Though I have felt the hatred and desire for reciprocal hurt that those who have witnessed terrorism often feel, and though I do not in the least excuse the 'terrible things' Tony was guilty of, I would find it hard to wish or visit vengeance on so troubled and vulnerable a head.

I didn't want to return to the bookshop after overhearing the things I had. To have done so would have seemed at least imprudent, if not perilous. It was possible, after all, that the proprietor had thought the shop was empty and that what he'd said to Tony, and then to whoever he'd spoken to on the phone, was not something he wanted witnessed. No doubt when I did finally leave the shop he noticed me and, who knows (depending on his reliability as a witness), might have recognised me again. But I very much wanted that copy of Conze's *Buddhist Meditation*. It was a book I already had, but having a tangible reminder of my encounter with Tony exerted considerable appeal. I could tell, even as I fled the shop, that this was something I'd want to write about – though as it has turned out I haven't done so for over a decade. The book was easily secured. A cousin, understanding my reluctance to go back, visited the shop the next morning and bought it for me. It sits beside me now, hundreds of miles from Lisburn, as I struggle with words to try to explain something of its significance.

Here is a volume touched by the pallid hand of a terrorist that reached into a space once occupied by Australian finches, their tiny delicate bones long since reverted to the dust that claims us all. His ghostly touch sits invisibly alongside the mark of the Buddha's mind, recorded now in writing, but originally held for centuries in the memories of monks, preserved unwritten in the intimate fastness of individual remembrance. When the book was published, I was a babe in arms, and the shelf it would one day sit on was within earshot of the breath of tortoises whose tiny plodding ghosts I sometimes imagine stalking the County Antrim gardens in which, so unexpectedly, they found themselves. Gotama and Tony, both someone's son, but their lives so very different – even if built of the same blocks of matter – lived in the same element of space-time, and were caught on the same wheel of life. In a shabby shop, in a dirty street, in an unremarkable town, I felt I'd stumbled through a portal that seemed to suck me into it and draw things beyond the possibility of any simple response to the request to 'tell me what happened'.

Conze's book contains translations from a selection of great Buddhist meditation texts, including Buddhaghosha's incomparable *Visuddhimagga* (The Path of Purity). Buddhaghosha composed his great treatise sometime in the fifth century, detailing methods and objects of meditation with a thoroughness and rigour still unsurpassed. Mindfulness of body, mindfulness of breathing, the recollection of death, these are all useful aids to calming the mind and focusing the concentration. But I add to them now another meditation that might, perhaps, be called 'Recollection of the ineffability of the ordinary', or 'Mindfulness of the mystery of everything'. This takes as its point of departure a small scuffed paperback book with an invisible handprint on its cover. It ends by following a path whose only claim to purity lies in its insistence on complication.

MIRACLES

The otolith sits on the flat of my hand, black, dense, heavy, compelling. Its thickly curved presence fits neatly in the palm. Curiously, its shape recalls a human ear. It is as if one had been used to make a mould, into which the tar of molten basalt was poured. Cooling, it settled into every nip and tuck of flesh to leave this eerie impression of a body part cast in stone. It has about it some quality that beckons touch. From the moment I saw it, before I knew what 'otolith' meant, before I had any idea what this object was, I wanted to pick it up, heft it in my hand, let my fingers close round it, feel its cool density grow warm in my grip. Now that I know what it is (or know enough about it to put some labels on it, for in truth it is part of a mystery that shrugs off words), that innate magnetism has been magnified. If it were smaller, I think I might carry it with me, put it on a chain, perhaps, and wear it round my neck, grow used to its hardness lumped against my flesh. Touching it, I can feel the lure of totems, talismans and charms.

'Otolith' comes from the Greek – *otos* for ear, *lithos* for stone – and at first I thought this pairing offered a perfect description. In this instance, though, the bare word 'otolith' needs to be prefaced by another, 'fossil', for the original material of this ear-like object has been swapped for the black stone that now occupies its form (not basalt, despite appearances, but some kind of calcareous limestone). It is witness to a stealthy eviction, a slow shift in substances over the millennia, as one thing gradually became another. Here is a transubstantiation that's at once believable and utterly astounding in the sheer unlikelihood of it ever happening and, happening, that this particular object, out of all the billions surrounding us, should be one of those that momentarily stippled my awareness with its presence.

Moving from etymology to actual meaning, the definition of 'otolith' is: 'a small hard object, made of bone or minerals, found in the inner ear of certain animals, the movement of which helps to maintain balance'. Otoliths are particularly prominent in bony fish (coelacanths, cod, trout, etc.), where they occur as milky white stones that can be as large as a pea. We too have otoliths, though they are so tiny by comparison that they are sometimes referred to as otoconia (ear-dust). Looking to ourselves, *Gray's Anatomy* defines otoliths as:

> Two small rounded bodies, consisting of a mass of minute crystalline grains of carbonate of lime, held together in a mesh of delicate tissues, and contained in the wall of the utricle and saccule opposite the distribution of the nerves.

Listen! There is poetry already resonant in such attempts to nail things down to the manageable particularities of precision. Within the literal, another voice is always singing. Why are we so deaf to it?

I often think, as I balance it on my palm (a ritual frequently performed), of this otolith's budding and beginning. I imagine a hardness growing out of nothing, a microscopic speck, like some tiny planet in a miniature cosmos, which gradually wound about itself a thicker cladding, drawing a dense mass to its presence with the incremental magnetic gravity of growth. This one began around thirty-two million years ago in the head of a whale, swimming somewhere in the ancient oceans that washed between primeval landmasses, starting to resemble the continental shapes we recognise today. 'Began' is the wrong word here (as is 'otolith', as I was subsequently to discover). 'Begin' means 'to come into being' and that long-dead whale, which flashed into and then out of existence all those aeons ago, was merely a staging post along the way. The story was long begun by the time of its brief individual efflorescence. The processes that laid down the substance of its bones were already ancient when it swam its way through the waters, animated by those innumerable microscopic transactions in the muscled labyrinths of flesh, wormed with nerves, that, together, fire a life. Secretly unfolding into the precise exactitude of concretion needed for the body's inner scaffolding, this stone rose's unseen blossoming, its unfurling into the bony tenting of a living head, was directed by forces whose origins were forged thousands of millions of years prior to their traceable impact on the intimate architecture of this individual creature.

In the act of holding it and writing this, I feel as if I'm trying to act as some kind of lightning conductor, providing a conduit so that the charge of meaning carried mutely in the otolith (let's continue to call it that for now) can find safe passage and be earthed through words. The trail of sentences, written first in black ink (before their electronic marshalling into print), is like a slow unpacking of its cargo, an attempt to bleed out significance and sense from the tiny incisions that are all we can puncture in the tough armour of the baffling phenomena around us. It is, I know, just a scratching at the surface, a peeling off of only the thinnest, most obvious layer, a thin trickle from a seemingly inexhaustible reservoir. With something as densely concentrated as this, I could write for all my life, trail out skeins of words, and still not discharge more than a fraction of the otolith's dark, compacted voltage. It is this laden plenitude, the potency of meaning so tightly compressed within it, which gives this object so much of its allure. It seems to offer the promise of revelation, of opening like a magic window, if its super-concentrate of presence can be diluted by the wash of words into a solution that's the right strength to nourish our imagination.

In considering the otolith, in trying to conduct its electricity through the wire of writing, I find two words, long cast aside as useless, surfacing insistently from whatever desolate region of the mind houses our discarded vocabulary: 'miracle' and 'miraculous'. This is a fossil doppelganger of what was once part of a whale's skull, bluntly pushing through the waters as the animal navigated through those ancient seas, as the planet itself swam through space freighted with the vanished lives of creatures, some of whom eventually gave birth to us. That it should be warmed, thirty-two million years later, by the flesh of another mammal as he navigates through the new ocean of language – for on this kind of time-scale our sea of words is something only just invented – are these not the circumstances of miracle?

Whenever I think of miracles now, I think of Brother Erskine, who denied them. He wasn't a brother in the monastic sense, though in appearance, at least, he could have played the part well enough. It would have been easy to imagine him clad, not in his customary black trousers and green blazer, but in a dark-cowled mendicant's robe, striding through some cloistered abbey, bright-eyed, purposeful, intent on doing God's business. Despite his doubts about miracles, Brother Erskine was a 'man of the cloth', as everyone in County Antrim used to call clergymen. And, for all his unexpected scepticism, he had an air of unshakeable faith about him. He had acquired the nickname 'Brother' because of his invariable habit, whenever someone was late for class, of saying, 'Come in, brother, take a pew'. At that point I was at an all-male school in Belfast where he was chaplain, so any latecomer could be so addressed. Perhaps the all-purpose 'brother' avoided the embarrassment of forgetting who was who. Or, since occasionally he added the individual's surname ('Come in, Brother Acheson/Brother Black/Brother Mitchell, take a pew'), maybe it was intended to soften the school's custom of addressing boys by their last name alone and to emphasise a Christian sense of love and, well, *brotherhood*.

Brother Erskine taught English as well as scripture, and it's his classes on Chaucer I most remember now, though the sometimes extraordinary length of the prayers he offered when taking services in the school chapel have also carved a less fondly remembered niche in memory. Standing in the pulpit, his eyes closed, his expression rapt into a frown of puzzled concentration, it was as though he forgot the several hundred boys in front of him as he laboriously thought his way through innumerable petitions to put before his God. A commanding but gentle presence, who maintained discipline without being feared, Brother Erskine always sat elevated in front of his classes by the simple, if uncomfortable, expedient of sitting on the back of a hard wooden classroom chair, his feet placed squarely on the seat. Thus perched, he read Chaucer in his booming, sonorous voice, used to filling sombre Ulster churches with its sound. The colourful bawdiness of *The Wife of Bath's Tale*, our set text, would no doubt have shocked many respectable churchgoers in Belfast in those more strait-laced days. They would have been surprised and disapproving to hear a Presbyterian minister repeating her frank appraisals of sexual appetite without a blush. But Brother Erskine handled the rumbustious Wife with unfailing humour, good sense and appreciative aplomb. His commentary on the text was expert and detailed; his delight in Chaucer's language was infectious.

He had been a tank commander in the war, and had seen action in North Africa. Sometimes he talked to us about the desert, man to man, urging us with understated drama to 'Go there before you die, brothers, stand in its vastness at night', and he would fall silent for a moment and gaze across the classroom as if the containment of its four walls had been dissolved by the dwarfing memory of some star-lit Saharan vista. Sometimes he spoke about the camaraderie of tank crews, and once about a tank that had run over a man during a training exercise. 'We pumped him full of morphine, brothers, but it was no use of course; he died.' He never spoke about battle, though, and we never asked. There seemed to be a tacit understanding, a kind of unspoken contract between him and us, as there was between us and the master who had been a paratrooper at Arnhem, that this was forbidden territory, not something to be talked about. It's odd when I think of it now – though it didn't seem so then – to imagine these decent, cultured men killing others, and of others trying to kill them. We simply took it for granted, something we'd grown up with through fathers, uncles, neighbours, teachers, that theirs was a generation that had gone to war.

One of the stories that had been established at school, a kind of folk-tale passed between generations of boys in the oral tradition that establishes the shared images and mythologies that help to bond a community together, was that Brother Erskine's manner of sitting in front of a class, perched high on a wooden chairback, was because it reminded him of a tank commander's vantage point in the turret. I don't know if this was true, or if it was the desert, or battle, or his experience as a POW, or his own reading and reflection, but something eroded his faith in what most churchgoers in Northern Ireland accepted without question then. Somewhere along the way his belief in miracles was lost. Whatever the intellectual equivalent of an otolith may be, our inner cognitive compass, Brother Erskine's shifted the alignment of his faith. His sense of theological equilibrium faltered and swung his steps in a direction that was at odds with traditional Protestant opinion. This was to result in a very public confrontation.

When I say that whenever I think of miracles now I think of Brother Erskine, this isn't because of any illicit attempt on his part to preach or proselytise in the classroom. It is because of the controversy he occasioned, outside the school, by questioning miracles. The incident happened in 1970, and if you look back at the newspaper coverage, particularly the correspondence that was generated, you can still see glinting, just below the surface of outrage, the raw nerve Brother touched. 'CHURCH HECKLERS STOP

SERMON' reads the headline for 19 January of that year in *The Newsletter* (Ulster's main Unionist paper, established in 1737 by Francis Joy). This was a shocking story. For a congregation to challenge a minister, for those in the pews to leave them, for people to abandon the time-honoured rituals of Sunday worship and demonstrate opposition within the church – such things were utterly unheard of in Northern Ireland's deeply conservative Protestant community. People were left stunned by such events.

What happened is simply told. It took place near the school in Knock Presbyterian Church, which at that point was without its own resident minister. (Knock is from the Irish *An Cnoc* and means 'The Hill'. The area of Belfast so named should not be confused with Knock in County Mayo, sometimes called Ireland's Lourdes, at whose famous shrine healing miracles are supposed to happen.) Trying to make the point that the Gospels shouldn't be regarded as histories or biographies, Brother Erskine, preaching one Sunday as guest minister at Knock, posed a number of key questions and answered them in the negative. 'Do we believe that Jesus really stilled the storm? Of course we don't.' 'Do we believe that Jesus fed 5,000 people with a few loaves? Of course we don't.' All went smoothly when the sermon was given at the early service. But when, later the same morning, it was given at the main service, some members of the congregation, forewarned about the sermon by those who had already heard it, interrupted at the crucial moments to affirm their belief in these miracles, saying that if Jesus was God he could do these things. Others showed their opposition with the blunt eloquence of shocking gesture, walking out without a word.

Newspaper coverage of the incident sparked a torrent of letters, most furiously asserting the literal truth of all biblical miracles. Brother Erskine, to our delight, was interviewed on a national TV programme, where he cut a reasonable, if subdued, figure, obviously reluctant to feed the controversy he'd started, despite the programme-makers having paired him with an almost rabidly aggressive literalist who championed uncritical acceptance of everything written in 'God's Holy Book'. The Presbyterian Church authorities in Belfast issued a robust assertion to the effect that 'miracle is an essential element in the Gospels'. Their view was that 'the word of God as set forth in the scriptures of the Old and New Testaments is the only infallible rule of faith and practice'. Almost lost in the enraged shouts of protest was the point Brother Erskine had been trying to make: Christ lived a real and human life and did not escape difficulties by becoming God when things got tough.

To its credit, the school took the matter in its stride and things continued as they always had done. We were aware that there had been a great fuss, having read the papers and watched Brother Erskine's performance on TV. He made a wry face in one class when the topic of miracle was mischievously introduced, and said he'd better not comment on that. No doubt some of the more rigidly pious boys (and some staff and parents too) disapproved of his stance. Perhaps some shared the anger, so evident in the newspaper correspondence, that a man of the cloth should attack the beliefs they held dear. This was thought worse than any attack from outside. It was seen as an intimate, unexpected betrayal by someone who should have been a trustworthy defender of the faith. But whatever disapproval there was, no attempt was made to silence Brother Erskine, either as teacher or as chaplain. He continued as before, helping us through Chaucer and taking services in the college chapel.

The incident gives a snapshot of the Ulster Protestant psyche at a crucial juncture in Northern Ireland's history. The way in which liberal theological views sparked a tirade of indignation did not just demonstrate the expected inflexibility of a highly conservative mind-set. It was also symptomatic of a type of outlook (though 'inlook' might be a more accurate locution) whose deep-rooted, violent intransigence, whose virulent denial even of the possibility of a different view from its own, was to be such a contributory factor in the tragic unfolding of events over the next thirty years. It was the minister of another Belfast church, this time First Presbyterian Church in Rosemary Street (where Brother Erskine's father had once been minister), who put his finger on the wider implications of the matter. According to the Revd D.G. Wigmore-Beddoes, the spirit of the outburst that followed Brother Erskine's sermon at Knock, and the tone of much of the newspaper correspondence it generated, 'has an all-too-close resemblance to the kind of emotion and intolerance that was responsible for last year's violence'. How little did anyone then suspect that 'last year's violence' was the grim herald that was to usher in modern Ulster's decades of agony.

Are there such things as miracles? Can the blind be made to see, the lame to walk, the dead brought back to life? Can the natural laws that enmesh and define us, out of whose patterns our form is cut, be trounced and evaded so that water will bear our weight, so that 5,000 can be fed on just a few loaves and fishes, so that Lazarus, lying four days dead in the tomb (his sister warning that 'by this time he stinketh'), can be raised and restored, the corruption of death put off, the decaying flesh made whole, the brain, stilled and cold within the skull, be warmed back to its edgy, animated state as if it had never been extinguished?

No, and no again.

Such things identify desire, not reality; they point to the depth of human longing that things be other than how they are, not at any instances of possible change. Which of us, when faced with regret, illness, death, the fact that time passed can never be reclaimed, has not sometimes *wanted* a miracle, wished that the hard realities that descend on us could be lifted, their gravity reversed? Such desperation, though a fertile bed for cultivating dreams, imaginings, thirstings after wizardry, is impotent. It cannot hatch our wishes into the irrevocable stream of what passes so that the waters of iron circumstance that cradle and confine us are somehow unlocked, diverted, magicked into wine.

I share Brother Erskine's scepticism about miracles. Indeed his dismissal of them was gentle compared to mine. Those who look to fatuous conjuring tricks for their salvation strike me as intellectually and imaginatively impoverished. To harbour the hope that life's difficulties will somehow miraculously disappear through divine intervention is surely not only unhelpful and unrealistic but theologically childish in the extreme. A deity that lifted from the shoulders of just a few of its creatures the burdens all others labour under might, in so doing, demonstrate superhuman power, but would also display a capriciousness sufficient to undermine the attribution of other traditional characteristics of deity – such as omniscience and all-encompassing love. To suppose a universe-creating God might sometimes choose that life, not death, attend someone mangled under tank-tracks, or that days after death a person could be made to live again, would be to substitute sleight-of-hand for anything sublime. It would also accord a significance to individuals so out of line with our apparent place in the scheme of things as to suggest a failure to perceive scale, a blindness to the minuteness and transience of our passing lives when seen against the backdrop of time and space. This was a point well made by Voltaire when he said that the human species 'is much less than a small anthill in comparison with all the beings that fill immensity'. He follows this comparison with a question:

> Is it not the most absurd of follies to imagine that the infinite being would invert the eternal play of the immense engines which move the entire universe for the sake of three or four hundred ants on this little heap of mud?

Even if we stick with the anthill of our own little planet and look only at the multitude of creatures that have flourished on it since creaturehood began, to suppose that, out of all the uncounted billions lost in the dust of their own annihilation, you or I might merit special treatment, suggests a bizarre failure to weigh the evidence. Unalleviated suffering, unanswered prayers, manifold tragedies and extinctions – predictably repeated across millennia – sit heavily on the scales. There is nothing that can shift them.

Brother Erskine was concerned that an insistence on miracles acts to make Christian teaching appear ridiculous. He feared that in throwing out the bathwater of unbelievable claims – the virgin birth, the stilling of storms with a word, the curing of the blind and the raising of the dead – the baby of ethical conduct would be jettisoned too. As he said in defence of his sermon at Knock:

> I was trying to develop the idea that young people are put
> off the church because we insist that they believe all sorts
> of incredible things.

He understood the Gospels not as literal records of what happened, but as writings intended 'to teach the Christian life', which he viewed as one of honesty, compassion, hard work and moral decency.

Though such a comparison would have been unthinkable in Belfast in the 1970s, it seems to me now, looking back at the point Brother Erskine was trying to make, that it comes across particularly well if you contrast the story of Jesus and Jairus's daughter with that of the Buddha and Kisogotami's son. The New Testament tells us that Jesus, on being told that Jairus's daughter was dead, said: 'Fear not, believe only, and she shall be made whole.' Amidst the weeping and wailing of the bereaved, he insisted that she wasn't dead 'but only sleeping'. And we're told that everyone 'laughed him to scorn, knowing she was dead'. Jesus is reported as going into the girl's room, taking her hand, and saying ' Talitha cumi' (a command to get up), whereupon Jairus's daughter arose and walked and the people were 'astonished with great astonishment'.

In Buddhist scriptures we read of a woman called Kisogotami whose infant son has died. Like Jairus, like any parent, she is distraught with grief. Carrying the tiny body with her, she goes to the Buddha, whose fame as a sage has made her hope for a miracle. She pleads with him, desperately hoping that he will somehow restore her son to life. The Buddha agrees to help, but only after she has brought him a handful of mustard seeds. Ecstatic with the expectation that a miracle cure is going to be effected through this easily available commodity, Kisogotami does not immediately realise the significance of the proviso the Buddha adds before she sets out on her quest. The seeds must be obtained from a family in which no one has died. She goes from house to house and is readily offered mustard seeds at almost every door, only to find that a mother or father, a grandparent or an uncle, a sister or an aunt, a cousin or a brother has died in the household offering them. At last, having fully realised that no family can evade death, that our finitude is inescapable and non-negotiable, she returns to the Buddha, becomes one of his followers and, so we are told, eventually attains enlightenment.

Who, cradling the body of their dead child, would not prefer a miracle to a lesson in the hard facts of mortality? But who, with any insight into the inextricably intermingled joy and woe of human experience, would expect an exception to be made to the scaffolding of rules that shore up the edifice of each event, that allow things – that allow us – to happen? What kind of deity would allow occasional, unpredictable, temporary reversals? This time I wasn't serious, it didn't matter, it was just a trial run. This time the bitter cup can turn to honey. Just this once, time can move backwards and things that have happened can be made to un-happen. You can be momentarily reprieved from pain and fear, disaster and disease. Death can be undone, though only for a while (Jairus's daughter, after all, didn't live forever). To foster the expectation of exception rather than rule, to allow that somewhere there are indeed miraculous mustard seeds that can change what, in our hearts, we know is unchangeable, is a denial of reality

MIRACLES

on the terms it dictates to us, and (this was Brother Erskine's
concern) a refusal to live within those terms in as decent a way as
we can manage. To imagine there are other terms is simply to in-
vite delusion, to fail to grasp what history teaches over and over
again.

And yet, despite my dismissal of miracles – miracles, that is, in
the childishly literal, picture-book sense that the hecklers at Knock
sought to defend – I find myself reaching for 'miracle' and 'miraculous' whenever the fossil otolith is cupped in my grip, its coolness
gradually warming as it absorbs for a while the passing warmth
of my body.

Consider the otolith again. In fact, it isn't one, though it was
labelled as such in the fossil shop where I found it (Stan Woods'
famous shop in Edinburgh's Grassmarket). Yes, it is approximately
32 million years old and, yes, it is from a whale. But, it's a 'bulla'
or petrosal bone, not an otolith, which would be nowhere near
this size and unlikely to be fossilised anyway. There are two of
these bullae, one on each side of the skull base, just in front of the
hole for the spinal cord. They form a kind of shell enclosing the
sound-conducting bones of the middle ear. Whales' petrosal
bones often separate from the rest of the skull after death and are
one of the commonest cetacean fossils. So, this stone-heavy, ancient object clasped in my left hand used to be part of the living
architecture of a whale, part of a skull that cupped within it a brain
that saw and sensed the world aeons before anything remotely
hominid appeared on it, aeons before language, before any notion
of miracle, before Ireland was a place, before 'Catholic' or 'Protestant' had any meaning.

If we could map all the tendrils of connection, the maze-ways
of cause and effect, that stretch between my holding this fossilised
whale's petrosal bone and its functioning in a creature that lived
long before humans evolved, would we be dealing with something

mundane or something miraculous? If, hefting its black density, its slowly warming coolness in my outstretched hand, I could somehow access the complete story of this one singular object, would it seem ruled or exceptional? Though the product of laws, though repeatedly illustrative of unbreakable links in the chain of events whereby one thing leads irrevocably to another, a sense of miracle seems also to attend it. To be able to hold this punctuation mark of almost eternity, a crystallisation of time, condensing within its lithic density an ancientness that dwarfs anything human, is to feel something of the weightless depths beyond our ordinary sense of gravity and equilibrium. Thinking about the origins of this object, about how it became what it was, about how what it was became what it is, about how in another 32 million years its atoms will be something else again and the world as changed as it was between the whale and our ephemeral now, jars our ordinary orientation, fractures all our everyday measures.

What words should we use to try to catch this kind of incandescent irruption of another sense of gravity and scale into the co-ordinates of the quotidian? Do we have a vocabulary adequate to the trajectories into which it nudges the imagination? Like Jonah swallowed by the whale, but this a far stranger, yet far more believable event, I feel engulfed by a gargantuan sense of otherness and reach for 'miracle' and 'miraculous' in an effort to describe it.

For David Hume, who provided the classic philosophical critique of miracles in Section X of his *Enquiry Concerning Human Understanding* (1748), 'a miracle is a violation of the laws of nature'. Nothing would ever be thought a miracle if, as he puts it, it 'happened in the common course of nature'. So, it wouldn't be considered miraculous if a man 'seemingly in good health, should die on a sudden'. However unexpected, however shocking, however terrible, such things happen. But it *would* be a miracle 'if a dead man should come to life' because 'that has never been observed in any age or country'. As Hume argues, there must be 'a uniform experience against every miraculous event, otherwise the event would not merit that appellation'. But 'uniform experience' is precisely what we take as proof. So, by definition, any miracle always has overwhelming proof against the fact that it ever happened. Hume's rebuttal of the concept of miracle is effective. How could there ever be convincing evidence that a natural law had been violated? Against the elegant cut and thrust of his argument, belief in miracles – in the naïve literalist manner of Brother Erskine's detractors – emerges looking bedraggled and discredited, pretty much indistinguishable from superstition or wishful thinking. It is an intellectually untenable, if emotionally understandable, belief. I have no wish to defend such an indefensible understanding of miracle, to suggest that the touch of Jesus's hand could magically reconfigure from a 32-million-year-old fossil the living creature, whole and un-dead, from which this remnant was cast. How can people believe such things could happen? Instead, I want to explore the possibility that there is another sense of miracle altogether, one that need not collide with Humean logic, or outrage morality, or reduce theology to a childish belief in tricks. This sense of miracle doesn't picture it as a violation of the laws of nature. Rather, it wonders whether nature and its laws might themselves be considered miraculous. This is a sense of miracle allowed by Voltaire who, like Hume, was dismissive of traditional understandings of this concept. In his *Philosophical Dictionary* (1764) he writes:

A miracle, in the full meaning of the word, is an admirable thing. In this sense everything is miraculous. The prodigious order of nature, the rotation of 100 million globes around a million suns, the activity of light, the life of animals are perpetual miracles.

The idea that everything is miraculous, that we are surrounded by miracles, is one that I suspect the miracle-denying Brother Erskine

would have warmed to in those desert nights when he stood awed
by the silent immensity of being.

We can often learn a lot from error. Without the mislabelling of
the whale's petrosal bone as an otolith, I would never have been
alerted to the existence of the fascinating mechanisms of equilibrium and balance in which otoliths and otoconia are involved,
the ways in which creatures sense acceleration and orientation,
know the positioning of their bodies in relation to other things.
Fish develop particularly large otoliths and scientists can read a
great deal from them. Seen through a microscope, fish otoliths
show concentric growth rings. For the first year, a ring is formed
for every day of the fish's life. After that, they are laid down more
intermittently, but yearly rings form throughout each piscean lifespan. From these annual registers the trained scientific eye can
read out date of hatch, growth rate, migration patterns, stress.
Indeed it has been claimed that virtually the entire lifetime of the
fish is recorded in an otolith.

Tethered in the intricate canals of the inner ear, the otolith
provides a sounding board and anchor, feeding the brain information about the body's whereabouts so that an even keel can be
maintained. Part of the complex mechanism that provides fish
with their sense of proprioception, otoliths are like an internal
compass from which the animal's own true north can be read – so
that its placement in the ocean, head up, head down, facing forwards, facing backwards, diving, upside down, will always instantly
be evident. An inboard Rosetta Stone of positioning, the otolith's
perpetual whispering discourse with the ear's other deep utricular
structures provides a moment-by-moment reading of co-ordinates
that only stops with death. Its automatic decodings provide a sense
of presence as continuous, as intimate, as essential to the integrity
of identity, as is touch or breathing. The otolith's signals, part of
that secret inner symphony that silently sounds out a sense of self,

are as much a constant as the weight of water pressure against a fish's skin. An otolith acts like a spirit-level, a little capsule from whose hard bubble angle, acceleration and elevation may be calculated. It helps hold a body in place, aligning it in the water, allowing it to wheel and turn and dart and pirouette with the effortless grace that holds us mesmerised whenever we watch fish in an aquarium.

In our own skulls there are tiny particles of calcium carbonate, chalk-like crystals located in the intricacies of the inner ear. These otoliths, though insignificant in size compared to a fish's, serve much the same function. By exerting pressure on the delicate receptor hair cells in the semicircular canals, they create an invisible Morse code that taps out to the brain information about acceleration and gravity as the hairs are brushed and bent and straightened by the otoliths' pressure against them. They form part of the intricate system by which the body reads itself and maintains its balance. Normally we only think of yaw and pitch and tilt, all the business of equilibrium, when it fails – when, for example, we become dizzy. But to know where our bodies are relative to other things around us is one of those essential constants of self-knowledge automatically provided (like a sense of temperature, or knowing where our fingers end) on which our fundamental sense of being is heavily dependent. Not only are these delicate mechanisms of poise intrinsically fascinating, whether operating in us, in fish, or in 32-million-year-old whales swimming through the ancient oceans, they also provide the essayist with an unexpected seam of metaphor.

The sermon I would like to heckle and walk out of in protest is not the one that denies miracles in the silly conjuring-trick sense that Brother Erskine properly objected to, but the one that obscures the miraculousness of existence, the moment-by-moment miracle of being in the world. Alas, this is a more insidious preaching than any single voice speaking from the elevation of a pulpit. The message is ingrained in many aspects of our culture: the programmes we watch, the books we read, the values we cleave to. In an Irish context, one form this deadening, wonder-denying preaching takes is the cul-de-sac mentality of politico-religious dualism that has done so much to create the country's fissures – fissures which, in turn, carve themselves deeply into the psyches of its people. It is almost as if, lodged like cankers in the archetypal skull of each tradition, deep in the inner ear of its own narrative and mythology, tribal otoliths of pathological dimensions have congealed, swelling to a monstrous size around grains of fear, recrimination, bitterness and hatred. Our sense of equilibrium and gravity has become deranged; our crazed proprioception has led us on a dance of death. When you walk into the flag-bedecked enclaves of each territory, read the graffiti, hear the innately adversarial vocabularies, know the repeated litany of violence, it is as if the whole country lurches drunkenly, now this way, now that, its fundamental bearings lost. The preoccupation with mundane savagery, local balance sheets of revenge and retribution, masks the incredible nature of being. This is the opposite of miracle; a determined clinging to skin-deep preoccupations, history narrowed down to what we can remember. The tribal otoliths embedded in Ulster's head and heart, tracking every move we make – hard, stony, unforgiving – are deadweights laying down layer after layer of warping remembrance in a daily ossification, a building of inner walls, that keeps the two communities apart. If you could extract and dissect them, our tragic, bloody, repetitive story could be read out of these cultural earstones. Biases are built into our very sense of balance. Here is orientation by unthinking opposition; Ulster says no and walks away from what it doesn't want to hear, blocks its ears and continues in its own closed orbits.

But, for all the repugnance of its sermon, this is a hard church to walk out of. Blood ties and the economics of loyalty and betrayal shackle us to its pews. Barring some miracle, in the childish sense of a conjuring-trick (which, alas, many people still think politicians or gunmen can deliver), education is the only way to slowly change the shape of these imprisoning otoliths, whose concentric circles, year by year, bind us to the past. In the long term, the solution to our 'troubles' is not political but spiritual, a kindling of broader visions, a learning how to see miracle (in Voltaire's sense) within the mundane. We need some equivalent of '*Talitha cumi*' that would bid our deadened sensibilities rise up, walk away from local bitterness and blinkers, remember that millions of years underlie us, not just the few short blood-soaked centuries in which our grievances are rooted.

Some 32 million years ago, the bone occupying this bulla, pushing out and filling each fold and curve of its dimensions, was held suspended in a whale's head somewhere in the oceans that clad our planet in an endlessly moving liquid mantle. Who knows where the whale that bore it swam, or what perceptions it sifted from the moments of its existence, what end it met, what sensations were generated within its brain? All this has gone. All that's left is this fossil remnant lying on my desk, black, hard, dead – but bearing within it, as so many things bear within them, latent and invisible, a massive voltage ready to surge into the electricity of wonder as soon as the imagination finds the requisite switch.

What sounds vibrated in the echo chamber of the delicately curled petrosal bones, cupped neatly, like praying hands, to create a little auditorium nestled snugly at the base of the skull, waiting to catch the whispering of sub-sea sonic? Did this whale sing like humpback whales, which, as Diane Ackerman reminds us (in *The Moon by Whale Light*), 'have been singing longer than human beings have existed'? What depths and distances momentarily accommodated its eerily entrancing sounds? How was its life linked to what went before, to what comes after? Think of the skein of time and events and sounds that connect the whale's listening and my listening to Brother Erskine's voice, deep and sonorous, reading Chaucer with an Ulster accent in that Belfast classroom thirty years ago. We sat before him and caught and decoded the sounds with our own astonishing apparatus of bone and blood, raised Lazarus-like from the planet's sleeping elements. Yet we never sensed the miracle of it.

When this bulla's whale swam in those ancient waters, were the links of encounter, memory and imagination already forged and set between it and me and a man of the cloth fighting in a desert as vast as an ocean? Or, do we all swim in a sea of infinite possi-bilities, history hatching every moment out of the intermingled laws of accident and design? Watching present-day whales, Ackerman talks about them navigating 'through a rich, compli-cated landscape at a stately pace, slow as zeppelins, majestic and alert'. Their pace of being led one of the observers whose work she draws on to suggest that 'whales teach us a new sense of time'. This is a lesson we badly need to learn in Ireland, where it some-times feels as if time has been forged into a loop and history grimly repeats itself.

Time, in which we're all embedded, moves rapidly away from each of its moments, like some endlessly fecund but un-nurturing mother who scarcely pauses to give birth before continuing on her way. Each instantiation of the flesh into a bounded, contained specific individual – whale, Brother Erskine, boys listening to Chaucer – will some day be ancient. Or, looked at another way, given what has led up to them, they should each be regarded as al-ready ancient. In space-time's oceanic deserts the journeys life traverses in all its diverse craft are truly amazing, if also daunting. We may possess navigational devices of surpassing elegance, econ-omy and precision – sight, hearing touch, taste, smell, our ability to take immediate bearings from the imperceptible movement of otoliths and otoconia brushing their little solidities against micro-scopic hairs. But there is also a sense of lostness that can be both inspiring and frankly terrifying: who knows where we really are, where we have come from, where we are headed?

With such scale shimmering all about us, is it not reasonable to claim that there are miracles woven into every moment? We may walk blundering and blind among them, too rarely seeing beyond the manageable horizons of the everyday, but, look closely, and what has happened, what is happening, can seem more miraculous than any mere conjuring trick that supposedly only reverses what we find unpalatable. We daily deal in the incredible. In her musings on whales, Diane Ackerman talks about them representing 'the monstrous grandeur of the unknown', and how they constitute a powerful instance of the 'magical realm' where 'the ordinary and the sacred meet'. That explosive, awakening meeting has the potential of happening repeatedly, or of never happening at all. Art, religion, science, music variously fail us if they do not keep us mindful of the fact that each of us, every denizen of the vanishing present, has navigated depths and distances as vast and as breathtaking as anything traversed by my extinct whale in order to have arrived at the abiding, unnoticed miracle of the here and now. The collision of the ordinary and the sacred (both terms are woefully inadequate approximations) happens with every breath.

'Go to the desert before you die, brothers.' I wonder how many of us have, how many of us will. Judging from what he said about its vastness, and by the air of still and stilling recollection that accompanied his every mention of it in that dingy classroom, I suspect for Brother Erskine the lure the desert held was that of wonder (and 'to wonder at', *miraculum*, is, of course, the Latin root from which 'miracle' is derived). It was, for him, a place that fostered belief in miracle of the encompassing sort identified by Voltaire, where the ordinary suddenly seems so suffused with a remarkable sense of specialness that it can seem to meet, if not become, something sacred. As such, I don't suppose it matters much whether we go to the desert, or the mountain top, the forest, or the ocean – wherever it is that will act to still us and instil in us a sense of amazement at the fact of being. Nor do such places have to be remote, inaccessible, or even places. My own desert is here, in reflections like this. Words provide grains of sand to create the rills and ridges of distance that stretch the vision beyond its customary confines, unfolding a space in which to gaze and ponder; an inner Sahara through which I try to navigate, ears tuned to wonder.

We go naked now to death, unaccompanied by the grave goods that used to cheer our ancestors on their way: food, weapons, tools. Our sense of gravity has changed. We map our fate in very different terms from those of previous generations. The hope of afterlife or resurrection has dimmed into uncertain abstraction, shadowy hopes and fears, whose coming true seems as impossible as the biblical accounts of conjuring-trick miracles. So we taste the bitter taste of extinction and seek whatever comfort we can find in the laws that rule us, rather than the exceptions that, if they existed, would deny who and what we are. Writing in the inaugural issue of *Irish Pages*, a literary journal edited at Belfast's Linen Hall Library (a new and promisingly intelligent voice in Ulster), Michael Viney – of *A Year's Turning* fame – contemplates his end:

> My ashes, I like to think, would settle with instant self-effacement into the beach at the foot of the hill, flying perhaps like a skein of wind-blown sand, then sifting invisibly among the fragments of other worn-out lives. At the middle of the beach, on a plateau, there is a drift of broken shells that get richer the closer you look: tiny scallop fans in pink and orange, minute cowries like rolled-up finger prints; curved tiles from the broken domes of sea urchins, violet and rose. Here I imagine a broody ringed plover might nestle down to lay her eggs, enfolding crumbs of my skull into the warmth of her white breast feathers.

Listen hard to that enfolding of skull-crumbs into feathers, or to the ringing of the fossil bulla when the notes of what it is are sounded. Can you hear the creak and groan of language as it struggles to say something that might catch, if only for a moment, the Saharas and Atlantics of miracle and meaning that inhere in the things around us?

Looking ahead to my own extinction, I toy with the idea of entering it with the whale's bulla locked in the rigor of my dead hand. As we meet the furnace and are reduced to ash together, my clutching it would not be meant to represent any hope of journeys still to come, where such a symbol of ancient life and listening might help me attune my hearing to new co-ordinates, re-establish a sense of orientation. Rather, it would act as full stop and anchor, celebrating at journey's end, as I will be dumb to, the sacred, the miraculous (call it what you will) looped indelibly, intriguingly, in hard concentric circles, into the invisible otoliths that are there at the heart of each seemingly ordinary moment.

MISTLETOE

If – impossibly – she was swinging there now, part of the view would seem unchanged. On her right, the familiar redbrick of the house. A tall hawthorn hedge, neatly clipped, still standing to her left. Ahead, the same copper beech tree that has grown in that spot for almost a century now. But this would give the first indication of difference, for the copper beech she used to see from her swing was only eight feet high. Now it's close to eighty. If she turned round she'd see the plum trees she ate fruit from every summer of her childhood, always careful to avoid the wasps that burrowed their way into the ripest plums, devouring them from inside, a buzzing, easily provoked core, writhing black and yellow around the stone. The plum trees are more gnarled, a little bigger, but still recognisably the same. Slow growers anyway and regularly pruned, they don't display the copper beech's dramatic index of time's passing.

Despite some seeming constants, though, almost everything has changed. The house she knew as home is now inhabited by strangers. On the other side of the hawthorn hedge, the wildflower-strewn field – where she and her sisters often played – has disappeared beneath the tar and concrete of a housing estate. Beyond the copper beech, just out of sight of the swing, the five mature chestnut trees she knew so well have all been felled. Almost continuous traffic now roars past on the quiet road they once shaded. Seventy years have passed since my mother sat on her swing in this secluded Irish garden, her firm, fifteen-year-old muscles pulling on the ropes. Her then unmet husband is now already dead ten years; her unborn sons have grown children of their own.

When I think of that moment now, the image that comes most forcefully to mind is of an empty swing. It's still gently in motion, suggesting that we've just missed someone, that they stepped out of the picture only moments ago. The scene is still suffused with a strong sense of their being there – like putting your hand on a rumpled bed and finding a patch still warm from where someone has been sleeping. Though strong, this sense of presence is illusory. The swing has long gone. The apple tree it hung from was cut down years ago. Almost a life-time has passed from when my mother sat there as a girl, confidently swinging into womanhood. Her muscles are now frail and wasted. The energetic arcs as she pulled herself high on the swing are a world away from the old woman who can't pull herself out of a chair unaided. Had the swinging girl been able to see her future self, she would have been shocked and disbelieving. Looking back, my mother laments her loss of youth and raw, animal vitality. She has reached the nadir of life's swing. Movement that was once so fluid, so easy, has become slow, laboured, filled with pain and discomfort. Now 'decrepit' is the word my mother chooses to describe herself. She pronounces it with angry disgust and a ghost of the surprise her earlier self would have felt had she been able to glimpse the future; it's as if she still can't quite believe how age and infirmity have overtaken her.

Despite her decrepitude, though, the seed she sows by telling me about this vanished time has taken vigorous root in my imagination. Looking back, I can see her dappled with light as the sunshine falls upon her through the leaves. The weight of her body, and the backwards and forwards motion of the swing, send tremors through the tree that shake loose some apple blossom. The petals fall on her dark hair like prophetic snowflakes, studding it with the white it will one day turn. The sun is always shining in this limbo-land of the imagined past. A voice has just sounded

there, calling my mother inside for tea. The grassy path leading to
the house shows soft indentations caused by her light tread. Released from the lithe pressure of her youthful body's running
weight, the blades are slowly bending back to their original position. Soon the hypnotic pendulum of the empty swing will stop.
The same iron laws that command bent grass blades back to up-
right rule that its motion must slow and return to stillness.

It's because of mistletoe that this moment from another life has
got entangled with my own, prompting me to try to resurrect it
here in words. Without my mention of mistletoe, my mother
would never have told me about her swinging. Without the weight
of symbolism associated with this strange plant, I'd probably not
have paid her account much mind. Now, it almost feels as if her
memory of the swing possesses some mistletoe quality of its own
– the sticky seeds of her remembering have fastened themselves
to the branches of my consciousness and sent their roots thread-
ing through a whole network of associations, drawing the sap of
meaning from unexpected places.

My mention of mistletoe was one of those serendipitous
things that could never have been planned and which seem unimportant at the time. It's only later their significance hits you. So
far as I know, we'd never talked about mistletoe until about a week
before last Christmas, when the topic cropped up in one of our
regular phone calls. Certainly in those long-ago family Christmases
in Ireland, when my brother and I were children, mistletoe never
played much part. It was the Christmas tree that always dominated,
claiming centre stage (though holly sometimes had a supporting
role in minor decorations). The imitation plastic sprigs that fell
out of crackers were the only mistletoe I recall from then. These
cheap plastic gimmicks meant nothing to us beyond the horseplay
they sometimes sparked – embarrassed cousins clumsily trying to
kiss, or avoid being kissed, beneath them. Things were very

different in my mother's childhood. She remembers decking the house with mistletoe and holly, but they never had a Christmas tree. It's interesting – though of course this didn't strike me then – that the way we marked Christmas was very different from what she was used to. It's easy to confer on traditions you grow up with a more ancient lineage than they have any right to claim.

Apart from one genus (*Arceuthobium*) which relies on its host plant completely, mistletoe is a semi-parasitic species. It photo-synthesises on its own behalf, but depends on whatever plant it's attached to for water and other nutrients. Its own roots penetrate the woody capillaries of deciduous trees (only very rarely will it grow on evergreens), suckling from their intricate tubing of xylem and phloem what the mistletoe needs for its own metabolic needs. This little vegetable vampire is propagated through the good offices of birds. The mistle thrush is named because of its liking for the berries, but many other birds will eat them too. The seeds are sheathed in a kind of sticky gel. This allows them to affix themselves to branches like limpets. Then, as they germinate, they slowly push their unfolding tendrils into the sap-filled heartwood of their living perch, merging with the nerves of apple, willow, lime and stealing from them whatever they need to flourish.

It used to be thought that mistletoe could *only* grow following excretion by birds, that the process of avian digestion and void-ing punched some essential code in the seed's germination sequence without which it would never open. Theophrastus (c. 372–287 BC) and Pliny (c. AD 23–79) both record this view. Though birds are largely responsible for spreading the plant, pass-ing through their bodies is not a prerequisite for growth. If the berries simply fall in the right place they can grow, as they can if they're placed judiciously by a human hand, or if seeds are wiped onto branches as birds try to clean the berries' stickiness off their beaks.

Mistletoe is evergreen and most visible in winter when the other leaves have fallen. Indeed – a sure instance of appearances being deceptive – it can look as if the life-force of a tree has

retreated in the face of winter's siege, concentrating its remaining
verdant garrison in the strange keep of what is, in fact, a clump of
alien, invasive foliage engaged in silent pillage. As parasites go,
mistletoe is relatively benign, though in cases of heavy infestation
it can kill. Mostly it seems merely to slow the growth of its host
tree, with whose lifespan its own is coterminous. But we should
not underestimate the extent to which mistletoe leeches material
from its hosts. It may only rarely bleed them dry, but its hold is
deep, tenacious, predatory – mistletoe growing on coffee bushes
yields almost as much caffeine as the plant it takes it from. Mistletoe bites its prey like some stealthy, ligneous mosquito, then extends its feeding tubes deep into the host's living substance and
sucks from there the rich juices of the tree's vital pith. Its berries
are like cuckoos in whatever nest's been colonised.

It's a long time since I passed a Christmas in Ireland, where
mistletoe is scarce and rarely seen other than in cut sprays – mostly
French imports – that go on sale from mid-December. Mistletoe
has been grown in Ireland's National Botanical Gardens at Glas-
nevin for over two hundred years. There are reports in the 1853
issue of *Notes and Queries* of it flourishing in the apple orchards of
the Flood family in Kilkenny and the fact that its presence there
dates from 'beyond the memory of the present generation'. From
elsewhere across Ireland, mostly in the south east, there are sporadic reports of its occurrence. However, it's not listed in Webb's
Flora of Ireland and is generally considered a garden escape rather
than a native species. Once a plant is flourishing, though, natural
processes soon take over and it's not always easy to distinguish between the indigenous and the introduced – as human colonisers of
Ireland and elsewhere have found.

In Wales, where I've lived for over a decade now, there are
some locales in which wild mistletoe is common. At a December
farmers' market in our town last year, one enterprising stall-holder
had secured a supply from Tenby, a picturesque village on the
Pembrokeshire coast. He was selling the heavily berried sprays
with the added attraction of oddity. They had been blessed by

Druids. These contemporary representatives of this obscure, archaic faith evidently did not know – or perhaps just didn't care – that their ancient Celtic forbears only considered sacred mistletoe that grows on oak – which it does extremely rarely, preferring other deciduous species. The Tenby mistletoe had all been culled from apple trees. Shortly after we hung our spray, laden with its crop of pale ripe berries, my mother telephoned. In answer to her enquiry about our Christmas preparations, I mentioned that we'd got some mistletoe. This is what prompted her to recall the swing.

The swing was just a simple loop of thick rope slung over one of the branches of an apple tree. My mother used to bring a cushion from the house, put it on the rope and sit there swinging, reading Shakespeare. She was fifteen, it was 1932, and she was studying *Hamlet* at school. Etta McKee, her passionate – but strict – English teacher, was slowly kindling a love of literature that would last a lifetime, pushing her to get her started, until she acquired her own momentum and became that wonderful thing, an independent reader. 'Through the process of reading', says Sven Birkerts in *The Gutenberg Elegies*, his meditative lament for the fate of reading in our electronic age, 'we slip out of our customary time orientation, marked by distractions and superficiality, into the realm of duration'. It's only in this realm, Birkerts believes, that we think about our origin and end, our identity and purpose. This realm of deep time that the act of reading engineers within the psyche is the place where, he says, we're 'prepared to consider our lives under what the philosophers used to call "the aspect of eternity"'. As my adolescent mother swung with Hamlet, adrift on the seas of Shakespearian duration, what thoughts were being kindled in the secret intimacies of her heart about the nature of her being?

On one of the apple tree's branches, clearly visible as she swung, was a bushy, pendent clump of mistletoe. As I looked at our freshly hung spray and told her about it, she looked deep into her memory and retrieved from over seventy years ago an image of mistletoe flourishing beside her swing. Strange to think that my Druid-blessed mistletoe from Tenby should have sparked a recollection of swinging in a County Antrim garden a lifetime earlier, with a clump of this same strange semi-parasitic plant closely attendant. You're supposed to kiss under mistletoe and pluck a berry every time you do. I can almost feel history's lips brushing tantalisingly against my cheek as I picture the swing's motion linking past and present, weaving gossamer connections I had not seen before.

Year by year the copper beech tree grew, flagging up time's passing in the swelling of its girth and span. The mistletoe provided a less obvious, but no less sure, marker of time's passing – one of nature's hour hands, its motion unnoticed by those who view the world at a hurried human tempo. In many ways it's a rather dull plant in appearance, lacking any showy display of flower or foliage. The leaves, narrow rather thickset ovals that all the books describe as 'leathery' (and which do indeed have a certain rubbery toughness), grow in pairs and are no more than two inches long. The flowers – appearing in February or March – are vanishingly small and easily missed. Modestly coloured in a green-tinged yellow, they crowd in little trios in the forks of the mistletoe's branching stems. The hanging bushes of the whole plant are rarely more than three feet long, so to talk of stems seems more appropriate than 'branches' – though the stems are hard and woody and certainly thick enough in places to outgrow the brittle boundaries of 'twig'. The berries – at their best around Christmas – are smooth, white and, if examined closely, marked with a strange, almost geometrical, design at the end opposite the stalk. Here, etched in miniature, there is a little mandala of four outward-facing black triangles clustered around the dot of what used to be the flower. Each berry contains one heart-shaped green seed in a slime of sticky gel. Mistletoe is strange rather than striking – or perhaps striking because it's strange.

As the mistletoe's invisibly incremental invasion of the apple's inner sanctuaries continued, as its suckers perforated the tree's defences and began to milk it of its riches, as its flowers and berries discreetly semaphored the passing seasons, as the morning dew beaded the berries' black triangle quartets with tiny droplets, what was happening around it? Beyond the swinging girl and her family, beyond their secluded garden, what was happening in County Antrim, in Ireland, in the world? As the earth spun on its axis and the mistletoe pushed its slow raping presence into its victim's marrow, what shape was history taking?

Things at that point are relatively calm in Northern Ireland. It's enjoying one of its intermittent lulls between storms. A dozen years have passed from the murder of police Inspector Oswald Ross Swanzy, an event which sparked terrible sectarian riots in Lisburn, resulting in hundreds of Catholic families fleeing the town as Protestant mobs went on the rampage seeking indiscriminate revenge for Swanzy's killing. The house with the apple tree and mistletoe, the swing and the copper beech is only fifteen minutes' walk from where the IRA gunmen shot their victim as he walked home from church one Sunday morning. The church bells are clearly audible from the garden. Perhaps the gunshots too would have reached the ears of anyone sitting on the swing. For the moment, though, the rampaging is over, the burnt-out properties have been restored, life is back to normal. The town's first cinema opened its doors only five years ago. Etta McKee, freshly graduated from Trinity College Dublin, has been teaching at the local school for only three years but is already making her mark as a 'formidable' character with a passionate love of literature. As my mother-to-be swings, my father-to-be is twenty-seven and at work in Belfast. They have each to negotiate the seemingly endless slew of chance which, altered just so slightly, might mean that they would never meet. The piece of German shrapnel that will shatter his leg in Egypt has not yet been forged into the bomb that will release it. The world is only seven years away from war, Northern Ireland only nine years from the worst German air-raid it would suffer, which left 900 dead in a single raid on Belfast. My mother, with her mother and two sisters, will be able to see the angry glow in the night sky as the city burns (the house is only eight miles from Belfast). As always when the sirens sound, they will take shelter in the tiny room under the stairs, this being viewed – I'm not sure on what authority – as the place in a house most likely to shield its occupants in the event of falling masonry. Outside, oblivious to the sirens and the ominous rumble of the aircraft engines, the dull thud of the bombs and the beating hearts clustered in the under-stair haven of their blacked-out house, the mistletoe will continue to hang from the apple branch, swaying gently in the breeze.

Or, leaving this violent near-future, go back in time to a few years before the moment when my mother sat swinging from the mistletoe-infested apple tree, reading *Hamlet* in the summer sunshine, lost in a fifteen-year-old's reveries. The scene is little changed, except the apple branch is bare, unhaired by the clump of mistletoe that will later mark it, as if we're seeing it in pre-pubescent form. To account for the mysterious presence of a plant growing not in the soil but in the high branches of a tree, folklore sometimes casts lightning in the role of mistletoe's progenitor. In this instance the part of lightning-bolt creator was played by two little girls. If we could use the swing more precisely to move back and forward through time, like a pair of dividers on a navigation chart, toggling its position to get an accurate temporal fix, a precise position, we could adjust it to bring into focus the exact moment when my nine-year-old mother and her sister Kay (eleven) took some berries from a sprig of Christmas mistletoe in the house and squashed them into a crack in an apple branch.

Swing forward through the years and they are both grown, married and with child, pale seed from other sources urgently deposited within the crook of their branched flesh, quickening into form. This new life will be even more dependent on their blood and breath than the mistletoe is on the apple they'd impregnated, their virgin fingers sticky with crushed berries. Swing forward through the years – children grow, leave home, marry, have children of their own. Swing precisely to the present. My mother is now in her late eighties, confined to a nursing home. It's only a mile from where she sat swinging as a girl. Now her hand shakes uncontrollably as she holds the telephone receiver and tells a distant son, who at that moment is looking at a berried spray of the plant blessed by latter-day Druids, about how, years ago, she and her sister deliberately infested the apple tree with mistletoe. It flourished, and soon they had a ready source of the plant for their Christmas decorations.

The etymology of mistletoe is interesting, though uncertain. Commonly, it's said to derive from the Anglo-Saxon terms for dung ('mistel') and twig ('tan'), so that literally it means 'dung-on-a-twig' – the rationalisation behind such a derivation being that the plant was seen to appear on branches after birds had left their droppings. The neatness of this account appeals, but its accuracy is suspect. There's a case for the Celtic term for moss, 'mwsogl', being somewhere at the root of it, or the Semitic 'mister', meaning secret place. Certainly the mossy resonance of secrecy would fit what must have seemed the mysterious appearance of mistletoe in the branches of its host trees. 'Mistl' can mean 'different' and 'teinn' a staff or twig, so mistletoe may also tap into the idea of a different twig, emphasising its alien nature among the boughs of apple, willow, ash, or whatever other tree becomes its host. It's also possible, if we bring the Welsh 'uchelwydd' or Breton 'uhel-varr' into play, that 'high branch' is contained somewhere in its spectrum of meanings. In Scots Gaelic mistletoe is called 'sugh an daraich', or 'sap of the oak', again suggesting the intimacy of connection between parasite and host and the particular importance accorded to the oak-grown variety. For centuries – going back to the earliest accounts of what people believed about it – mistletoe has been regarded as having potent curative properties. Pliny reports that the Gauls at the time of Julius Caesar called mistletoe by a name that in their language meant 'all-healer'. Following this thread in his fascinating article on mistletoe in the *Bulletin of the History of Medicine* (1939), Leo Kanner notes that:

> McAlpine's *Gaelic Dictionary* cites for mistletoe the word *an t'uil*, which means 'cure-all'. The Irish designation is *uile-iceach*, from *ule*, 'all, whole, universal', and *ic*, 'healing remedy'.

Another suggestion is that mistletoe stems from the Old English word 'mistion', defined by Dr Johnson in his great *Dictionary of the English Language* (1755) as 'the state of being mingled'. Add to this 'tod' or 'toe', meaning bush, and we have another derivation that emphasises the intermingling of mistletoe and its host.

In the end, though, however we unravel its origin and etymology, whatever fossils of meaning we discover laid down in the strata of human utterance over time, precisely how the sound 'mistletoe' – and its shape upon the page – came to convey the enormous cargo that they do, is likely to remain as mysterious as the plant itself. The process of naming occurs in some secret mossy hollow of the psyche – 'Where words and water make a mixture/Unfailing till the blood runs foul', as Dylan Thomas puts it. Our language is like dung on the twig of the real, it percolates through the world as surely as mistletoe percolates through its host trees, drawing out the nutrients it needs in order to make sense of things. Our wordy foliage – 'girl', 'swing', 'tree', 'mistletoe', 'Ireland' – grows on the branches of experience as mysteriously as *Viscum album*.

The fact that my piece of Tenby mistletoe was blessed by Druids and that in modern Irish mistletoe is known as 'Druids' weed' (*Druidh lus*) is a reminder that mistletoe carries with it a far weightier symbolic cargo than the seasonal highjinks of kissing under it suggest. This is a plant that people have pressed into play in order to say something about how life and death stand in apparently indissoluble relationship. It has been used to parse whole grammars of fear and longing. Mistletoe has acted like a kind of mysterious living word. We have harvested it wherever it grows, taken cuttings and used them to try to give voice to our hopes and dreams and imaginings. Through it we have tried to utter some response – inchoate, incoherent but deeply felt – to the impress of things upon us.

Just how big a role mistletoe played in the sacramental life of the Druids is hard to determine. If we rely on Pliny for our information about this ancient cult we get a theatrical account of sombre priestly figures clad in white, cutting the sacred plant with golden sickles and catching it on white cloths spread beneath the trees (it was thought that if mistletoe ever touched the ground any power it had would instantly be lost). At some point in the proceedings two white bulls were offered to the gods, their slaughter marking the beginning of a sacrificial feast. It's hard to know what credence to give such accounts. As J.A. McCulloch points out (in a sober article in the *Encyclopaedia of Religion and Ethics*), Pliny's description of Druids has become 'the foundation for much speculative nonsense'. Thus, lurid accounts developed of their sacrificing white-clad virgins by moonlight and engaging in cannibalistic feasts, the human flesh spiced with mistletoe berries. We should remember that Pliny's compendious work – *Historia Naturalis* runs to thirty-seven volumes – although a treasure-trove of information, mixes the real and the fantastic indiscriminately. Reading about dog-headed people who communicate by barking should alert us to the fact that Pliny does not provide a straightforward documentary account. Certainly his claims of druidic cannibalism are nowhere substantiated by other classical sources.

As Stuart Piggott puts it in his level-headed study, *The Druids* (1968):

> We have Druids-in-themselves, whom we can never reach,
> but for whom we have literary evidence from which we

infer our Druids-as-known. There has also been a process of manufacturing Druids-as-wished-for going on since Classical times.

I guess there's a similar trinity at work in almost any act of re-membering. In this instance, for example, as I try to salvage her youthful image from the past, there's my mother-in-herself as she once sat on the swing reading Shakespeare, the clump of mistletoe just above her. No matter how familiar, how close it might seem, how impeccable my sources for reconstructing the moment – I know the garden well myself, I have talked with my mother many times about this little shard of history – my construction of my mother-as-known will always be a long way distant from the em-bodied girl who sat there, animated by the warm particularities of whatever she sensed and thought and felt. I can no more reach my mother-in-herself than I can the Druids-in-themselves. We are all marooned in our aloneness, however close our relationships might be. I hope I can at least resist the urge to manufacture history-as-wished-for, though in wishing our loved ones well which of us would not, if we could, change the fabric of time for them?

Whatever significance mistletoe held for Druids, it's clear that this is a plant to which a great weight of meaning has been at-tached over the centuries. It has been used to articulate deeply held anxieties and hopes. Beliefs about it are very ancient and can be found spread across a culturally diverse area. It was not only the Druids who felt its strange allure, nor was it only the oak-grown variety that offered, or was invested with, the huge weight of sym-bolic potential evident in the plant's accumulated lore. This mytho-logical efflorescence is easy to dismiss as merely ridiculous, a crop of ignorance and superstition, but for all the credulity it betokens, it tells us something important about ourselves. We are a meaning-generating species and need only the littlest platform on which to begin the process. Just as oysters secrete pearls around the grains of sand that cause them irritation, so we secrete our myths and legends around even the most unlikely grain of experience. It's fascinating to see what we choose as the cores around which to weave our stories and our symbols. Who would have guessed that mistletoe would foster such a rich narrative brood? Interestingly, many of the traditions attached to the European plant (*Viscum album*) came to be transferred to the American mistletoe (*Phoradendron serotinum*), which is very similar in appearance and habits but sufficiently dissimilar botanically to warrant a different name. As people left the old world for the new, an invisible cargo accompanied their material possessions. Myths migrate just as surely as the individuals who carry them.

Mistletoe has been placed in cradles to guard against children being stolen and replaced with fairy changelings; it has likewise been hung above doors to ward off witches and deny entry to evil spirits. It was seen as an aphrodisiac and as an antidote for poison. It was thought able to open locks and to extinguish fire. Wands fashioned from its wood were thought proof against werewolves and lightning. It was considered to cure epilepsy (no less a figure than Robert Boyle – founder of the Royal Society – recommends its usage for this ailment). Mistletoe has been found placed in the coffins of the ancient dead; it has been used to try to ensure a good harvest, fatten cattle, aid in conception, fertility and birth. It was thought to bring good luck and be efficacious against nightmares (so was placed under pillows). It has been offered as a cure for everything from headaches to leprosy and bubonic plague. Galen and Dioscorides both recommended the curative powers of mistletoe. Sir John Colbatch's *Dissertation Concerning Mistletoe* (1719) went through six editions and was translated into French and German; its recommendation of the plant as 'a most wonderful specifick remedy for the cure of convulsive distempers' found a wide and receptive audience. Throughout our existence on this planet, we seem to have reached out to mistletoe, hoping to find in it some solace for life's ills.

Kissing under the mistletoe can trace its roots back to ancient Greece and Rome, where it seems to have been used in Saturnalian festivals and in ancient marriage rites (the Druids, too, saw mistletoe as having an intimate connection with fertility). Indeed, it's been suggested that the custom of kissing under the mistletoe may go back to ancient Babylon, where the plant was sacred to the goddess Mylitta. Female devotees of her cult were supposed to give themselves once in their lives to a stranger. This sacred coupling was performed in the temple precincts under a spray of mistletoe. Who knows, perhaps my mother performed a similar rite in her fifteen-year-old's imagination as she swung in her reverie with *Hamlet*.

Though we would, quite rightly, dismiss as superstitions almost all of the beliefs that once held sway about this plant, it's interesting how constant our search for consolation is – even though we radically alter the terms by which something is accorded credibility as a source of solace. Thus in Christian times the mistletoe's pagan associations were slowly translated into terms more palatable to this newly emergent myth. It came to be seen as the shriven remnant of the tree from which Christ's cross was made. Indeed mistletoe began to be called 'wood of the cross', or 'holy wood', or *lignam sanctae crusis*. Having been the means of Jesus's execution, the tree supposedly shrivelled, died of shame, and was then transmogrified by the Christian imagination into a plant that pours down peace and good fortune on all who pass beneath it. In these post-Christian times, when it often seems that illness has replaced sin as our main affliction, it's interesting to see how mistletoe has come to be viewed as an anti-cancer drug (it's also used to treat high blood pressure, as a diuretic and a styptic). Though we deride the fantastic claims made for the plant – that it opens locks, cures epilepsy, puts out fires – the symbolic pool our era drinks from sometimes seems more limited than it need be. Has our rationality made us lose the knack of quenching our thirst for meaning at the many strange oases nature offers?

The most imaginatively coherent myth associated with mistletoe is found in the Norse tale of Baldur, whose death represents the onset of winter and the dying of summer's light and warmth. The story goes like this. Freya, goddess of love and wife of Odin, possesses the ability to see the future, but is powerless to change it. She foresees that her beautiful son Baldur, god of sunshine, will die at the hands of an unknown assailant. Desperate to avert such a disaster, Freya resolved to go round all of creation and extract sworn undertakings from its elements and creatures that they will not harm her son. Oaths are sworn by trees and by animals, by earth, fire and water, by stones and by metals, by illness and by sleep. All promise that they will do no injury to Baldur. Eventually, her task complete, it seems to Freya that she has enwrapped her son in such a protective cocoon that he has been rendered invulnerable. But Freya had considered one plant too insignificant to trouble it with an oath. Loki, god of evil and darkness, discovers that this plant is mistletoe. He fashions an arrow from its wood and tricks the blind god Hother into throwing it at Baldur, who dies. Such is the sorrow of Baldur's wife, Nanna, that her heart breaks asunder. The bodies are placed in Baldur's ship, which provides the funeral pyre for their cremation. There the story ends in the Prose Edda, the great epic associated with Snorri Sturluson. But in the older Verse Edda, Baldur is resurrected and the sun shines again.

Like all such stories, the myth of Baldur, however fanciful it sounds to modern ears, carries within its colourful cast of characters many prosaic truths: our strong attachment to those we love, our desperate, impossible wish to preserve them from all harm; the vulnerability of what we cherish; the inevitability of injury and death; the lure of some unobtainable nostrum of immortality; the wheel and turn of the seasons with their appointed times for growing, reaping, dying, sowing; the fact that darkness treads on the heels of light. Mistletoe came to be seen as instrumental not only in the death of sunshine, but also in its rebirth. The winter berries were viewed as the stored semen of the gods. As a token of the promise of Spring's returning fertility, its evergreen sprays came to be used as midwinter decorations.

J.G. Frazer devotes much space in *The Golden Bough* to dis-
cussing the mythologies associated with mistletoe. 'From time im-
memorial', he says, it 'has been the object of superstitious
veneration'. According to Frazer, we can never put ourselves completely in the standpoint of what he dubs 'primitive people' – no
more than we can reach what Piggott dubbed 'Druids-in-
themselves' – so our theories about their beliefs and the legends
in which they're embedded 'must therefore fall far short of certainty'. The 'utmost we can aspire to', Frazer argues, is 'a reasonable degree of probability' that our interpretations are correct. We
may not be able to unravel the intricacies of the Baldur myth, trace
out its origins, map its development, decide if some historical kernel of actual midwinter human sacrifice lies beneath the mytho-
logical embellishment. Frazer is right to be cautious. But we can
be certain, surely, that the story's enduring appeal, the reason it
has survived and come down to us, lies in the truths it conveys
about the hard facts of life, about the nature of things, about what
we think of our being 'under the aspect of eternity'. On one level,
Baldur's story is fantastic; on another, it's as ordinary as the patch
of mud that develops underneath a swing. It shows the places
where we put our emphases.

When I look back at the girl on the swing, my inclination is to
act Freya-like, somehow exact a promise from the time that lies
ahead that none of its denizens will harm her. I know this is irra-
tional, impossible, ridiculous. Her decrepitude stands witness to
the fact that she has already fallen victim to time's arrows. And of
course it may be only in my imagination that she's sitting happily,
swinging in the sun, enjoying the warmth of a vanished summer's
day, entranced by the beauty of Shakespeare's prose, excited by
the prospect of imminent adulthood, protected for the moment
from all the tragedies that overtake our lives as we bid goodbye to
those we love and in our turn take our leave in death's darkness. I
hope the image holds at least some echo of what really was, rather
than merely conjuring some easy, lulling idyll that is no more than
a lie. I can no more put myself completely in the standpoint of my

mother than I can of those 'primitives' who so fascinated Frazer. From what she has told me, though, this was a happy time. But, however comfortable any moment may be, we are all on the swing of history, plummeting through time. We do not know when mistletoe arrows may rain down upon us, steal away our happiness, or our very existence, as surely as the plant on the branch above the swing stole the apple's precious substance.

Even in the seeming idyll of a carefree swinging girl, it doesn't take much to see why we crave the balm of some kind of magic all-heal. Before any mistletoe arrows wound her – the premature death of her father, a sister's polio, the suicide of an uncle, the sectarian poisons raging in Ulster, the war that is about to engulf the world – consider the seemingly innocuous word 'swinging'. For all its innocence, its connotations of childhood reverie, of playgrounds and fun, the word is already bloodied before we utter it. It comes to us with the violence of a genealogy that reminds us of life's savagery. 'Swing' is derived from the Old English 'geswing', as in 'sword geswing', a stroke with a weapon, and from 'swengan', to shake or shatter. In a world of sword cuts and hangings (another darker sense of swing), of shakings and shatterings, it's natural to try to find some succour that might swathe us in its armour.

Once the arc of our little swing through history is given the harder push of time-in-the-raw, it takes us to astonishing destinations, at once breathtaking and terrifying. It is no great effort to swing the image of my mother back to her nine-year-old self planting the mistletoe with her sister, and then to swing things forward eighty years to her frail and weakened presence as an old, decrepit woman. But the swing of time is not bounded by anything so manageable as the limited frames of individual lives. Push harder and we'll easily break the temporal barrier of our lonely, bounded lives. Push! Her parents enter the picture, push on them and their lives flash past, dissolving into shadowy figures beyond them – parents, grandparents, great-grandparents – soon we've swung through a whole genealogy and reach unknown faces, the anonymous unnamed crowds of strangers who are our bloodline. There is no safe containment – time gave no Freya-prompted oath not to terrify us with its magnitude. We are penetrated by the distant past and the distant future as surely as the apple was penetrated by mistletoe. Suddenly ahead not just the copper beech tree, no plum trees reassuringly at our backs. Instead the awesome amplitude of time as we swing back to the dinosaurs and beyond and forwards again in a dizzying loop to who knows what far-chilling destinations. With gentle swinging backwards and forwards, the copper beech tree waxes and wanes in size like a familiar wooden moon showing us who we are on a scale we can make some sense of. But it takes only a little more exertion to sweep it off the canvas and to unreel history towards the molten birth of the planet or to the sun's eventual supernova. Push! There is the gentle idyll of the pretty girl reading on a swing; push again and she's incinerated by the furnace of the millennia.

As it happens, around the time my mother sat swinging, Mary Leakey had just begun her work in Tanzania's Olduvai Gorge, not far from which she was eventually to find a trail of hominid footprints 3.7 million years old. Push on the swing of time and all of recorded history goes by in a flash. We're flying through the aeons, back to whoever paced those ancient steps, the blood warm and precious in their veins. Then swing forward through the countless generations that led from them to us, and beyond to those for whom we will someday be just as remotely ancient. Backwards. Forwards. Is there any habitable sense in time's stupendous arc? Can we somehow affix ourselves like mistletoe to our branch of history, draw from it something to help us weather the great storm of being in which we're marooned, weave some safety net of meaning below the terrifying gallows-drop of our life-swing?

In one view of our situation, we keep swinging into and out of existence on the cosmic roundabout of samsara that's posited by

Eastern thinking. The Buddha, the great spiritual doctor for humankind, offers the all-heal of his *dharma* by which we may find a way to peace. On another view, the apple tree contained a serpent, Eve plucked the fruit and our species was enmeshed in sin that took the sacrifice of God's only son to cure. New stories map the slings and arrows, the swings and roundabouts, of outrageous fortune by a naked singularity that peopled existence with galaxies and stars, with atoms and with evolution. We may think we've moved a long way from the cartoon deities of the Norse Eddas, but each winter Baldur dies, and each moment we step closer to the looming dark. Our need for balm is as raw and urgent as anything the mistletoe-seeking Druids felt.

Frazer is one of several authors who suggests that the famous golden bough in Virgil's *Aeneid* is mistletoe. Virgil himself mentions mistletoe (*Aeneid*, VI, 205), though he nowhere makes clear if it is, in fact, identical to the golden bough – that magical talisman by which Aeneas compelled the dread ferryman Charon to transport him to the underworld so as he could speak to his dead father and learn about the future. Mistletoe's nature seems to fit it nicely for the task of allowing the living to pierce the realm of death and draw from it some of its secrets. Certainly the way in which the plant takes on a golden tinge when it withers makes it a plausible candidate. This golden colour may also be behind the belief that it helps in the discovery of more durable treasure in the earth, the gold of the leaves supposedly corresponding to the location of real gold. It may not seem like riches to others, but looking at the shadows thrown by the clump of mistletoe beside my mother's swing, I feel that it has helped me to locate a seam of some precious material which, without it, I might never have discovered.

It could, of course, be fool's gold. What I read as the stickiness of meaning, the viscous promise of symbolism, suggestiveness and sense, may be no more than the treachery of birdlime. Perhaps all my mistletoe can offer is entrapment in a sticky mess of words that issue in no destination beyond themselves. It's as well to remember the Roman proverb, '*Turdus malum sibi metipsi cacat*' – the thrush excretes its own doom – a saying spun because of the way in which the same plant that birds help propagate was used so often to trap them (mistletoe berries were the principal ingredient of birdlime, a kind of avian flypaper spread on branches to catch the unwary). The saying is applied when someone does something that boomerangs and injures them (as when an essayist's words fail to gel into anything coherent).

Mistletoe is sometimes found growing in regular linear patterns across quite wide spans of countryside so that, seen from the air, it appears as if someone has placed a giant ruler above the trees and, using it as a guide, has scattered mistletoe seeds on the land below. These patterns of growth may be interrupted by rivers or bare fields but otherwise trace such straight lines across the map that an area may look scored with numerous abortive stretches of narrow green freeways hanging from the branches of the trees. It's thought that such lines correspond to the flight-paths of flocks of fieldfares and redwings that have gorged on the berries and evacuate in mid-air. In the end, do our attempts at finding a meaning for our fleeting existence leave any more intelligible marks upon the planet than these faint green lines that stop as suddenly as they started and seem to lead nowhere?

On New Year's Eve last year I took a handful of berries from my Tenby mistletoe and crushed them in a likely looking crack in the apple tree in our garden. If a plant takes and grows there it will give me enormous satisfaction. Though I hope I am not prey to the foolishness of superstition, I hope I am not blind to the unlikely places in which the ore of meaning lies waiting to be mined. To stay the cancer of forgetting, to reverse – if only for a moment – the iron law that says bent grass stems must straighten and swings stop swinging – that is gold indeed. I don't believe mistletoe can ward off evil, or heal all ailments, or open locks. Nonetheless, I know I will treat any sprigs of this mistletoe-to-be with more than ordinary respect. I know already that they will have about them something of the potency of relics.

ROOM, EMPTY

Curiously, it's only as absence has taken hold that I've become aware of the room's presence. Before that, it was just there – so much a part of things I rarely thought about it. 'Presence' may be the wrong word to use, though, since it suggests something alive and close at hand. Why use the wrong word? Because, although I know it's neither, the room *feels* like something living and sufficiently nearby for me to hear its breath sounding gently in time with my own, like the softest of echoes, an intimate haunting, as if some silent companion was standing at my shoulder poised to shadow my every move. So, in one sense, 'presence' does fit well enough. But despite these symptoms of live proximity, I know this is only a spectral presence, and of a place not a person, and of a place that – for all its apparent closeness – is hundreds of miles from where I sit writing this. I know that if I whipped round quickly now there would be no trace of what seems so close, so tangible. All I would see behind me would be the ordinary constituents of whatever happened to be there at that moment making up the scene, not some unnerving hallucination. It's not as if some limping doppelganger has been born into substance to stalk me. There is no such disfigured embodiment of the mind's invisible preoccupation lurking at my side. Yet I still feel something akin to the prickling of the scalp that supposedly betokens such theatrical hauntings.

Like 'presence', 'curiously' also risks pointing in the wrong direction. For why should it occasion any puzzlement or surprise when imminent loss kindles the desire to remember, to hold on to, to try – impossibly – to not let go? As absence gains the ascendant and becomes the room's principal feature, it is surely not curious in anything but a superficial verbal sense that presence follows the arc of its trajectory instead of falling away and diminishing. Yes, the two words sound dissimilar notes and may seem to travel in different directions. To say that a sense of presence is born as absence increases may, in consequence, sound odd. But in the less clear-cut transactions of the psyche, where things are bound in more complex relationship than anything such verbal dualism can parse and unravel, absence and presence operate more like systole and diastole than straightforward antonyms that just cancel each other out with the mechanical precision of mere opposites.

Such misleading impressions corrected, let's start again with something simpler, more concrete, less prone to error: an empty room. For it is this, not some apparition of a person, that has come increasingly to haunt me. It's as if the room in question, though not dead (if rooms can die), has already given up its ghost (if rooms have ghosts) and that ghost, seeking some familiar habitation, has decided to take refuge in my consciousness.

For much of its history, the room in question has held people. That, after all, is its function – for it is what most households call a 'living room' or 'lounge' or 'sitting room', though in the middle-class Protestant Ulster of the early 1940s, which is when it first came into being (it being relatively young for a room), they preferred the genteel pretensions of 'drawing room'. It's only in the last year or so that human occupancy has become increasingly rare. Now, the room is nearly always empty.

But, again, the word that first comes to mind to describe this new state needs to be honed, refined, corrected before it will work. Left on its own, 'empty' will botch the job of conveying meaning as surely as 'presence' and 'curiously'. It must likewise be fine-tuned and qualified. For the room is as full of furniture and ornaments as it ever was. It is carpeted and curtained. The television sits as it always has done on a sun-faded table in the corner. There are photos and paintings on the walls, books on the bookshelves, a fire set ready in the grate. The clock on the mantelpiece, if there were anyone to look at it, still shows the correct time. Spiders have left their cobwebs looped loosely from ceiling to wall. They sway gently in the draught admitted by an ill-fitting window, tiny near-invisible hammocks waiting to ensnare.

When I say the room is empty, I mean that it is empty *of us*. You won't find us sitting there of an evening as we used, invariably, to do. The cradling hands of walls, floor and ceiling that cupped the sound of our voices like invisible water, now hold only silence. Names once spoken here every day are almost never heard. It's as if a drought of sound has taken hold, making the room an aural desert. Dust slowly settles and accumulates on surfaces that were once kept polished. The windows let in light and darkness to fall equally unobserved by any human eye upon the books left neatly stacked and long unopened on a small table by the door. The chairs are unburdened with any weight except of cushions. There is no one there now. There will be no one there for days. The room is in that strange, silent interregnum between lives.

Our time in this room is rapidly drawing to a close. Soon, I know, it will belong to someone else, another family will take up residence – and then I will never set foot here again. Perhaps, when that happens, when the house is sold and this room, like the others, becomes part of some stranger's private territory, its ghost will finally be laid to rest and I will stop recalling the room with such persistence that I sometimes feel I'm there, sitting on the green settee in the fading light of an autumn afternoon, with the fire lit and the garden reflected in the silver orb of the circular mirror above the mantelpiece. That sense of presence is so like being there that I can see the precise way in which the mirror's slight concavity distorts, making it seem as if the flames from the hearth are bestowing on the reflected grass and trees a mirage-like shimmer of summer warmth. I have looked at that reflected image so often, sat there so many times, that the experience comes back pitch perfect, even though I've not been there for almost half a year.

Or, perhaps the transfer of ownership when it comes, underscoring the fact of our loss and absence, will merely make the recall of this place more vivid and arresting and its ghost will become a constant companion – until it is as much a part of the way things are as the room used to be, and so at that point will finally sink into the silt of unconsciousness and this haunting limbo of absent presence will be ended. Maybe the only way to be rid of such ghosts is to get so used to them that they just fade away, banished by that exorcism of routine which dulls our noticing of so many things; constant presence leading in the end to the absence of not noticing.

This drawing room, now so unused to people, was the main room in the house my parents built at the start of their married life together. Like other inhabited places it can be read in very different ways. To strangers it would appear unremarkable, almost two-dimensional, untextured beyond the immediate impress of things upon the eye. Such a perspective would register only the surface information of shape, colour, number, but be blind to the depth of association that is, for us, so densely woven into this place and all its constituent objects that it almost feels as if their contours have run into ours and vice versa, so that to separate family and room causes a painful sundering of things bonded to the flesh. To strangers, this is just a room. Shorn of all the invisible nuances of narrative, it would appear with a sparseness that would be so alien to us that, if we could witness the manner of its appearance in their mind's eye, we would probably not recognise it as the same place we know. And of course in many ways it *isn't* the same place. To strangers it can be a room in the simple sense of 'an area within a building enclosed by floor, walls and ceiling'. They may note its dimensions, the colour of the carpet, the number of chairs, but we can never regain such innocent shallowness of perception. To us, it is much more than an anonymous rectangle of enclosed space. Here, every object speaks to us, offering a way back into our experience of time. Everything in and of the room – the space enfolded by it, the views from its windows, the noise the door makes when it shuts, the dusty smell of the curtain fabric – constitutes a threshold, invisible to others. Crossing it takes us back into the tangle of stories woven by the time we spent here, growing up, growing older, living, dying.

To us, this is a place made dense with memory and meaning because of the role it played in the unfolding of our lives. It is heavily clad with the particularities of our family's history. The room has seen babies arrive, grow up, leave home. It has celebrated birthdays and Christmases. It has hosted family gatherings and parties, welcomed grandchildren, held within its walls a whole catalogue of conversations. It has heard whispered endearments, squabbles, questions, plans. Conversations about gardening and God and holidays, about cars, cancer and the choice of wallpaper, gossip about neighbours, plain unexciting news of how a day was spent, arguments about the political situation as Northern Ireland descended into its terrible period of 'troubles'. It has witnessed laughter and tears and the odd disjointed dialogue of dreams as people dozed by the fireside with inane TV dramas playing unwatched in the background. My father lay here in his coffin before the funeral, the polished wood of the casket held for a while, like a sudden shocking cataract, in the glassy eye of the mirror. My mother's wheelchair sits unused in the corner. Now, with her failing health having led her to a nursing home, and my brother and I no longer living in Ireland, the room – like the house – is unoccupied. The garden is tended by a gardener who posts me his bills. A cousin occasionally looks in to lift the mail and water the houseplants. Essentially, though, the drawing room is now possessed of an emptiness so rarely broken that visiting has taken on a sense of intrusion, almost violation and trespass. The room has acquired a heavy sense of liminality, of imminent transition from one phase to another, as if it is poised to slough us off like old, unwanted skin. New characters are waiting close by in the wings of contingency. Our part here is drawing to a close. There are no stage directions, but it's clear enough that the remaining scenes, whatever they contain, will not require our presence.

According to the great Buddhist philosopher Nagarjuna, who flourished sometime in the second or third century,

> It is because of emptiness that all things and events can be established; without emptiness, nothing can be established.

I find myself remembering his words as I think about our empty drawing room. Looking for a way to understand the sheer power of the vacancy it now presents, it is the concept of *sunyata* – emptiness or voidness – that suggests a tentative scaffolding for understanding.

But can an empty room really be seen through the frame provided by *sunyata*? Is this not to mis-apply a complex philosophical concept to a trivial setting? Is it not to confuse metaphysical and mundane senses of 'emptiness', merely exploiting the accident of the same word having different levels of meaning? I would argue that the metaphysical is so tightly embedded in what we take to be the mundane, that the philosophical is so close-threaded all through the everyday, that it is impossible to separate them. Unless we address the intimacy of such interconnection, we risk marooning our reflections in realms of artificial abstraction that are irrelevant to the hard realities our lives must negotiate.

Perhaps something of the depth and, yes, the *creativity* of absence that is now so evident in this empty room, can be grasped if we emphasise what, at first sight, may seem just like loss. Without us there to read the script, to translate the argot of our accumulated signals, dropped like leaves as the seasons of our lives progressed, any talk about the contents of this room, or the space enclosed here, will have little purchase on the significance of things, on the way our time happened here, on the particular intricacies of our experience. In fact it could be little more than bland inventory, the registering of mere appearance, a superficial list. It is only the rosetta stone of intimacy that can conjure the story-generating wealth of associations out of every object, angle, space. And these stories will die with us. Our passing marks their end. The layered memory of being in this room gives us access to the strata of time laid down here for a while and to all the fossils compacted in them. These fossils are inaccessible to anyone beyond the small circle of my immediate family. For me, having been in this room so often means that the invisible contrails of personality and presence left behind by those who lived here seem almost to have solidified into something tangible. All of this accumulated history vanishes with us. No one will be able to read the room as we read it – just as we will be unable to read the text that will be written by the lives of whoever comes here next.

Contrasting the very different ways that I and some stranger would experience this room calls back to mind the old philosophical conundrum of unwitnessed existence. This is the suspicion that, without the warming presence of our being there, things cool into the absence of non-existence; that a tree, for example, only exists if there is someone there to see it. I know the drawing room is still there now, this moment, that it is real, that it exists independently of me or any of its erstwhile occupants. Even though no one is there now to summon it into presence, I have no doubts about its current and continuing existence. But it is there only in the sense of its raw physicality. What *does* depend on us – though not on our actually being there – is the unique particularity of its presence. Without us to conjure our stories out of the inventory of objects, dimensions, shapes and colours that is all a stranger could access, they vanish. They don't exist without us. Who but myself could hit the correct resonance in the tuning-fork of recall that would summon from that threadbare patch of sun-warmed carpet by the French window a small boy being taught to sit cross-legged to listen as his mother read a story? Who but one of us would be prompted by the blue cloisonné vase sitting on the mantelpiece to recall a holiday in Donegal, a passionate affair, a carefully chosen gift? Or who could reconstruct from the clutch of photos on the coffee table the lives behind the courtships, marriages and travels pictured? All of these things vanish, to be replaced by others. One set of lives moves on, another takes their place. If we, or any of our things, were permanent, if the cargo our lives loaded into this room was something fixed and static, it would soon become a deadweight, something that would besmirch the unsullied emptiness whose serial virginity allows the rich play of life to happen. And does that not introduce into the icy face of loss a hint of the kind of warming shimmer that the drawing room's mirror interpolates into every scene it holds? Is it merely an illusion, a distortion?

There is no abiding presence. Everything passes. We live surrounded by process rather than permanence. For Buddhists, the three marks of existence (the *trilakshana*) are *dukkha, anicca* and *anatta. Dukkha* refers to the cluster of circumstances, from the profound to the trivial, that make us unhappy with our lot, it is the raging fire of our dis-contentment, our dis-satisfaction, our dis-ease with the way things are. For who could stand content, satisfied, at ease – however lulled by comfort – in a world of such pain and horror, underlain by death? *Anicca* refers to impermanence, the fleetingness of things. *Anatta* points specifically to the impermanence of the self, the fact that we, as the individuals we imagine ourselves to be, in fact are woven from a series of passing circumstances behind which there is no perduring core. Or, to put this another way, everything is empty. Emptiness rages unstoppably through all that we experience. Every object, every place, every person is like a lit fuse leading from what burnt out before it to whatever fizzles into being next. It is *sunyata*, emptiness, that provides the oxygen in which the conflagration of existence burns.

In the same way that it's easy not to see that we are mostly made of water, or that the universe is mostly space, so the fact that the drawing room, and all our places, are, have been, will be mostly empty is easily forgotten when thinking about how filled with our lives they have been. The familiarity of place acts to corral and tame the unnerving nature of what surrounds us. But time, space, death, *sunyata* cannot be contained for long. In fact they cannot be contained at all, whatever lulling fictions we may drape upon them for a while. Sixty years ago there was no house here, no drawing room with its mirror and chairs and ornaments and pictures, no walls or ceilings ready to provide anchorage for the swaying hammocks of spiders' webs and a safe haven for our voices. Then, there were just fields, some trees, a barbed wire fence. Horses and cattle used to graze at the exact same coordinates where, years later, we would sit and watch TV, as – years before their grazing – unknown prehistoric creatures loped across an unmapped landscape still aeons removed from any sign of human intervention. Millennia from now, something equally alien will no doubt occupy the spot in which we pitched the temporary encampment of our drawing room. Some sense of the scale and diversity of occupancy that a place can boast over the vast span of years that time allows is given in Jeremy Gavron's *An Acre of Barren Ground*. With admirable imaginative finesse, Gavron maps a small section of the network of stories spun by the different occupancies – plant, animal, human – of a single London street. He suggests something of the enormity of narrative that can issue from even one small patch of earth once we begin to unravel the lives of its diverse inhabitants across the centuries. His book hints at the infinitely malleable void underlying what is today a busy city street, an emptiness that underlies every place and that holds everything within its temporary enclosures.

Back in the 1940s, when a house was being built, it was the custom in Northern Ireland's Protestant heartlands for the builders to fly a Union flag from the chimney as soon as it was erected, a sign of approaching completion and a signal for money to change hands. Thinking of the fireplace and its flue, a sooty artery running from the drawing room's hearth to the once be-flagged chimney, I picture a column of smoke rising from this place, visible for a while beyond the roof-tiles, then vanishing into the immensity of the night sky that dwarfs the house and the town and the nation and the world with its peppering of far distant stars. Our lives seem not dissimilar to smoke. The fire of being generates us for a while, then we are gone. The grazed grass and the shading trees, the livestock in the field that preceded the house, the prehistoric creatures that preceded them, whatever will come next, have no more claim to ownership, to permanence, than have we, or the spiders or their parasitic mites, or the insects struggling weakly in their webs seconds before they are obliterated by death. We are all part of the smoke of forms that has blown across this place and that time will fan into new, but never more than passing, instantiations of being, whether bacteria, birds or people. We come, we go, creatures of a moment – the horses, the builders, the families, all the life clustered in this particular place, teased out by the updraft of time moving us inexorably towards dispersal. In familiar places, as in unfamiliar, we are surrounded by unnerving, yet inspiring, vistas if only we raised our eyes from our everyday preoccupations to look at what's there all around us. If truth be told, the spiders' webs, like our rooms, like the Union Jack flapping in the gentle breeze of a forgotten summer, are shackled to emptiness, forged from emptiness, though they shield us from it for a while.

Being haunted by the empty room and its liminal sense of incipient absence, the looming fact of new occupancy, of time moving on and ejecting us from these well-known purlieus that yet contain all the numen of utter otherness, has made me ask, as I did not think to ask before, what *is* a room? Of course at one level I know the answer well enough, but beyond the familiar, ancient tropes of shelter and habitation, I find it now prompts more general thoughts about *enclosure* and how much we rely upon it (how often we are duped by it). Walls, ceiling, floor, windows are cupped around a space and hold it for a while (it's interesting that 'room' can mean both space and its interruption by enclosure, its division by walls). And this division of the invisible is only temporary. At some point the walls will be taken down, or fall down – no house stands forever – and the drawing room's space will then merge with the space around it, from which it has never really been separated. Then something else will occupy this mysterious emptiness, the space that we have tried to hobble into the domesticity of the familiar, trying to incise on it the contours of something that can be known, recognised, dealt with.

We live lives of temporary enclosure within the void. At a different level, in a different tempo, atoms and cells do much as a body does, as a room does, as a planet does. All demarcate, divide, enclose, release. We are interruptions in nothingness, transitory enclosures of space in time and time in space that will soon release their hold, let free again what has been momentarily confined. Which is not to say some essential kernel is ejected to take up habitation elsewhere. Such comforting illusions of persistence cannot survive the realisation that every enclosure opens – kernels too – that nothing can be cocooned in its particular substance for long. Nothing is more than a flicker within the stupendous containment of *sunyata*.

As I struggle to accommodate Nagarjuna's thinking on emptiness with the (dulling?) fullness and familiarity of rooms and houses, a picture comes unbidden into mind of birds' nests. Every year in the hedges and bushes of the garden that, even as I write this, I know is being reflected in the mirror above the mantelpiece, thrushes and blackbirds built their nests. And, for a while, these little twiggy enclosures held a precious clutch of eggs that hatched into nestlings, that grew into adult birds, that mated and produced another generation whose singing would, for a while, be loud enough to be heard by anyone sitting in the drawing room. For the most part, though, the nests are empty, just damp twig bundles in the hedges that will rot and fall, joining eggshells, leaves and droppings in the rich detritus of the garden's humus, that melting pot of organic enclosures. And the birds themselves, life cupped in the nest of their hollow avian bones and feathers, are likewise only the most evanescent of enclosures. Their song-filled beaks can peck no permanence into the whirl of processes that leave life's signatures transiently rippled across the fabric of space-time, like the patterns of wind playing on some immeasurable expanse of water.

What this room encloses will be spilled, set free, as surely as what a bird's nest encloses, as surely as beneath the crudities of what meets the eye, enclosures constituted by cells and atoms, likewise decay, disperse, reform. The silver cigarette box on the table by the window, the blue cloisonné vase, the circular mirror above the mantelpiece which has pictured so much of what has passed here on its distorting reflective surface, the room itself – these enclosures are all as temporary as the coffin that once lay here, as the secret chambered intimacies of our bone and blood, the pocketing embrace of flesh, which weaves its substance round us, spinning mind and its meanings out of membrane and mucous. Everything will be spilled, gathered up in different containers, spilled again.

As rooms go, the human cargo carried by this one has been modest. Just a single family's occupancy, so it has only witnessed parents, children and grandchildren in its sixty-year history. In *Home*, a book which tells 'the story of everyone who ever lived in our house', Julie Myerson unravels the history of the 130-year-old house she lives in at 34 Lillieshall Road in London. She uncovers a fascinating cast of characters and unearths – or imagines – at least part of the vanished happenings that used to fill the rooms she and her family now occupy. Myerson wonders if, perhaps, 'in the end, we all of us have one compelling thing in common', namely 'that we inhabit spaces and know we aren't the first to do so and that we won't be the last either'. She talks about the way in which her family's occupancy of the house has blotted out that of the people who came before them, and reckons that this is maybe 'a necessary element of domestic living, the only way we can co-exist comfortably with each other's past lives'. If it wasn't for such blotting out, 'we'd be stifled by years of emotional history every time we passed through a doorway or climbed the stairs'. Though she's trawling for the stories that are shoaled in the history of a house that's over twice as old as my parents' house, this is still just a tiny segment of the bloodline our species trails out across its diversity of habitations, a fragment snipped from the perplexing umwelt of *Homo sapiens*, our innumerable temporary enclosures. Counting family members, friends, tenants, neighbours, miscellaneous visitors and builders, a tally of all the people who have ever been in our house, or in 34 Lillieshall Road, the total would probably not go much above a few hundred. Little compared to the thousands who have been in rooms in ancient public places. Nothing at all compared to the billions who have sojourned in the great room of Planet Earth.

What is happening now with our empty County Antrim drawing room is like a rehearsal in miniature of the manner in which the world is sloughing off our presence. Thinking about the liminal, haunting state of the room, and of our increasingly precarious, near fugitive status in it, the fact that we shall soon be gone from it forever acts as a reminder of our temporary sojourn in every room we occupy in the strange house of existence – whether it be the room of mind, body, cell, corpse, coffin. All of them, in truth, are empty. For a while, the drawing room gave us the illusion of permanence and security, in the same way that our personality and body do, but they are all temporary enclosures only. Things pass, we pass, emptiness remains to enwrap other forms and provide the invisible breath that animates every particular. The room of the self, of identity, is at once as strong, and as fragile, as the rooms we occupy. Enclosure, and the dissolution of enclosure, seem so deeply engraved on our experience that we could be forgiven for seeing this dichotomy as a fourth mark of existence. Curiously (or maybe not), the *world* seems most present when we feel the imminence of our absence from it. Things may ultimately be empty, but they appear swollen with a fullness that is breathtaking.

The haunting presence of the empty room prompts – I was about to say a *memory* of a far more ancient site of habitation, but it's just the memory of a painting, someone's imagined reconstruction of the past. The painting is Zdenek Burian's rendition of a late Palaeolithic hunters' encampment (one of the wonderful illustrations he contributed to Josef Augusta's *Prehistoric Man*). The hunters have built crude lean-to hide shelters against a rocky outcrop which provides the more robust habitation of a cave. A busy scene is pictured. A giant elk is about to be butchered, firewood is being gathered, tools are being made. But it is a scene in the middle of the painting that remembrance highlights. Here, an animal skin has been pegged out on the ground. A women kneels on it, scraping. It's not because it brings back to mind the ur-rooms of our species – the caves and lean-to shelters, our earliest nests – that memory has selected this painting as I think about the empty drawing room. Instead, memory has selected an image for its own operation. As my thoughts return to the empty drawing room and all that it holds, it is as if the room's objects and dimensions act like pegs that hold the skin of memory spreadeagled on their frame while it is scraped of the fat of recall. Held by them, it falls into a particular shape and texture and so will provide a particular cladding against the cold of forgetting. And it occurs to me that this recollection is garmented by that fabric, and that its wordy walls make a kind of conceptual room that tries to contain the real one. Building it, it is easy to forget the extent to which it is bound to select and distort, bound to scrape the hide of the past in one way and not another. And it is also easy when working closely with words not to see the extent to which they too rely on emptiness and absence. After all, it is the space between letters, words and sentences (as it is the silences between notes in music) that allows us to weave the magic of our meanings.

Rooms sometimes seem like ears, cocked at various angles to catch the different sounds that time makes in its passing. From our drawing room's listening post on time, we heard snatches of the larger, less personal history that was hatching beyond the confines of the family. As Northern Ireland's turbulent decades unfolded, the windows were shaken every now and then by explosions and the TV screen carried images of mayhem only a few miles away in Belfast. Mostly, the bombs were safely distant. But several times they exploded close enough to almost shatter the room's glassy eardrums. Sirens sounded regularly on the road as the army's bomb squad raced to incidents. Soldiers on foot patrol walked down the road, guns at the ready. To begin with, this was an utterly incongruous sight – weapon-laden squaddies in our quiet suburb. But we soon grew used to it; routine can render invisible even the grim accoutrements of violence.

Beyond this little corner of the world, preoccupied with its own bitter conflict, the history of other nations was happening, the story of the world and of our species was unfolding, the saga of the universe was telling itself to anyone who could listen. Just as the metaphysical is tightly embedded in the mundane, so the universal is riveted to the local, however much our parochial preoccupations may blind us to it. Whether we are Palaeolithic hunters or essayists or terrorists, at root we occupy the same perplexing place, we are part of the same great tapestry of space-time woven on the loom of *sunyata*.

How different things might have been if we had walled our spaces differently. Theodore Zeldin has observed (in his *Intimate History of Humanity*) that 'individualism has flourished most in places where people can afford to have a room of their own'. There seems little doubt that not only do we build according to our predilections, but that our built environment has a wide-ranging influence on our lives. In Ireland, even up to the sixteenth century, houses tended not to feature corridors. Instead, as William Magan notes of his ancestral home, Umma-More, 'rooms led directly into each other, for the reason that privacy was of no importance'. What different perspectives are facilitated – and frustrated – by the manner of our enclosing the spaces we inhabit! Would it be possible to think or write a reflection of this nature in the kind of room Magan describes? And the Ireland of a nomadic, cattle-herding Celt would have been very different to the Ireland of a present-day inhabitant of Belfast. The country falls into different declensions when framed by the walls and windows of a city tower block and the branches of a simple bothy, abandoned as easily as it's built.

Sometimes I think of Ireland as a kind of room and picture the country emptied of each generation and its artefacts, then emptied of us altogether, and realise that our vision of it, the way we read the texture of our habitation here, with all the old sores of enmity celebrated, tightly clasped in the vice of tribal memory, would be as invisible to a visitor as our lives are to a stranger in our drawing room. Nations are also only temporary enclosures. Even Ireland's long, blood-soaked remembering will release its bitter cargo as time conjures new habitations out of emptiness.

At the back of all our history – local, national, international, global – is our absence. For the most part, we are not here; the world is without our presence in it. 'Not to be here, not to be anywhere' (to quote from Larkin's magnificent poem, 'Aubade') is our overwhelming reality. Or, to spin this in a different key, *other* presences, not ours, are what characterise things. Filled with the transient warmth of presence, though, this is easy to forget. I'm reminded of the story of Nan-in, a Japanese master during the Meiji era (1868–1912), who received a visit from a university professor eager to learn about Zen. Nan-in served tea. We're told that he poured his visitor's cup full, and then kept pouring.

> The professor watched it overflow until he no longer could restrain himself. 'It is overfull. No more will go in!' 'Like this cup', Nan-in said, 'you are full of your own opinions and speculations. How can I show you Zen unless you first empty your cup?'

Often, our cup of experience is so full of what happens moment by moment that we don't notice how things are framed by our absence, how they are underlain by emptiness. The mystery of space tends to strike us, if it does at all, only when we encounter the very large or the very small – galaxies or atoms. At the meso-level of rooms and lives and ordinary business, there's a tendency not to see the emptiness that enfolds us. Filled with our everyday preoccupations, we need to perform some equivalent action to the emptying Nan-in saw as necessary, before we can begin to appreciate the nature of what's around us. Interstellar space and the body's inner spaces, the microscopic world of cells and molecules and atoms, the inner emptiness of things, suggests a different calibration to the crude measures of our unaided senses, a calibration that cannot measure emptiness but that might suggest how we are measured out of it. Pascal famously suggested that 'The universe is an infinite sphere whose centre is everywhere, its circumference nowhere'. Emptiness partakes of such dimensions, if you can call them dimensions. It is a close bloodbrother of space.

In *The Pearly Gates of Cyberspace*, her history of space from Dante to the Internet, Margaret Wertheim includes a comment on the outlook of contemporary physicists that hints at some of the points of overlap between physics and Buddhist philosophy. Physicists, she says,

> believe that in the end there is *nothing but space*, with even matter being just space curled up into minuscule patterns. In this vision, space becomes the totality of the real – the ultimate underlying substance of everything that is.

The drawing room in its potently empty state, its liminal anticipation of change, has the feel of space curled up into minuscule patterns. It is a place where, for a short while, emptiness seems so tightly scrolled into the interstices of all its objects and dimensions that one can almost feel *sunyata* coiled like some ontological ouroboros at the heart of vases and chairs and spiders' webs and mirrors and reflected gardens and everything that is. As absence has become the dominant colour of its aura, emptiness has become tangible.

Garma Chang (in *The Buddhist Teaching of Totality*) sees *sunyata* as the core of Buddhism, the teaching that most distinguishes this great spiritual tradition from others. It is also, he reckons, the teaching that is hardest to comprehend, and easiest to misrepresent. He reminds us that the Sanskrit term *sunya*, as well as meaning 'empty', also means 'cipher' or 'zero' and this, he thinks, is the key to avoiding the misunderstanding that equates *sunyata* with something nihilistic. 'Zero', says Chang, 'is both nothing and the possibility of everything. It is definitely not something nihilistically empty, but rather it is dynamic and vital to all manifestations.' Extrapolating from this, *sunyata* does not mean 'complete nothingness' but is, rather, something 'serenely vibrant' that 'has both negative and positive facets'. A zero may have no value in itself, but it is something which, placed behind any integer, multiplies its value. This sense of boosting value, of allowing things to happen, of enabling quantity and scale, of letting space be massively increased or lessened according to the presence or absence of zeros, is something that can usefully be brought into play when we are trying to grasp the way in which *sunyata* leans its weight upon us.

Sunyata's etymology also suggests connotations of swelling and expansion. Since it is derived from the root *sui*, 'to swell', *sunyata* implies 'relating to the swollen' – nicely underlining the way in which fullness and emptiness, absence and presence, the metaphysical and the mundane, the history of the universe and local history are all entwined, however much we may like to hone such concepts into separate and separating categories. And the idea of

swelling emptiness suggests another intriguing isobar linking Eastern and Western thought. We could think of the Big Bang as a
kind of systolic–diastolic ballet – on a cosmic scale – between
emptiness and fullness, between the absolute emptiness of a naked
singularity and the swelling outwards of its evolving universe.
Everything we experience today was, some fifteen billion years
ago, compacted into the one-pointedness of this original singularity, no bigger than a spider's web. Consider what physicist Paul
Davies has to say about the expansion of the universe from that
originative point of mysterious concentration (this is from *Super-
force: The Search for a Grand Unified Theory of Nature*):

> The expansion of space is nothing but a continual
> swelling of space. Every day the region of the universe
> accessible to our telescopes swells by 1,018 cubic light
> years.

The swelling fecundity of space, its near infinite amplitude, provides an interesting parallel to Nagarjuna's thinking on emptiness.

It is, of course, perilously easy to give emptiness a cosiness
wholly alien to the icy exactitudes of Buddhist philosophy. As we
think we glimpse it glinting beneath things, around things, in
things, in the familiar surroundings of a drawing room grown
strange and estranging, we should bear in mind the great monk
Mahakashyapa's warning about forming an attachment to *sunyata*.
He says that it's 'better to believe in the reality of a self as great as
Mount Sumeru than to cling stubbornly to a belief in emptiness'.
Zen teaching develops this insight of its original Patriarch in the
saying that 'Even false words are true if they lead to awakening;
even true words are false if they breed attachments'.

For a time, some fugitive traces of us will remain in the empty
drawing room, even after it has been colonised by others – dust
made from our skin particles, a fallen hair or two, a nail clipping,
perhaps some residue of breath. But we will soon enough be
scourged from its presence completely as we will likewise be
scourged from time and space, and our absence shall then be

absolute. 'The world-space in which we dissolve', Rilke asks in his second Duino Elegy, 'does it taste of us afterwards?' Perhaps some fugitive flavour will remain for a while, but it will soon enough disperse into the void. Recognising (in Sonnets to Orpheus, II.1) 'how many places in space were once inside me', Rilke feels that 'many a wind is like a son'. Such a feeling underscores how intermixed with emptiness we are. Yet it is the sense of being orphaned that usually prevails, rather than any warm glow of parenthood.

I picture time passing here, where I sit trying to word into sense some idea of the drawing room's potent emptiness, of our existence-amidst-*sunyata*, and time passing there, with the clock's unheard gentle whirring as the batteries power its hands around their slow, unwitnessed orbit. I think of the spiders' webs marking with their equally minute movements the passing of the slightest draught, and of the garden held reflected in the distorting orb of the mirror. Perhaps, at this precise moment, a bird is flying across the lawn, or a twig is falling from a disused nest in the hedge. And I cannot decide if the words I have assembled here to try to describe the impact of absence, the fullness of emptiness, have prised open the drawing room's haunting liminality just enough to point, albeit tentatively, in the direction of some kind of awakening, some hint of meaning, or if they simply represent the blindness of attachment.

WAXWINGS

'Memory is a filament around which our sense
of the world has crystallized.'

Bruno Schulz

Sometimes I think of the past as a shower of rain that's fallen
on a life. The wet sheen of the present perpetually drains into
memory, from where it can be recalled – though never with the
same glistening freshness of its original moments. A proportion
of the water of immediate experience – which dries so soon into
history – simply evaporates; we can never call it back. Some of it
is stored straightforwardly enough in memory. A few of the
droplets, though, seem to possess a special property. They slowly
percolate through the mind, mostly unnoticed, even apparently
forgotten. As they do so, they take on a weight they did not
previously possess. Eventually, this heavy water reappears, defying the gravity of memory's imprisoning absorbency. It emerges
into the mind again and demands a place in our present reflections. Such irresistible rising damp, the past's tangible echo fountaining within, turns our attention back to the time that minted
it. But we see things now through a liquid lens that's been distilled and clarified for years in the deep chambers of the psyche.
The slow drip-drip of countless associations and influences, the
touch of a whole slew of time's varied denizens, the gentle abra-
sion of unseen reflection, has patiently ground this lens into its
unique torque of concavity and thickness. The view it offers is
magnified, distorted, changed – seen as through a film of newly

discovered oil rather than through the pristine clarity of the original water.

I'm not sure how well this metaphor works. It can certainly be misleading if too much emphasis is placed on transparency, the aqueous limpidity of water. Recall – or rather reconstruction – inclines more to the turbid than to anything translucent. Oil, not water, should be stressed. So, if the image of some kind of glistening dewdrop is threatening to form on the mind's delicate leaves, virginal, pellucid, it should be shaken off immediately and replaced with a drop of oily liquid streaked and stained with locality, nationality, religion, age, class, gender and other less readily labelled opacities. It's likewise misleading if the image of the past as 'a shower of rain that's fallen on a life' is taken too literally, suggesting that the varied climate of experience is always that of downpour. Neither of these readings is intended. What I'm looking for is a way of picturing those fragments of the past that – for whatever reason – come back to haunt us in a special way. (Or perhaps the truth is that they never really leave us.)

Another metaphor for the way in which memory seems to operate dispenses with the liquid parallel and instead sees it as something that chops and dices the present, salting away some bits of its flesh for later savouring, throwing away others. How this selection is made is unclear, but decisions about what to keep and what to jettison rarely seem to follow any of the obvious contours of priority or value by which we would consciously map our experience and mark on it what matters and what does not. Again, as with the droplets that become heavy water, some of these salted-away pieces of preserved-present-soon-turned-into-past seem to have a special property. They mature in a way that confers upon them a greater density than that of other memories. This exerts a powerful gravity that can summon the mind back to the exact co-ordinates traced out by these pieces and make it tarry there, as if temporarily corralled.

This metaphor emphasises the transformation of experience as much as its preservation, for we don't live staccato lives that jerk from one discrete moment to another. Time doesn't happen in diced, separate pieces. Rather, it unrolls its continuance in an unbroken carpet that smoothly bears our steps upon it until the final moment when it stops. But memory can't keep pace with this. It's not some gigantic anaconda that can swallow whole in one great ongoing gulp time's unfolding body. It's more like some small rapacious carnivore that bites and slashes from its quarry whatever gobbets of its flesh can be claimed as the huge carcase lumbers past, invulnerable to more than piecemeal attack. Some of the gobbets are obviously memorable, others obviously trivial. The ones that intrigue me are those that become interior talismans. They often seem unimportant, but the mind keeps returning to them – as if they are possessed of a special magnetism. This rarely happens immediately, indeed the pieces may seem forgotten. But at some point, unerringly, the mind is drawn back to them. It starts to finger them as if they were a rosary, until the texture of the beads is smoothed and utterly familiar from repeated telling.

The gobbet-talisman that concerns me here is one that memory tore from an afternoon that passed some forty years ago. It has been a long while trickling through the hidden strata of the psyche. Remembrance has held it mostly dormant in its great reservoir of recollection; it has surfaced into present awareness no more than a dozen times since it was first laid down. But it has recently emerged again with a new and pressing urgency – converted, so it seems, into droplets of precisely that type of heavy water that ruptures memory's containment and floods the mind again.

In *Translations*, Brian Friel points out that:

> It is not the literal past, the 'facts' of history, that shape us,
> but images of the past embodied in language.

It's clear that we're moulded not only by what happens to us, but also by the way in which the raw weight of actual events is subsequently measured out, preserved, presented, thought about. And language's preservation and presentation can edge so subtly into distortion that it's easy not to notice. Friel is right, I think, to stress how important it is to 'never cease renewing those images' – because 'once we do, we fossilise'. Such fossilisation is like being caught in a sudden ice age. It freezes the water of history into sharp, angular, unforgiving shapes that penetrate and puncture the present, leaving caustic ice crystals burning at its core. This is certainly true at a national level. Think of how often Irish history has frozen into imprisoning images that bear little resemblance to what actually happened. Yet it is these images that have acted to shape the beliefs and actions of many individuals, setting up patterns of rivalry and retribution that have blighted lives, moulding a history – and a continuing, self-perpetuating image of that history – that few would have chosen. At an individual level too, it seems important to keep under review the images our memory feeds us of our own past lives, if only to make us recognise how hard it is to reach 'the literal past', how elusive and complex are 'the "facts" of history', and how our image of our lives, ourselves, sits on far less secure foundations than we might suppose.

How far does my image of an afternoon in 1966 match what actually happened on that day? It would be nice to think that there's a straightforward one-to-one correspondence between recall and event, that what I set down here by way of description is simply a truthful record of what happened and that any divergence between image and actuality is due only to the time that's passed, or to my deficiencies as observer and chronicler. But I suspect the difficulty I have in setting down a clear account, where the contours of the words fit snugly across the topography of the moment, is much more deep rooted than anything that can be accounted for simply by appeal to individual fallibility or the mere span of time that has elapsed between then and now. It has more to do with the intrinsically unequal relationship that exists between actuality and utterance, between experience and accounts of that experience.

If I could be transported back there now, pen and pad to hand,

I might be able to catch more detail, but would that enable me to give a significantly more accurate verbal fingerprint of the way in which I was touched by reality in that place on that day? Even supposing I could go back in time with a camera, it would be naïve to imagine that I would thereby be able to capture or create some faithful imprint of the moment that would show it undistorted, uncut, complete in all the rich fullness of its original occurrence. As Eugene Goodheart puts it (in his essay 'Whistling in the Dark', *Sewanee Review*, 2005):

> Photographs are lies. They fix moments in the past in which what was really felt and experienced is unrevealed. All surface and seduction, they present a beautifully composed past that tells us nothing of the real life of the moment.

I'd not go as far as that. I think photographs can tell us a lot – and I wish I had one at hand right now to prompt my hazy recall. But Goodheart is right to warn of their propensity to mislead. It's not usually a case of photographs lying, more of our misperceiving what they offer. In this they are very similar to the verbal images which Friel warns us to keep under review. For all its robustness as it rains down upon us, the 'real life of the moment' is a fragile enough thing when it comes to its representation. It is easily bent out of shape or made to wear entirely different colours from the hues of its original livery.

The image I wish to renew/review here has become increasingly powerful as the strata of time laid down on top of it, far from acting to obliterate – as they so often do – have instead compressed its components into the hard fossil shape, the heavy water, that has worked its way to the surface again and is what I'm turning in my hands as I write this essay. But the actuality so 'preserved' (in fact transformed) is weak, unclear, elusive. When I try to flesh out the moment on these fossilised bones of remembrance, the grafting fails to take and I am left with something skeletal rather than a properly embodied form. The image has all but eclipsed the actuality out of which it was born.

At one level it's easy enough to describe what happened. It's 1966. I'm eleven years old and visiting my cousins in Ballynahinch, a small County Down market town about twenty minutes' drive from where we lived in Lisburn, County Antrim. Their house occupies a sloping site on a steep rise of land just outside the town. Its elevation means that from the front there's a view across fields and woodland to the Dromara Hills, and beyond them – on a clear day – to the Mourne Mountains. More immediately, the house overlooks the Ballynahinch River and Montalto Estate, in whose demesne deer can sometimes be seen grazing. But that afternoon, a wintry Saturday, it's not the view from the front of the house that catches our attention. Instead, all eyes are focused on something at the back. Usually the view from here does little to lure the eye. The land rises so steeply that it makes the rooms at the back seem rather dark. The gradient so angles the lie of the land as to make it appear that the garden is looking into the house rather intrusively. What, laid flat, would have been a pleasing enough little vista of flowerbeds, shrubs, grass and vegetable patch, seems instead to loom and overshadow.

We're gathered in a cluster, standing in a bedroom – myself, my cousin Sue, our mothers and perhaps one or two other figures too. It's odd that we're there. Bedrooms are considered private – normally we'd sit in the lounge or kitchen, or more likely play in the garden whilst the adults talked inside. Almost immediately outside the window we're so intently looking through is a dry-stone retaining wall – maybe five feet high – which runs beside the narrow path at the back of the house. Sloping steeply up from the wall is a part of the garden dominated by a dense growth of cotoneaster. These tough, evergreen shrubs have fanned out here to cover a rectangle of ground maybe ten feet by eight. The cotoneasters are laden with berries. There are so many of them that the room seems almost back-lit by their bright red glow. And there, feeding on the berries, is what holds our attention and explains why we're standing there silently, not moving, gazing so hungrily out: a small flock of wax-wings. There are perhaps six or eight birds, gorging on the berries, systematically harvesting the rich abundance of the small red fruits. The waxwing – by which I mean the Bohemian waxwing of Europe (*Bombycilla garrulus*), not the American cedar waxwing – is a rare winter visitor to Ireland. A native of northern Scandinavia, even in those exceptional years when many fly to Britain, few continue on across the Irish Sea. The last such 'irruptive' year, as ornithologists term such mass influx, was 1947. Even to someone with no interest in ornithology, these migrants are very striking birds. Crested, with bright red spots on each wing and a vivid band of yellow across the tail – all this set against a background hue of subtle chestnuts, they are strikingly different in appearance from any native Irish species. Everyone gathered in that room had some interest in birds, and this was the first time that any of us had seen a waxwing, so we were transfixed. The plumage of a waxwing is so striking, so resplendently emblazoned with an exotic mix of colours, that they seem to burn with presence. They're so real they don't seem real at first. Until the eye absorbs their opulent brilliance and the astonishing fact of seeing such rarities seeps in, the mind reaches for artificiality (are they bits of coloured plastic?), deception (garish decoys?), or captivity (aviary escapees?) to account for the presence of these plump crested beauties. And then the fact sinks in with the satisfying heaviness of undeniable authenticity: we were seeing waxwings! As R.S. Thomas puts it, 'Ah, but a rare bird is *rare*', it comes 'When one is not looking, at times one is not there'. But that afternoon in Ballynahinch the timing was perfect – we were looking and the birds were there, and so the epiphany happened.

In *The Peregrine*, his brilliant visual meditation on these rare and beautiful raptors, J.A. Baker invites readers to look at the bird as it's typically illustrated in a standard field guide:

> Large and isolated in the gleaming whiteness of the page,
> the hawk stares back at you, bold and statuesque, brightly
> coloured. But when you have shut the book, you will
> never see that bird again.

Just so with waxwings. Illustrations show a plump, sleek bird so richly coloured, and with its trademark crest so prominent, that it outshines any other species on the page and seems far bigger than birds of about the same size that we're used to seeing – starlings, blackbirds, thrushes. Fixed there before the eyes in its technicolour perfection, this two-dimensional shadow, however accurately the artist has contrived to catch its shape and form and colour, does little justice to the 'real life of the moment' in which the birds appear. There's a world of difference between a living creature and some lines drawn on a page, or between the incredible fullness of any conscious moment and the dull notation of time and place and circumstance by which our words fossilise experiences into those images of whose adequacy Friel is rightly suspicious.

As an eleven-year-old boy standing in that bedroom looking out at waxwings, I was innocent of the complexity of moments and how difficult it is for memory to fix them into history. Such realisation only dawned on my horizons decades later. Even now, squinting against its brightness, I'm not sure how adequately I recognise the potency of the sun of being which beats down so burningly on all those readily flammable links we weave between reality and representation. Back then, I believed in the straight-forward accuracy of perception, the reliability of memory, the possibility of description, the authority of books and the uncom-plicated purity of history as a truthful record of what happened. Such faith is no longer open to me. This doesn't mean that I've gone from one extreme to another, from naïvety and trust to scep-ticism and doubt, simply that as I've grown up, grown older, the extent to which we rely on and accept approximations has become much clearer. A good description remains valuable, worth working for, though it is inevitably incomplete and thus inaccurate. Though our words will always omit, misrepresent, ignore, overemphasise, there's an important distinction, never to be lost sight of, between trying to be accurate and not bothering (or, still worse, trying to deceive). Books, for all their fallibility, can be massively authoritative. And yet with history, as with birds, it's often the case that once we close the book we will never see that image until we open it again, so little likeness does it bear to what it is attempting to portray.

I lack the incandescent prose of a great nature writer like J.A. Baker, whose descriptive prowess is peregrine-like in its ability to scythe through the flocks of our quotidian vocabulary, stoop on a moment and catch it in word-talons of astonishing strength and sharpness. But though I lack his lethal verbal brilliance, is there anything wrong with the admittedly pedestrian description of seeing waxwings that I've given? Why should I present this as something problematic? Does it not suffice well enough to give a picture of that moment? The problem is that if you press gently on any of the apparent '"facts" of history' that my account seems to offer, they soon warp out of focus. Were this merely something that affected my recollection of waxwings one distant boyhood day in an Ulster garden, it would be of little consequence for anyone but me. My waxwing moment is a very little '"fact" of history'. It's not as if I'm trying to recall some epochal battle in which the fate of civilisations was decided, or give a verbatim account of the words of a Buddha or a Christ, or recount a great statesman's conversation, or the way in which a revolution in scientific thinking began. This is just a vanished afternoon in the life of one of those millions of anonymous people who make up history's crowd scenes, the uncounted and unnoticed. As such, is it worth paying it attention or worrying about the pedigree of its description?

The fact is that my image of the waxwings, my recollection of this moment, for all its seeming insignificance, carries with it a germ of uncertainty that can unravel far more fabric than the few threads that are all this instance can claim for its own depiction. When I interrogate my experience, I find my memory of the waxwings far less certain than I used to imagine. When I ask other witnesses, their testimony does not always chime in harmony with mine. It has become increasingly clear that my picture of what happened is not only an impoverished reflection of events, but that the reliability of some of its basic elements is suspect. If, as I suppose, this is the case not just for my memory of one particular afternoon, but rather that it's symptomatic of the manner in which human recollection happens, many of the full stops that I used to imagine punctuated history, morph into question marks or rows of non-committal dots. Concise sentences that once conferred 'facts' with the authority of certainty run together, blur, become unfixed ...

Looking more closely at that winter afternoon in 1966, the simple lines of the quick sketch I've offered tremble, shake themselves like a wet dog and settle into new arrays of possible combination. What once seemed fixed and certain deliquesces and becomes fluid, elusive, more like a shifting mirage than a definite, solid moment. To begin with, I'm not sure if it really was 1966. I think I was about eleven. But perhaps I was nine or twelve or eight. Looking back, it's not as if the years automatically arrange themselves into a neat calendar in which every memory falls into its correct chronological niche. It would be more accurate to what's held in memory – though not, of course, to the actual event – to say 'a winter afternoon sometime between 1963 and 1967'. Nor am I absolutely certain that it was an afternoon. This was when we customarily visited our cousins, but maybe that Saturday we went in the morning instead (if it was a Saturday – weekends were the norm, but there were exceptions; usually it was Saturday, but occasionally we made a Sunday visit). 'Winter' is conveniently vague, covering several months of possibility. I have no idea whether our visit was in November, or just before Christmas or sometime in February.

I'm surer about place than about time and could take you now to the room where we stood, point out the cotoneasters where the birds were perched – though perhaps they've since been uprooted and cleared. The house was sold following my aunt's death and I don't know who lives there now or how much of the original house and garden they've preserved. I'm certainly not sure how long the 'moment' lasted. Did we stand there looking at the waxwings for only a few seconds, a few minutes, a quarter of an hour? Did we tire of watching, leave the room and then come back again? When asked about the waxwings, my cousin Sue remembers them – but her image has them perched in a laburnum tree, not on cotoneaster bushes. When I mentioned this difference between our two recollections she reminded me that a laburnum grew just above the cotoneasters, so the birds could have perched there first and then flown down. She remembers the birds keeping to the vicinity for several days. Once she mentioned the laburnum tree, it came back into my image of the scene. Prior to this I had no memory of it and wonder now if it can be thought of as something I've been prompted to remember, or if it is an interloper cast by the imagination from the ore of Sue's account. I can 'see' it as clearly as I 'see' the cotoneasters; it has become as real for me as they are.

My uncertainties about date and time are matched by uncertainties about people. Who does the 'we' who saw the waxwings refer to? I know I was there. My mother and her sister, my Auntie Kay, were there (this is mum's recollection; Kay – like her husband and my father – died long before it occurred to me to ask them about the waxwings). My brother has no memory of being there; I suspect it was term time and that he and my older cousin, Brian, were away at boarding school. Were our fathers there? Sue thinks they might have been, I'm not sure but guess they weren't. Not infrequently they were away fishing at the weekend – at Loughan Island or Lough Island Reevey, or one of half a dozen other venues dotted through the Ulster countryside. Sometimes when my mother visited her sister in Ballynahinch, my father – if he wasn't fishing – drove on to visit his brother, a country doctor who lived in a village only a few miles away, so perhaps he was there that day. I know I watched the birds from the bedroom and that I was in a group of watchers, not alone. But I have no idea now, and there is no way now to find this out, who was there, who stood next to whom, who said what (if anything), what anyone was wearing. I'm not sure exactly how many waxwings there were, where exactly they perched, whether they made any sound or showed any awareness of our watching (bird books describe them as 'unafraid of humans'). I don't know who saw them first and summoned the rest of us to watch. Sue raised the possibility of our being telephoned in Lisburn specifically to come over and see them. I don't recall the weather that day, or what I was thinking, or what anyone said or did afterwards. The event – rather the re-call, the image of the event – warps into a cloud of unknowing. Yet somewhere in that cloud it stands in its unadorned, unaltered actuality, however little of it I can bring to mind. The bright sheen of the moment has long since drained away and what's left of it has been transmuted into this curious heavy water that has returned to haunt me, droplets from some inner Sargasso bearing with them a dense weedy tangle of time and place and memory.

In a comment that fits so well with what Brian Friel says about them that the two might be adjacent pieces in the same jigsaw, Susan Moeller suggests that images have 'authority over the imagination'. This can be found in her book *Compassion Fatigue*, a study of the way in which the media present human disasters and tragedies. For Moeller, 'images cannot help but simplify the world'. What matters, she argues, is 'the *quality* of their simplicity'. If – ignoring Friel's warning – we fail to keep the images that define us under review, if we fail to check the quality of the simplifications that we rely on, we risk a fossilisation of the spirit that will poison us. It's a sad feature of Irish history, of the histories of many nations, that highly toxic simplifications often crystallise in the mind, warping the present into shapes that cripple its denizens.

Clearly my image of the waxwings is a simplification, an approximation, and one of dubious enough quality. The more I subject it to attempted review and renewal, the more it seems at risk of losing its hold on that slope of credibility that any memory must climb if it is to distinguish itself from forgetfulness or fabrication. Does it matter that the picture I've carried for years of this long-vanished afternoon in Ballynahinch is one that's so incomplete, so unreliable, so little able to retrieve intact what I know I witnessed? My image of that moment, once assayed, yields so few specks of gold from the rich mother lode it was mined from that its value is surely suspect. Seen in isolation, this might seem entirely unimportant. What of it if a boy forgets some birds? But what is a self if it is not composed of the moments it inhabits? And what is history if it is not the story of our selves? If eviction is threatened from their territory, where will they then find shelter and sustenance? If memory's moorings are loosened, if the habitations that we quarry out of time are found to have leaking roofs, ill-fitting doors, walls dangerously aslant because of subsidence, what will hold us to ourselves?

In 'Theology of Fields', a fine essay that appeared in the Autumn 2006 issue of the *Harvard Divinity Bulletin*, Reginald Gibbons offers a fascinating meditation on the spirituality of childhood. But he's clear that what he's describing is childhood:

> not as it was in itself, nor as it was to me then, but as
> the elusive, mostly lost, intermittently lit place it is to
> me now.

Gibbons suggests that such a current image of childhood is like Hades, the ancient Greeks' post-mortem underworld, which is 'populated by shades, and is itself a shape of shadows'. He develops the idea of Hades acting as a metaphor. It shows, says Gibbons, how

> people and places seem to us in our memory, irrevocably separated from us by time, so robbed of substance by that distance that they seem nearly transparent.

In retrieving my waxwings from this inner Hades, can I breathe colour back into their plumage without destroying it? Is it possible to restore to more than shadows the people who stood there watching them, without allowing imagination to weave up details that do not correspond with reality? How much of our view of time past, of our own intimate history, is distilled from the uncertainties of Hades-dwelling shades? Closely examined, the images held in memory seem formed from something more mutable, more intangible, than the metal of the original experience. Looking at how this memory is born out of shadows, how the image that I've erected from this waxwing moment stands on such a flimsy foundation, one that is so different from the reality of what happened, I can't help wondering, beyond the ambit of my own insignificance in the scheme of things, how much of what we regard as history and treat as a solid record of events is likewise rooted in something far more nebulous than what happened.

Waxwings are so called because of the bright red patch on either wing (a feature usually, though not always, missing in the females). These patches, as *The Observer's Book of Birds* explains, are 'composed of sealing-wax-like tips to the quills'. This association with wax is fortuitous in the context of thinking about memory, for it brings to mind the classical image of how we remember. From Aristotle and Plato through to Cicero and Quintillian, there's a tradition of seeing memory as the pressing of sense impressions upon the mind's soft retentive wax. They leave their signatures there like footprints, from which we can track and reconstruct the trails we've taken. Looking at the famous passage on memory in Plato's *Theaetetus* (191 C-D), Frances Yates summarises this conception of how we remember things:

> Socrates assumes that there is a block of wax in our souls – of varying quality in different individuals – and that this is 'the gift of Memory, the mother of the Muses.' Whenever we see or hear or think anything, we hold this wax under the perceptions and thoughts and imprint them upon it, just as we make impressions from seal rings. (*The Art of Memory* [1966], p.35)

So, that little fingerprint of six or eight (or seven or nine?) waxwings pressed the weight of their rare and colourful presence against my memory-wax, imprinting on it an echo of their form, a kind of instant fossilisation, so that a trace was left of these beautiful creatures long after they had gone. Although there's a simple and appealing elegance in this notion of memory working as a kind of interior script which delicately embosses our experiences upon its accommodating surface, such an image assumes a more straightforward equivalence between experience and memory than is warranted. Of course Socrates allows that the 'block of wax' we possess is of varying quality. Perhaps my own is made of particularly inferior material. But does anyone possess a memory of such regular and reliable verisimilitude that whatever is laid down upon it will be an exact imprint, something that precisely traces out the shape, the form, the texture of the original?

The wax in that flock of remembered waxwings, though it brings this classical image first to mind, soon discards it in favour of another, less obvious, association – that of *cire perdue*, the so-called 'lost wax' process. This is a technique for casting bronze and other sculptures in which the shape is first made using soft, pliable wax. When it hardens, the wax is coated in clay, leaving a small drain hole at the base. The clay is then fired. This melts the wax, which is 'lost' – pouring out through the drain hole. The hollow clay mould can then be filled with molten metal. When it cools, the clay is cracked and chipped away, leaving the hard metal echo of the original waxy form. This image appeals because it involves the complete loss of the original substance, and its replacement by something that has taken shape via several stages, rather than the ghost of the original claimed by an automatic process of continuous imprinting. In the case of memory, though, it is more as if the metal of experience is what is lost, to be replaced with something far less durable.

Thinking about the waxwings as they appear to me now, they seem to have been moulded by something that approximates more closely to the *cire perdue* process than to imprinting onto any inner block of wax. But the clay mould into which my memory of them has been poured, and out of which I retrieve my images of them again, is not one that clings faithfully to the outlines of their shape alone. Instead, it follows various loops and pockets of association that pull its contours away from any straightforward shadowing of the appearance of the birds themselves. And it is certainly not metal that has been poured into this mould of many meanderings, but rather some composite, mercurial substance that bears within itself all kinds of shadings, emphases and absences. No amount of sculpting will render it smoothly uniform. Moreover, the mould is not cracked and disposed of but continues to hold something that seems reluctant to set into any final, solidified form.

The waxwings were seen at 'Gorse Hill', a potent place of childhood, whose name – even now – immediately conjures a rich cocktail of memories. Much of the mould into which the waxwings were poured, and out of which I retrieve them again, was shaped from the clay of this house and its garden. It is clay that is so laden with associations that they pockmark any vessel constructed from it and leave their imprint on anything it holds.

Gorse Hill was the house built shortly after World War II by my mother's sister, Kay, and her husband. A modest but comfortable bungalow on the outskirts of Ballynahinch, it was home to cousins very close in age to me and my brother. We played there with them often, roaming the secret nooks of Kay's beautifully landscaped garden, planted out – though we were innocent of such horticultural sophistication then – with a treasure trove of rare and beautiful species.

Any memory formed in the crucible of Gorse Hill will inevitably be coloured by it. Remembrance of things here will be ruled by the monarchies of specific place and time, with all their foibles, not by any democracy fairly elected only from the constituency of a particular moment. The indefinable, over-arching sense of a happy family home; the photos on the walls; the books on the shelves; the warmth from the open fire; the sweet aroma left perfuming the air from my Uncle Brian's pipe tobacco; the gun cabinet on the wall displaying shotguns and rifles, a flintlock pistol, a luger taken from a dead German officer – my uncle had fought in the war and been awarded a Military Cross for laying communications lines under fire; the dried-flower arrangements done with such artistry by Kay – these and other features crowd against everything that happened here. They are the fingers in the hand that holds the waxwings.

A few years after seeing the birds, as Ulster lurched into conflict, the guns were removed to a police barracks for safe-keeping. The empty, glass-fronted cabinet became an unlooked-for symbol of the Troubles, bleakly underscoring the fact that decent people could no longer safely have firearms about the house, no matter how lawful and non-belligerent their reasons. And in those violent times, when Ulster's riven polity was repeatedly disfigured by acts of sectarian hatred, I remember a party at Gorse Hill attended by an eminent public figure. He arrived with armed bodyguards, as exotic in their way as waxwings, but displaying a darker, deadlier allure.

The waxwings carry the mark of these and scores of other

associations, woven together from the countless times I visited this house. Sometimes, when we were children, we stayed with our cousins overnight and were taken with the novelty of a house with no upstairs, and of eating breakfast in the kitchen – in contrast to the dining room that was invariably used for meals at home. Instances that happened years before and years after seeing them hedge that waxwing afternoon with a foliage as dense and richly fruited with memories as the cotoneasters were with berries. Gorse Hill, like every place (whether named or unnamed), hosted a particular unfolding of time. The waxwings are just one tiny notch upon the pole of duration measured out here in the lives of my aunt and uncle, my cousins, in my own life and that of my immediate family, and in the cast of other characters who came and went over the years, in the plants in the garden, in the stones weathering unseen, imperceptibly, in the rich County Down earth. Sometimes I think a memory like that of the waxwings acts as a tiny fold in the immense fabric of time. What falls on either side of it is of such length as to make any mark we try to leave upon it vanishingly infinitesimal. The only reason such things can be seen at all is because of the magnification afforded by our individual existences, our focusing on – our fusing with – the minute areas that define us.

In *The Snow Leopard*, Peter Matthiessen describes the purpose of meditation as being:

> To pay attention even at unextraordinary times, to be of the present, nothing-but-the-present, to bear this mindfulness of now into each event of ordinary life.

I warm to that idea and wish I could implement it more successfully in my own life. Yet to be of the present is surely also to be of the past, since one is so instantly minted from the other. Perhaps paying such keen attention as Matthiessen here proposes might help to fix things more precisely in the memory as well as making the present more present. Paying attention to my image of the waxwings – a very different exercise, of course, from paying attention to the birds themselves – makes me wonder where to clip the wings of the moment, where to draw the boundary of this, or any other, experience. This was not a thought that troubled me when I was there in that back bedroom at Gorse Hill as a boy, gazing entranced at the spectacular resplendence of the waxwings' plumage. But now it is no longer clear to me what moments consist of, where they begin and end, and the suspicion grows that in 'each event of ordinary life' we are dealing with something gargantuan and stupendous. That all the cuts and clips we make, our crude abbreviations, are for convenience only and do not remotely reflect the way things really are.

In *Memory* (1957), Ian Hunter suggests that in investigating the recollection of childhood experiences, 'our greatest difficulty lies in obtaining authentic recollections'. Hunter raises the possibility that what appear to be memories may in fact be instances where an account is based on stories of an individual's past which the person concerned 'has heard so often that he has come to believe erroneously that he can actually recollect the event concerned'. Though naturally I realise that my own certainty can provide but little guarantee, I'm clear in the case of the waxwings of what my own memory of them is – and I'm mindful of its paucity – and what the stories told by others are. To my mind, the 'greatest difficulty' in dealing with this recollection is not knowing whether or not it's 'authentic' but in determining what nature of a thing it is and how far it is possible to trace out its lineaments.

Is my recollection of the waxwings a thought? A memory? Is it an outcome, at least in part, of the imagination? To what extent does it store, complete and undistorted, aspects of the actual perceptions of that moment as it happened on that day? To what extent does it consist of aspects of that moment that only occurred to me long after it took place? What proportion of my image of the waxwings is made up of sources other than the immediate impress of things upon the senses – and does the presence of such sources invalidate or augment the reality of the birds? Am I dealing with a record – the faithful, if incomplete snapshot of an encounter with given things the way they really are? Or with something that only dawned upon the mind after journeying through the complex filtration of influences that Gorse Hill exerts upon me? Are the waxwings as I have them now something woven together from strands taken from my personality, from a familiar place, or from how a single moment was perceived? It is certainly nothing as simple as I used to imagine such things were. I've come to see it as a complicated hybrid involving elements from all of these – and no doubt other – sources, and as a hybrid that stands not as a unique instance but as an exemplar for how all our remembering is done.

Peter Matthiessen refers to the Tantric discipline of *chöd* – overcoming feelings of horror by attempting to embrace and accept what one fears. This is done 'the better to realise that everything in the universe, being inseparably related, is therefore holy'. In the course of his arduous journey from Kathmandu to the Crystal Mountain, Matthiessen performs what he terms 'some mild *chöd* of my own' by forcing himself to look over the edge as he walks along a narrow mountain trail which skirts a bone-chilling drop of several thousand feet. A waxwing is no snow leopard and Ballynahinch is no Tibet, but there is a chilling enough precipice ringing this moment – as every moment – once you pay it some attention, see through the mask of the accustomed, notice what our cosy abbreviations are linked to.

Through the delicate hollow bones of that flight of waxwings, through the warm hidden tubing of their symphonic networks of veins and nerves, through the secret chambered universe of cells that's held so deftly in these little feathered blocks of meat, the presence of this species flows. The life expectancy of a wild bird of this size is five years at most, and often half that or less. But like the steps in a fantastic ladder the generations reach back, short-lived individual by short-lived individual, into the deep reaches of time, until they touch the archaeopteryx – the link between birds and reptiles – and, beyond that, their 150-million-year-old bloodline blurs into Mesozoic uncertainties, where 'waxwing' is but a distant possibility, a potential name and form waiting to unfurl from seeds sown far further back in time than language, in a place that is billions of years removed from the utterance of such intricate sounds as 'waxwing' or 'Ballynahinch'. Thinking of the waxwings' ladder through time, and the one on which my own life constitutes a tiny rung, that moment of encounter in Ballynahinch seems like a pinprick flash of coincidence, two blinks of sentience brought into momentary proximity on their respective species-ladders that snake uncertainly through the aeons. How far into the future will the stepping stones of waxwings lead? I wonder, sometimes, if any of the descendants of the birds I saw that afternoon will, decades on from that fleeting moment, be witnessed by any descendants of mine, somewhere, somehow, unbeknownst to either. The past reaches forward, always, to touch the present, often in unexpected ways. Or, reaching back, perhaps I and the waxwings are descended from individuals who, centuries before that afternoon, looked one another in the eye before moving on into their unknown futures.

Looking at the waxwings – or rather looking at the image of the waxwings now lodged in my mind – a realisation dawns of the contiguity of bone-chilling precipices all around. An awesome plenitude leans against the illusion of each apparently discrete and separable moment. It's as if, fountaining out of the waxwings' crests, there's a spiralling, sparking nerve that snakes through time and place, wakening more and more of their elements, pushing things towards Matthiessen's notion of inseparable relation. I picture it uncoiling like some tendril of raw energy, flashing from the birds to the cotoneaster berries, down the steep slope of Gorse Hill's garden, along the road towards Drumaness, Clough, Seaforde, Dundrum, Newcastle, the Mourne Mountains and the sea. Shooting across the waves, it reaches right across the far horizon, until it loops the globe, beading together on its nerve-thread a groaning multitude of other places, other lives, the interlacing trajectories of other stories, each one, like the waxwings, laddering back to incomprehensible ancientness and forward into the uncertain future. Then it returns, through Lisburn, Hillsborough, Annahilt, weaving through Country Down's drumlins, until it powers back up Gorse Hill's drive to meet the waxwing crests again, coming full circle to the fulcrum of this image. The little tableau of birds feasting on red berries explodes into a trillion intricate connections, tracing out a scale of things the mind is not calibrated to measure beyond the crudities of rudimentary metaphor. The momentary and the momentous are fused together in such a way that it stalls comprehension and leaves us reeling in wonder and in terror at the nature of existence.

The extravagance of connection that's implicit in this, as in every, moment is astounding. We can follow a few of the links in its latent, unseen networks in all sorts of ways, find different entrances into the same dense maze of interrelationships that cascade away from any of our plodding attempts to plot them. We could start with the berry-fed droppings of the waxwings as they gorged on the cotoneaster berries. They will have added their small weight to the garden's humus. That then feeds the plants, nudging them to produce flowers and fruit. The chemical elements of substance are passed from receptacle to receptacle in a kind of inorganic reworking of the passing of waxwing life from bird to bird. Or, we could trace the life of one individual bird, from egg to end, watch where it travels, what other stories might be glimpsed unfolding as it flies over the Ulster countryside, across the sea and back to its native Scandinavia. Or, looking inside Gorse Hill, we could consider the links that spiral out from one of my uncle's rifles, or from that wartime luger. A dark nerve that soon connects with the sorrow of millions, the breath of holocaust and horror reaching into even this happy place. The shiny iridescence of the links in these incredible chains of connection also become evident in considering the different ways in which the waxwing moment was perceived by all who witnessed it, how it was laid down in their minds, and where their stories led to – which other stories they linked to – as they moved on from that afternoon. Or, changing perceptual gear, another set of links comes into sight if we think about how the moment might have appeared from the perspective of the waxwings, rather than the waxwing watchers. Given that 'the sensory experience of birds extends far beyond the sensory experience of humans' – a point stressed by Frank Gill in his magisterial *Ornithology* (1990) – what we experienced and what they experienced would have been very different. Birds can see almost into the ultra-violet part of the spectrum, their hearing range vastly outpaces our own, they have senses we do not possess – being able to navigate and orientate themselves by reference to forces we are blind to, such as the earth's magnetic field and small shifts in gravity or barometric pressure. And of those individual manifestations of waxwing life, their bodies vanished, long cindered into dust, all the particulars of what they sensed dispersed, the only trace is whatever has been passed down through their fleeting generations – crest and colour packed in the fragile, yet durable, egg of continuance that has rolled down the gradient of the years from that moment, drawn by the same irresistible gravity of time as surely as the descent of our own genes through the generations.

In *Birds of the Grey Wind*, looking at the strange life-story of the cuckoo, Edward Armstrong muses that it's 'like a theme of a Hardy novel' because it displays 'a record of inscrutable forces playing with their blind, impotent victims'. The waxwing moment did not cast anyone in the role of victim, though we are all helpless in the grip of being, but it does seem imbued with 'inscrutable forces'. Perhaps it is only through a novel of Hardy-like dimensions that some justice might be done to mapping them, that the sense of having touched the nerve of the real might be properly conveyed.

Once, when we were too young to do so with any sensible level of safety, my cousins, my brother and I were target shooting with a powerful air-rifle on the small front lawn at Gorse Hill. This was some years before the waxwing sighting, though again I'd be hard put to place a definite date on things. Without a daily diary the precise co-ordinates of time slip easily from mind. I remember it as a sunny afternoon, but I know my childhood tends to appear bathed in a golden light whenever I look back on it now. We had, at least, enough sense not to point the gun at each other, or at the house, or to shoot towards the road. But we didn't know about the perils of ricochets and there was stone behind our cardboard targets. Someone else was taking aim as the rest of us stood – far too close – to one side. Seemingly at the same instant as they fired, there was a high-pitched zing and the pellet lodged in my leg. Sometimes now I think of my image of the waxwings as a kind of ricochet of memory, something that lodged with surprising force in the mind's unsuspecting flesh, a deflected shot, something coming from an unexpected direction, an unintended outcome of this moment. Unlike the pellet, which was soon dug out, the waxwings seem to have lodged in me permanently – or rather with as much permanence as my fleeting presence can bestow on anything. The image of this moment has become part of me. It is a section of clay in the mould within which the self's mysterious and complex wax is held. *Cire perdue* reversed, this speck of hot metal, a tiny meteorite from the past, shapes a small area of the psyche into the form it now bears. Here, the birds have taken on an almost mythological status. It's as if they've become tiny feathered unicorns, fantastic unreal harbingers of another world – but I know that even the dullest sparrow, if we pay it close attention, possesses just such incandescence and skirts a similarly sheer drop into the abyss of everything. There's no need to journey thousands of miles, or to scale some distant peak, in order to perform 'some mild *chöd* of our own'. Any moment carries that potential so long as we pay it the attention that it warrants.

I know I saw waxwings one afternoon in Ballynahinch when I was a boy. But, equally, I know that the sighting I experienced then was very different from the Hades-like shadows in the image of this moment that somehow ricocheted into my mind and came back to haunt me forty years later. It is that perplexing image – some droplets of memory's heavy water – that has been the subject of this memory-meditation, this attempt at a phenomenology of remembering (in the writing of which, of course, the original image has been renewed and altered). It is an image which certainly seems to have wielded considerable authority over the imagination. As to the quality of the simplification that it offers, though I hope it does not belong to that great tribe of garish reductions that render our world so vulgar and demean so much, I know it is far from adequate. It fails both on the micro-level of remembering the fine details of the moment and, an altogether more spectacular failure, but one that it shares with almost all memories, on the macro-level of not glimpsing the plenitude of existence in which that moment, like every moment, was embedded. Whatever its limitations, I hope it will stay in mind, if only as a stumbling block to trip up any image of the world I might construct in which there is no room for the periodic irruption of feathered unicorns and their unexpected epiphanies. It's easy for images of self, or of Ireland, or of the world, to settle like stones of seeming certainty, promising a clear-cut view of things, 'the "facts" of history' laid out as neatly as cadavers. But if we look carefully at any of the little moments from which our lives are woven we can, I think, find waxwings perched on all of them with their bright promise of subversion, resurrection, terror.

ACKNOWLEDGEMENTS

A writer's life is not the only one affected by what he does. Writing claims time in abundance and demands quiet and solitude. I'm grateful to Jane, Lucy and Laura for putting up with the demands my books make on them. Their support is invaluable. I hope I never take it for granted.

Various readers along the way have commented on individual essays and helped me see more clearly what my writing is attempting and how it might be bettered. Correspondence with four key authorities on the essay form – Richard Chadbourne, Lydia Fakundiny, Graham Good and Lane Kauffmann – has been particularly useful in this regard. I'm grateful to them for the time they've lavished on an unmet writer's work.

Many of the essays in *Words of the Grey Wind* have appeared in some form in literary journals, or in *Irish Nocturnes, Irish Willow* or *Irish Haiku*. The editors responsible for guiding them into these published places have provided invaluable encouragement and feedback. I'm indebted to the editorial skills of Elizabeth Davies, Dan Latimer, Margaret Kouidis, Karen Beckwith, David Gardiner and Willard Spiegelman.

Patsy Horton, Michelle Griffin and their colleagues at the Blackstaff Press have shown an admirable mix of insight, patience, determination and efficiency. Without their efforts, *Words of the Grey Wind* would not have seen the light of day.

I'm grateful to Jack Foster for writing the Foreword. It's an honour to have so well respected a commentator on Irish literature stand as scholarly sentinel at the book's beginning, beckoning readers across its threshold.

Michael Benington graciously granted permission to use his painting 'Eiders in a Gale'. The aptness of a Benington cover should be evident from the Dedication. Michael is son of the man who taught me how to dissect owl pellets (see 'Meditation on the Pelvis of an Unknown Animal') and who kindled my fascination for kingfishers, waxwings and other birds. That Edward Armstrong, author of *Birds of the Grey Wind*, was a relative of Michael's – a discovery made only shortly before *Words of the Grey Wind* was published – adds another pleasing loop of unexpected connection.

Any shortcomings in the book are, of course, my sole responsibility as author.

The author and publisher gratefully acknowledge permission to include the following copyright material:

'A Tinchel Round My Father' is from *Irish Willow* (ISBN-10: 1-888570-46-6 / ISBN-13: 978-1-888570-46-5) published by The Davies Group, Publishers, Aurora CO USA, 2002, and appears here by arrangement with the publisher.

'Ferrule' is from *Irish Nocturnes* (ISBN-10: 1-888570-49-0 / ISBN-13: 978-1-888570-49-6) published by The Davies Group, Publishers, Aurora CO USA, 1999, and appears here by arrangement with the publisher.

'Kingfishers' is from *Irish Nocturnes* (ISBN-10: 1-888570-49-0 / ISBN-13: 978-1-888570-49-6) published by The Davies Group, Publishers, Aurora CO USA, 1999 and appears here by arrangement with the publisher.

'Linen' is from *Irish Nocturnes* (ISBN-10: 1-888570-49-0 / ISBN-13: 978-1-888570-49-6) published by The Davies Group, Publishers, Aurora CO USA, 1999, and appears here by arrangement with the publisher.

'Meditation on the Pelvis of an Unknown Animal' is from *Irish Nocturnes* (ISBN-10: 1-888570-49-0 / ISBN-13: 978-1-888570-49-6) published by The Davies Group, Publishers, Aurora CO USA, 1999, and appears here by arrangement with the publisher.

'Miracles' is from *Irish Haiku* (ISBN-10: 1-888570-78-4 / ISBN-13: 978-1-888570-78-6) published by The Davies Group, Publishers, Aurora CO USA, 2005, and appears here by arrangement with the publisher.

'Swan Song' is from *Irish Haiku* (ISBN-10: 1-888570-78-4 / ISBN-13: 978-1-888570-78-6) published by The Davies Group, Publishers, Aurora CO USA, 2005, and appears here by arrangement with the publisher.

'Table Manners' is from *Irish Willow* (ISBN-10: 1-888570-46-6 / ISBN-13: 978-1-888570-46-5) published by The Davies Group, Publishers, Aurora CO USA, 2002, and appears here by arrangement with the publisher.

'Train Sounds' is from *Irish Willow* (ISBN-10: 1-888570-46-6 / ISBN-13: 978-1-888570-46-5) published by The Davies Group, Publishers, Aurora CO USA, 2002, and appears here by arrangement with the publisher.

'Witness' is from *Irish Haiku* (ISBN-10: 1-888570-78-4 / ISBN-13: 978-1-888570-78-6) published by The Davies Group, Publishers, Aurora CO USA, 2005, and appears here by arrangement with the publisher.

The author also wishes to acknowledge the following journals in which some of these essays were first published: 'Mistletoe' appeared in the *Southern Humanities Review*, 41.4 (2007); 'Room, Empty' appeared in the *Southwest Review*, 91.3 (2006); 'Waxwings' appeared in *An Sionnach: A Journal of Literature, Culture and the Arts*, 3.2 (2007).

Excerpt from 'No Rootless Colonist' by John Hewitt taken from *Ancestral Voices: The Selected Prose of John Hewitt* ed. Tom Clyde (Blackstaff Press, 1987) reproduced by permission of Blackstaff Press on behalf of the Estate of John Hewitt.